MW00720343

1997

JANUARY
M	T	W	T	F	S	S
		1	2	3	4	5
6	7	8	9	10	11	12
13	14	15	16	17	18	19
20	21	22	23	24	25	26
27	28	29	30	31		

FEBRUARY
M	T	W	T	F	S	S
					1	2
3	4	5	6	7	8	9
10	11	12	13	14	15	16
17	18	19	20	21	22	23
24	25	26	27	28		

MARCH
M	T	W	T	F	S	S
					1	2
3	4	5	6	7	8	9
10	11	12	13	14	15	16
17	18	19	20	21	22	23
24	25	26	27	28	29	30
31						

APRIL
M	T	W	T	F	S	S
	1	2	3	4	5	6
7	8	9	10	11	12	13
14	15	16	17	18	19	20
21	22	23	24	25	26	27
28	29	30				

MAY
M	T	W	T	F	S	S
			1	2	3	4
5	6	7	8	9	10	11
12	13	14	15	16	17	18
19	20	21	22	23	24	25
26	27	28	29	30	31	

JUNE
M	T	W	T	F	S	S
						1
2	3	4	5	6	7	8
9	10	11	12	13	14	15
16	17	18	19	20	21	22
23	24	25	26	27	28	29
30						

JULY
M	T	W	T	F	S	S
	1	2	3	4	5	6
7	8	9	10	11	12	13
14	15	16	17	18	19	20
21	22	23	24	25	26	27
28	29	30	31			

AUGUST
M	T	W	T	F	S	S
				1	2	3
4	5	6	7	8	9	10
11	12	13	14	15	16	17
18	19	20	21	22	23	24
25	26	27	28	29	30	31

SEPTEMBER
M	T	W	T	F	S	S
1	2	3	4	5	6	7
8	9	10	11	12	13	14
15	16	17	18	19	20	21
22	23	24	25	26	27	28
29	30					

OCTOBER
M	T	W	T	F	S	S
		1	2	3	4	5
6	7	8	9	10	11	12
13	14	15	16	17	18	19
20	21	22	23	24	25	26
27	28	29	30	31		

NOVEMBER
M	T	W	T	F	S	S
					1	2
3	4	5	6	7	8	9
10	11	12	13	14	15	16
17	18	19	20	21	22	23
24	25	26	27	28	29	30

DECEMBER
M	T	W	T	F	S	S
1	2	3	4	5	6	7
8	9	10	11	12	13	14
15	16	17	18	19	20	21
22	23	24	25	26	27	28
29	30	31				

WE'MOON '97

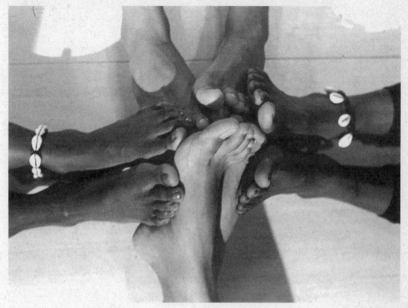

© Rita DeBellis 1996

WOMYN IN COMMUNITY

GAIA RHYTHMS: AN ASTROLOGICAL MOON CALENDAR, APPOINTMENT BOOK, AND DAILY GUIDE TO NATURAL RHYTHM FOR WE'MOON

 published by
Mother Tongue Ink

WE'MOON '97: GAIA RHYTHMS FOR WOMYN
© Mother Tongue Ink 1996

P.O. Box 1395-A
Estacada, Oregon 97023 USA
Phone: 503-630-7848
E-mail: wemoon@teleport.com
URL: http://www.teleport.com/~wemoon/

Earth ▢ *Antiga 1987*

Created by the **We'Moon** Matrix
Creatrix and Crone Consultant: Musawa
We'Moonager and Graphics Editor: Beth Freewomon
Writing Editor: Amy Schutzer   Contributor Hag: Laura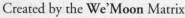
Production Gal, Databaser, and Admoonistrator: Linda Meagaen

Front cover art by Christine Eagon. Back cover art by Rita DeBellis. See "Cover Notes" on page 187.

Distributed directly by Mother Tongue Ink and by our other fine distributors: **USA:** Abyss, Bookpeople, Ingram, Ladyslipper, Moving Books, New Leaf, Pacific Pipeline, Small Changes, and Vision Works. **Canada:** Dempsey (Vancouver). **International:** Airlift (London), Bookpeople (Oakland, CA), and Rotation (Berlin).

Astro-data reprinted with permission from Astro Communications Services, Inc., P.O. Box 34487, San Diego, CA 92163-4487.

This **We'Moon** is bound to lay flat! If you prefer spiral binding, some copy shops can trim and add a spiral binding to individual books.

Disclaimer: any herbal or astrological information herein should be used with caution, common sense, and the approval of your health care practitioner, astrologer, and/or other sources you trust.

Printed with soy-based ink on 100% recycled paper made from de-inked newspapers and magazines, with a minimum of 50% post-consumer fiber, no chlorine bleach used in this process. By using this paper, we save about 97 trees and 51 cubic feet of landfill space.

To order this book directly from Mother Tongue Ink, see page 186.

$13.95 ISBN 0-9510661-8-8

TABLE OF CONTENTS

I. INTRODUCTION

II. MOON CALENDAR*

*Moons feature herbal lore by Colette Gardiner, astrological predictions by Gretchen Lawlor, and holy day descriptions by Dánahy Sharonrose.

III. APPENDIX

We'Moon '97 is dedicated to Terri Jewell (1954–1995).
A Black lesbian feminist poet, writer,
We'Moon Contributor, and editor of
The Black Woman's Gumbo Ya Ya (Crossing Press 1993),
an anthology of quotations by Black women.

"...We are all here, calling out to and reaching one another,
gathering at one another's feet and sharing sustenance that has kept
us alive and moving in the directions we must go."

© *Terri Jewell 1993, excerpted from her introduction*

What do I expect?

I expect magic between us, I expect love. I expect us to
blossom, and to go to seed~to seed new visions, new dreams.
I expect gentle interactions, full of care and respect. I expect
to move in an aura of cooperation, of 'what can I do?' and
'yes, let's explore that.' I expect to be amused by our weak-
nesses as well as our strengths~I expect to laugh heartily over
any little thing. I expect ease, flow, and joy in my life. I
expect to put some effort into creating my life the way I
envision it. I expect to live in peace and harmony. I expect
peace and harmony to live in me.

I expect a group life, a group bond, a group spirit to
emerge. I expect to value, to treasure the group. I expect to
move with the group, to create together our way. I expect to
make an effort to enter into the group energy. I expect to make
myself open to what we are creating. I expect to offer myself
in word, feeling, and action to the growth and well-being of
the whole. I expect the whole to live in me. © *Lee Lanning 1995*

WHAT IS *WE'MOON*?
A HANDBOOK IN NATURAL CYCLES

We'Moon: Gaia Rhythms for Womyn is more than an appointment book. It is a way of life! **We'Moon** is a *handbook in natural rhythm*. As we chart our days alongside other heavenly bodies, we begin to discover patterns in how we interrelate. **We'Moon** comes out of an *international womyn's culture*. Art and writings by we'moon from many lands give a glimpse of the great diversity and uniqueness of a world we create in our own image. **We'Moon** is about *womyn's spirituality* (spirit'reality). We share how we live our truth, what inspires us, how we envision our reality in connection with the whole earth and all our relations.

We'moon means "we of the moon." The moon, whose cycles run in our blood, is the original womyn's calendar. Like the moon, we'moon circle the earth. We are drawn to one another. We come in different shapes, colors, and sizes. We are continually transforming. With all our different hues and points of view, we are one.

We'moon means "women." Instead of defining ourselves in relation to men (as in *wo*man or *fe*male), we use the word *we'moon* to define ourselves by our primary relation to the natural sources of cosmic flow ("we of the moon"). Other terms we'moon use are *womyn, wimmin, womon, womb-one*. **We'Moon** is a moon calendar for we'moon. As we'moon, we seek to be whole in ourselves, rather than dividing ourselves in half and hoping that some "other half" will complete the picture. We see the whole range of life's potential embodied by we'moon, and do not divide the universe into sex-role stereotypes according to the heterosexual model. Instead, **We'Moon** is a sacred space in which to explore and celebrate the diversity of she-ness on earth. The calendar is we'moon's space. We see the goddess equally in the sun and the moon, in the earth and the sky.

We'moon culture exists in the diversity and the oneness of our experience as we'moon. *We honor both.* We come from many cultures, from very different ways of life. At the same time, we have a culture of our own as we'moon, sharing a common mother root. We are glad when we'moon from many different cultures contribute art and writing. When material is borrowed from cultures other than

7

your own, we ask that it be acknowledged and something given in return. Being conscious of our sources keeps us from engaging in the divisiveness of either *cultural appropriation* (taking what belongs to others) or *cultural fascism* (controlling creative expression). We invite every we'moon to share how the "Mother Tongue" speaks to her, with respect for both cultural integrity and individual freedom.

We'moon look into the mirror of the sky to discover patterns regarding how we move here on earth. Like all native and natural earth-loving people since ancient times, we naturally assume a connection with a larger whole of which we are a part.

We show the natural cycles of the moon, sun, planets, and stars as they relate to earth. By recording our own activities side by side with those of other heavenly bodies, we may notice what connection, if any, there is for us.

Gaia Rhythms: The earth revolves around her axis in one day; the moon orbits around the earth in one month ($29^1/_5$ days); the earth orbits around the sun in one year. We experience each of these cycles in the alternating rhythms of day and night, waxing and waning, summer and winter. The earth/moon/sun are our inner circle of kin in the universe. We know where we are in relation to them at all times by the dance of lights and shadows as they circle around one another.

The Eyes of Heaven: As seen from earth, the moon and the sun are equal in size: "the left and right eye of heaven," according to Hindu (Eastern) astrology. Unlike the solar-dominated calendars of Christian (Western) patriarchy,

© *Margaret J. Copfer 1995*

I Will Hold You

the **We'Moon** looks at our experience through both eyes at once, with stars for our third eye. The **lunar eye** of heaven is seen each day in the phases of the moon as she is both reflector and shadow, traveling her 29-day path through all of the zodiac. The **solar eye** of heaven is apparent at the turning points in the sun's cycle. The year begins with Winter Solstice (in the Northern Hemisphere), the dark renewal time, and journeys through many seasons and balance points (solstices, equinoxes, and the cross-quarter days in between). The **third eye** of heaven may be seen in the stars. Astrology measures the cycles by relating the sun, moon, and all other planets in our universe through the *star signs,* helping us to tell time in the larger cycles of the universe.

Measuring Time and Space: Imagine a clock with many hands. The earth is the center from which we view our universe. The sun, moon, and planets are like the hands of the clock. Each one has its own rate of movement through the cycle. The ecliptic, a band of sky around earth within which all planets have their orbits, is the outer band of the clock where the numbers are. Stars along the ecliptic are grouped into constellations forming the signs of the zodiac—the twelve star signs are like the twelve numbers of the clock. They mark the movements of the planets through the 360° circle of the sky, the clock of time and space.

Whole Earth Perspective: It is important to note that all natural cycles have a mirror image from a whole earth perspective. The seasons (summer/winter, spring/fall) are always opposite in the Northern and Southern Hemispheres. Day and night are at opposite times on opposite sides of the earth, east to west. Also, the waxing crescent moon in Australia faces right (e.g., ☾), while in N. America it faces left (e.g., ☽). The **We'Moon** calendar, produced in the northwestern United States, has a Northern Hemisphere perspective regarding times, holidays, seasons and lunar phases..

Whole Sky Perspective: It is also important to note that all over the earth, in varied cultures and times, the dome of the sky has been interacted with in countless ways. *The* zodiac we speak of is one of the many ways that hu-moons have pictured, counted, and related to the stars. In this calendar, we are using the tropical zodiac.

◻ *Musawa*

INTRODUCTION TO THE THEME: WOMYN IN COMMUNITY

Community is not a new idea. It is human nature, Gaia nature. Community is the natural tendency of all beings to group together organically into patterns that form a larger whole—whether mineral, plant, animal, or human, in inner or outer space. Ions do it. Molecules do it. Cells and organisms do it. Societies and solar systems do it. We'moon do it.

The earliest form of human society was tribal. Most people lived their whole lives in closely knit communities that were integrally connected with the natural world around them. *The 'web of life' was not a concept—it was a practiced reality. People felt deeply held in place by each other and their environment in ways we can barely re-imagine. (The Mother Culture) flourished for thousands of years in kinship-based tribal groups across the globe...What seems to have been intact in all those settings were the concentric circles of interconnection: the campfire, the extended family, the tribe, humanity, nature and the mystery of Spirit.* *

Over the past 5000 years, as the ancient Mother ways were usurped, the context for community was uprooted. The power dynamics shifted from all being parts of one whole—with the Earth as our universal Mother—to the fragmented, alienated, isolated individuals of modern technological society. Community values of cooperation, mutual respect and trust were eventually replaced by the rule of divide and conquer, resulting in the mutually destructive cycles of violence and abuse, power over and disempowerment. *Womyn are re/membering the cellular structure of original community and seeking ways to circle back into connection. The missing core in all our self-searching may be community: our ability to trust each other enough to inter/act and stay bonded as we learn how to reweave the web of the world.*

In the Western world, the isolated nuclear family has been one of our primary models for learning about relationship. As we come together in community, we bring with us the dysfunctional patterns of our cultural conditioning. It is not easy to undo the centuries of shame and blame that have taught us to turn against ourselves and each other. *These cycles of 'failure' reinforce the idea that patariarchal values are all that work.* We are not raised with community skills.

© Betty La Duke 1993

When the natural dynamic wisdom of the living whole is missing, we have to expend a tremendous amount of knowledge and energy to reconstruct the interrelation of each tiny strand of the web with every other.

It's time that true community values replace dysfunctional family values! We need to be gentle with ourselves and one another as we learn new ways of responding that are more supportive of our growth. What a miracle it is when one individual can accept the different parts of herself, or two individuals can sustain a healthy relationship with one another, or three or more individuals can share a common purpose.

Ecosystems show us that only in community can different species survive and grow to full maturity. The diversity that comes from supporting the growth of each species' full development enhances the whole community. These same ecological principles are at work in communities based on consensus. *To lose any part of ourselves, to still any voice, to devalue any contribution makes the picture incomplete and destroys the wholeness of the system.* If people can learn what Nature knows about flourishing in community with all our relations, life on earth will thrive.

11

The Tower is the Tarot card we associate numerologically with **We'Moon '97** (97=16=the Tower in the Major Arcana). Community is a power greater than the individual ego, capable of toppling the tower of patriarchy and its power-over politics that permeate all our relationships. Ideally, in community, the whole is greater than the sum of the parts, differences are a source of strength, not divisiveness, and everyone stands to gain by the empowerment of all its members. Community is based on common bonds—the same land, neighborhood, culture; a common purpose, vision, task; an affinity to one another, a sense of belonging, shared values and commitments, a heart connection. *Community is the extension of relationship from the personal to the collective. People give to the community and the community gives back.*

Traditionally, 'women's role' has been to relate, to take care of others, and to create family and community. In most cultures, womyn's community persists in some form or other (the moon lodge, quilting bee, womyn's support groups, etc.). Over the last three decades, womyn's communities have emerged from (and encouraged the growth of) various liberation and civil rights struggles, especially the womyn's liberation movement and the creation of lesbian culture. In this **We'Moon,** we explore womyn's experience of community in our lives today.

What are the ways we'moon come together? Who is the **We'Moon** community we draw from? What motivates community? These and other questions were asked in our Call for Contributions for the **We'Moon '97: Womyn in Community.** One of the concerns that motivated this theme was the difficulty of actually living and working in community. Where are the strengths ... and stuck points? What are the tools for community that have been found to be most helpful? There is a growing body of resources for community building coming out of living and working together: in intentional communities, the consensus process, recovery and support groups, cooperative work projects, collectively run businesses, womyn's lands, spirit-centered circles, indigenous peoples' cultures and we'moon communities as varied as the ones represented in this **We'Moon.**

This year our contributors include African-American, Australian, British, Canadian, Chinese, European-American, Hawaiian, Indian, Native American, Puerto Rican, Scottish and Swedish we'moon. Some forms of community represented within are the Beijing International Women's Conference, the Michigan Womyn's Music Festival, the Indigenous Women's Network, African-American and British theatre groups, Camp SisterSpirit in Mississippi, and H.O.M.E., Inc. in Maine.

Although **We'Moon** comes from and goes to a fairly diverse group of womyn, it is produced by a community of predominately white lesbians of mixed class backgrounds, ranging in age from our twenties to our fifties—living on land with wholistic earth/goddess/womyn-loving feminist politics. We believe it is important to acknowledge our own cultural biases as well as to reach beyond them. We honor the uniqueness of each culture as expressed by we'moon in that culture rather than represented by others 'borrowing' from it. Our common 'Mother Tongue' is each womyn's own experience—as it is embodied in our different lives.

Like Sappho, who lived on the island of Lesbos, in a womyn's community, and wrote love poetry to womyn for all the world to see, we love womyn and want to express the great strength, beauty and creativity of the diverse worlds we are in touch with that we'moon create together.

We need to find the center of the circle again—in ourselves, in the earth, in our communities—and reconnect with the source of wholeness. When we find the center in each one, we are naturally drawn to the center of all. When we learn how to create ways of being that nurture and sustain us in a balanced relation to one another, seeds of community start to sprout and leaf and blossom and fruit again. Womyn, the givers of life, the nurturers and sustainers, the creators and transformers of culture are leading the way. This is the revolutionary potential of womyn in community. □ *Musawa 1996*

** all italics are editorial comments by Christina Baldwin © 1996,
based on her book* Calling the Circle *(Blue Water Publishing, 1996)*

How to Use This Book: Key to the *We'Moon*

Below and on the following pages you will find terms and symbols, with explanations, keyed to their uses in **We'Moon**. See "Signs and Symbols at a Glance" (p. 223) for an easy fingertip reference.

Astrology Basics

Planets: Planets are like chakras in our solar system, allowing for different frequencies or types of energies to be expressed.

Signs: The twelve signs of the zodiac are a mandala in the sky, marking off 30° segments in the 360° circle around the earth. Signs show major shifts in planetary energy through the cycles.

Glyphs: Glyphs are the symbols used to represent planets and signs.

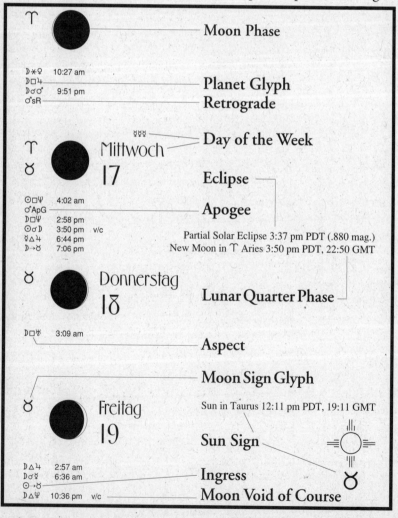

Moon Phase

Planet Glyph

Retrograde

Day of the Week

Eclipse

Apogee

Partial Solar Eclipse 3:37 pm PDT (.880 mag.)
New Moon in ♈ Aries 3:50 pm PDT, 22:50 GMT

Lunar Quarter Phase

Aspect

Moon Sign Glyph

Sun in Taurus 12:11 pm PDT, 19:11 GMT

Sun Sign

Ingress

Moon Void of Course

Features of the Calendar Pages

Sun Sign: The sun enters a new sign once a month (around the 20th or so), completing the whole cycle of the zodiac in one year. For a description of sign qualities see "Sun Signs" (pp. 19–22).

Moon Sign: The moon changes signs approximately every $2^1/_2$ days, going through all twelve signs of the zodiac every $29^1/_5$ days (the sidereal month). The moon sign reflects qualities of your core inner self. For descriptions of these energies see "Moon Signs: Transits" (pp. 23–25).

Moon Phase: Each calendar day is marked with a graphic representation of the phase that the moon is in. Although the moon is not usually visible in the sky during the new or dark moon, we take some artistic license with her representation. For the days before and after the *actual* new moon, we use miniscule crescent moon graphics. For more information about the moon see "The Eight Lunar Phases" and "Where's That Moon?" (pp. 26–28).

Lunar Quarter Phase: At the four quarter points of the lunar cycle (when the moon is new, waxing half, full, and waning half) we indicate the phase, sign, and exact time for each.

Day of the Week: Each day is associated with a planet whose symbol appears in the line above it (e.g., DDD is for Moon: Moonday, Monday, Luna Day, lundi, lunes). Each week the names of the days of the week are in one of four languages (English, German, French, Spanish). You will find Monday through Friday on the left-facing page, Saturday and Sunday on the right-facing page.

Eclipse: The time of greatest eclipse is given, which in general is not the exact time of the conjunction or opposition. For lunar and partial solar eclipses, the magnitude is given, in decimal form (e.g., .881 mag.), which denotes the fraction of the moon's diameter obscured by the shadow of the earth. For total and annular solar eclipses, the duration of the eclipse, in minutes and seconds, is given. For further information see "Eclipses 1997" (p. 199).

Daily Aspectarian

For each calendar day there is a listing of symbols that indicates a variety of planetary movements and relationships. Following are explanations of the various symbols found there.

Aspects: The little squiggles that show the angle of relation between different planets are aspects. An aspect is like an astrological weather forecast for the day, indicating which energies are working together easily and which combinations are more challenging. See "Signs and Symbols at a Glance" (p. 223) for a brief explanation.

Ingresses: Arrows, between planetary and sign glyphs, indicate planets moving into new signs.

☽ v/c—Moon Void of Course: The moon is said to be void of course from the last significant lunar aspect until the moon enters a new sign. The time just before the moon changes into a new sign is a good time to ground and center yourself.

ApG—Apogee: This is the point in the orbit of a planet or the moon that is farthest from earth. The effects of transits at this time may be less noticeable immediately, but may appear later on.

PrG—Perigee: This is the point in the orbit of a planet or the moon that is nearest to earth. Transits with the moon or other planets when they are at perigee will be more intense.

sR or sD—Retrograde or Direct: These are times when a planet moves backward (sR) or forward (sD) through the signs of the zodiac (an optical illusion, as when a moving train passes a slower train which appears to be going backward). When a planet is in direct motion, planetary energies are more straightforward; in retrograde, planetary energies turn back in on themselves, are more involuted.

Other Useful Features of the We'Moon

Annual Predictions: For an astrological portrait of this year for you, you might want to turn to Gretchen Lawlor's prediction for your sun sign. These are located in the calendar pages around the month of your birthday, on the same page where the sun enters a new sign (see p. 17 for an overview for 1997).

Time Zones: All aspects are in Pacific Standard/Daylight Time. To calculate for your area, see "World Time Zones" (p. 29).

Ephemerides are tables that show the exact position of heavenly bodies in degrees, using tabulations of latitude and longitude.

Planetary Ephemeris: Exact planetary positions, for every day, are given in the Ephemeris (pp. 204–209), showing where each planet is in the zodiac at noon GMT (Greenwich Mean Time).

Asteroid Ephemeris: Exact asteroid positions for every ten days are given (p. 203), showing where sixteen asteroids are in the zodiac at midnight GMT.

Month and Year at a Glance Calendars can be found on pp. 210-221 and p. 2, respectively. Month at a Glances indicate daily lunar phases.

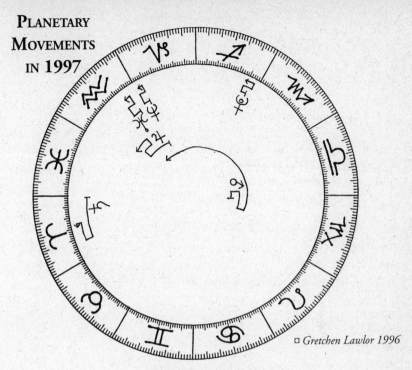

¤ *Gretchen Lawlor 1996*

1997 Overview

Between November 1995 and April 1996 three of the astrological giants—Saturn, Uranus, and Pluto—moved into new territory. This was a time of profound change as we each struggled to find our balance in a new order.

In 1997 we are still in the very early days of a new world. Uranus moves with lightning speed in Aquarius, creating new technology and accelerating the speed and quantity of information available to each of us in all aspects of our lives.

Uranus and Pluto support each other in cocreating new social frameworks. We are experiencing the breakdown of our belief systems, moving us from philosophical or nationalistic isolation to a global outlook. It's painful, even frightening, to admit the inadequacy of our current perspective.

With Saturn in Aries, commit to some bold new effort. Be accountable, in some simple way, for its progress and upkeep.

¤ *Gretchen Lawlor 1996*

YEAR OF THE FIRE OX
February 7, 1997 to January 27, 1998*

The year of the fire Ox is time for hard work. Ox works hard plowing the fields. Success is attained through diligent labor and conscientious effort. Begin by putting your affairs in order, especially your home. Stick to tried and true methods, routine, and conservative actions. Wild new concepts will not be well received. (Save them for next year—Tiger year.) Fire Ox year is not a time for laziness. Those who won't work won't eat.

Oxen and all cattle are blessed by the goddess Kwan Yin because of their gentle, peaceful nature. The ancient Chinese harnessed the ox, but didn't milk it, for they honored this hard-working, strong animal. The golden-haired Ox god, Nia Wang, protected cattle from epidemics. In Buddhism, the white ox symbolizes contemplation and wisdom. Some translations refer to Ox as Buffalo or water Buffalo. Patient, diligent Buffalo correlates to the Western sign Capricorn.

© Susan Levitt 1996

*Chinese New Year begins the second new moon after Winter Solstice.

□ *Tracy Litterick 1989*

Anatolian Ancestors

© A. Kimberlin Blackburn 1989

SUN SIGNS

There are twelve signs in the zodiac, marking off 30° segments in the 360° circle of the sky. As seen from earth, the sun travels through one sign every month, coming full circle around the zodiac in a year. What sign the sun was in when you were born is your *sun sign*. The zodiac starts at Spring Equinox when the sun moves into the sign of Aries. There are different *elements* associated with each sign (*air*—mind, *fire*—spirit, *water*—feelings, *earth*—body) and each element is in a different *modality* (*cardinal*—initiating, *fixed*—sustaining, *mutable*—transforming). These qualities are italicized at the beginning of each sun sign description.

♈ **ARIES** (March 20–April 19). A *cardinal fire* sign ruled by Mars. Aries we'moon love adventure and believe that they are destined to achieve success and make a huge impact on the world. They are passionate, direct, and ruled by their hearts. They are extremely independent and require an environment that allows them to express their creativity and nurture their personal growth. But they must not allow their idealism or enthusiasm to turn into indolent daydreams. In Chinese astrology, Aries the Ram correlates to the magnificent Dragon.

♉ **TAURUS** (April 19–May 20). A *fixed earth* sign ruled by Venus. Taurus we'moon are creative and talented, sensitive, humorous, and caring. They love making friends and creating networks and contacts. They are determined and often strive for things they desire, regardless of circumstances. Yet they have patience. They can be frugal if necessary, but prefer the luxuries of the materially rich life if they can afford them. They must avoid being too stubborn or narrow-minded. In Chinese astrology, Taurus the Bull correlates to the wise Snake.

♊ **GEMINI** (May 20–June 21). A *mutable air* sign ruled by Mercury. Gemini we'moon possess a sunny disposition, are bright, open, and cheerful. They are full of charm and alert in action, and dislike hidden agendas. They find people and crowds exciting for they love parties and are not loners. Because of their carefree nature, they need ample room for self-expression. Gemini we'moon like to tell you what is on their minds. Care must be taken that they do not let their quick opinions alienate others. In Chinese astrology, Gemini the Twins correlates to the popular, fun-loving Horse.

♋ **CANCER** (June 21–July 22). A *cardinal water* sign ruled by the Moon. Cancer we'moon have a gentle, patient, and graceful nature. They are artistic and creative, and have exquisite taste, especially in decorating their home. With a tendency to be introverted, Cancer we'moon resolve problems by contemplating in seclusion. They make decisions based on their accumulated experiences as well as their highly developed intuition. A negative trait could be overindulgence or overspending on luxuries. In Chinese astrology, Cancer the Crab correlates to the kind, artistic Sheep (Ram, Goat).

♌ **LEO** (July 22–August 22). A *fixed fire* sign ruled by the Sun. Leo we'moon are quick-witted, alert, romantic, playful, and extremely talented. In addition to being mentally active, they are full of physical stamina. They are uninhibited and express themselves fearlessly in all areas of life. They are generous and sensitive, and love to help others. They win trust easily and have strong leadership potential. But problems could develop from their being too self-centered and forgetting the big picture. In Chinese astrology, Leo the Lioness correlates to the ingenious, brilliant Monkey.

♍ **VIRGO** (August 22–September 22). A *mutable earth* sign ruled by Mercury. Virgo we'moon possess a sense of duty and pride. They are equipped with keen judgment and sharp wit, and are good planners. They can predict the outcome of any situation and act accordingly. They are quick and flexible. They are perfectionists who care what others think of them. They desire praise for doing a great job. Care must be taken because their criticizing tendencies may drive away others. In Chinese astrology, Virgo the Virgin correlates to the impeccable Rooster.

♎ **LIBRA** (September 22–October 23). A *cardinal air* sign ruled by Venus. Libra we'moon are honest and trustworthy, and make excellent friends because they are always on your side. They won't hesitate to make sacrifices for people and ideas they believe in. When they fall in love, they fall hard. They are dedicated to their partners and therefore are selective in the beginning stages of dating. Care must be taken to remain balanced and not go to extremes. In Chinese astrology, Libra the Scales correlates to the loyal Dog.

♏ **SCORPIO** (October 23–November 21). A *fixed water* sign ruled by Pluto and Mars. Scorpio we'moon make great friends and hurry to the aid of people they love. They have a strong sense of responsibility, and once their mind is set on something they don't easily change their direction. They are devoted to their chosen paths and careers. They don't like to be alone and will actively look for their "other half." Psychic and intuitive, they are attracted to the shamanic and otherworldly. Care must be taken to not become too intense in interactions with others. In Chinese astrology, Scorpio the Scorpion correlates to the sensual Pig (Boar).

♐ **SAGITTARIUS** (November 21–December 21). A *mutable fire* sign ruled by Jupiter. Sagittarius we'moon are clever, sharp, athletic, and humorous. They are observant and quick to take action. They are popular in social circles for they adapt easily to different environments, and their quick wit and broad smiles win admiration wherever they go. They trust their instincts over logic and reality. They are free souls who love adventure and travel. Being in nature is healing for them. Care must be taken to not become scattered or irresponsible. In Chinese astrology, Sagittarius the Archer correlates to the clever Rat.

♑ CAPRICORN (December 21–January 19). A *cardinal earth* sign ruled by Saturn. Capricorn we'moon are hardworking, methodical, independent, and ethical. Noted for their perseverance in attaining their goals, they get the job done. They are self-reliant, and believe deeply in what they are doing. They achieve success step by step. They believe that as long as they apply themselves, they will be recognized and rewarded. They must watch out to not become bitter or frustrated, for their temperament can hinder the success of their endeavors. In Chinese astrology, Capricorn the Sea Goat correlates to the patient, diligent Ox.

♒ AQUARIUS (January 19–February 18). A *fixed air* sign ruled by Uranus. Aquarius we'moon are courageous, sensitive, determined, and charismatic. They aim high and pursue their goals with passion. They stand out in a crowd because they are freethinkers and do not conform to the actions of the masses. Once they make a promise or declaration, count on them to pursue their goal with vigor and speed. They must take care that their loner attitude does not prevent them from seeking assistance when they are faced with an endeavor that requires the resources of another. In Chinese astrology, Aquarius the Water Bearer correlates to the daring, impulsive Tiger.

♓ PISCES (February 18–March 20). A *mutable water* sign ruled by Neptune. Pisces we'moon are intuitive, romantic, friendly, and adaptable. They long for companionship and dislike being alone, so they make every effort to conform. Their kindness and diplomacy make them welcome in social circles. They appreciate and strive to create peaceful and harmonious environments. Because they love peace and beauty and dislike making enemies, they tend to avoid arguments and conflicts. Care must be taken that their fear of conflict does not make them weak or indecisive. In Chinese astrology, Pisces the Fish correlates to the gentle, diplomatic Rabbit (Cat).

© Susan Levitt 1995

□ Emma 1994

© *Mara Friedman 1994*

MOON SIGNS: TRANSITS

Every two and a half days the moon shines her light through one of the twelve signs. This monthly cycle of the moon through the signs is reflected in subtle shifts in our feelings, moods, responses, and expression. When we attune our activities with the lunar flow, we become a channel for the wisdoms of the natural world. Approach each moon cycle as a journey and a teaching.

When the moon is in the same sign as our natal moon sign, we can look within more clearly, center in with our intuitive self, and reconnect with our primary mode of emotionality. Follow the moon around your birth chart, and try to cooperate with and utilize the energies offered with each sign.

During the year, each sign occurs only once as the dark/new moon, and only once as the full moon (except for the periodic doubling of signs); e.g., there is just one full moon in Leo, usually in February when the sun is in the opposite sign of Aquarius, and one dark/new moon in Leo during August when the sun is also in Leo. Expression of a sign is stronger at these times, so watch and celebrate.

23

♈ MOON IN ARIES—This initiating fire sign awakens our creative urges. Our physical energy increases, and restlessness fuels our explorations. We may be quicker to express feelings, attitudes, and desires. Try new approaches, and discover new outlets. Spirit is moving, so channel moon in Aries with your vital willingness to be and to do.

♉ MOON IN TAURUS—Earthy, appreciative Taurus concentrates our energies on the physical plane. This is a good moontime to beautify surroundings and acquire belongings. Our senses are keen, and our intuitive touch can inspire works of art, massage, or lovemaking. We find extra patience to stand our ground. Tend to body needs and pleasures.

♊ MOON IN GEMINI—Plan on play during airy, communicative Gemini. Watch for opportunities for witty verbal exchanges! This is a good time to put energy into friendships, to attend meetings, or study some interest by yourself. Let your curiosity keep you on the move and in the moment.

♋ MOON IN CANCER—Our sensitivity rises to the surface during this watery moon of the Great Mother. Cancerian love for inclusiveness and nurturance feeds our inclinations toward home affairs, family needs, and solitude with ourselves. Tend to emotional needs and healing spaces. Use long baths or walks to center yourself. Cook and share good food.

♌ MOON IN LEO—A generous warmth and vitality comes more easily during this fiery sign of the proud heart. Use Leo's energetic and extroverted energy to inspire self-confidence. Let any dramatic outbursts entertain and feed your creative appetite. Leo generates feelings of being special. Bring home treats for your inner child.

♍ MOON IN VIRGO—Process-oriented and earthy Virgo gets us motivated in the material world. Virgo favors focused intent and self-improvement, so direct your agenda accordingly. Use your critical eye, or someone else will. While cleaning up your act, assess and shore up projects. Tend to health and dietary needs, and address the stress factors in your life.

♎ **MOON IN LIBRA**—Venus-ruled, airy Libra is a mentor of the arts. Beauty, harmony, cooperation, and poetic flow are her gifts. It's a good social-gathering time when the moon entertains Libra. Both friendly attractions and love connections can be delightful. Balance bonds within yourself and significant others in your life.

♏ **MOON IN SCORPIO**—We are intuitive and intense when this fixed water sign surfaces each month. This is a good time for dowsing out the mysteries, using divination and ritual. There is a tendency toward self-absorption; taking private space assists our deep reflection. Intimacies may lead to personal disclosures. Our masks come on or off as passions well up.

♐ **MOON IN SAGITTARIUS**—Fiery Sagittarius inspires our independence, free expression, and gregariousness. Teaching, preaching, and promotional activities come easier during this extroverted sign. Time to move our bodies, so enjoy dance, sports, and travel. With our philosophical, high-minded aspirations, leaps of faith come easily! Keep a sense of humor.

♑ **MOON IN CAPRICORN**—We can ground our intentions with right action in the material world during earthy Capricorn. Let your strength of will and commitment to purpose rise up to meet the occasion. While feelings may be guarded now, channel your ambitions with effort and diligence toward duty. When in doubt, assume importance. Seriously.

♒ **MOON IN AQUARIUS**—Airy Aquarius catalyzes intellectual pursuits and the exchange of ideas. This is a good time for networking with friends, or for community activism. Leave room for impulsiveness. Expect some unique outpourings during this unconventional and offbeat sign. Create with the insightful, visionary qualities of Aquarius. Spread the word.

♓ **MOON IN PISCES**—Our feelings and sensitivities flow during this changeable water sign. When not seeking solitude, we may feel the urge to merge into heart and spirit space. Our moods may be influenced by unconscious motivations or old hurts that surface now. Trust your tears. Channel the intuitive, imaginative energy of Pisces. Let the impressionable poet express herself.

© Sandra Pastorius 1995

Lunar Rhythm

Everything that flows moves in rhythm with the moon. She rules the water element on earth. She pulls on the ocean's tides, the weather, female reproductive cycles, and the life fluids in plants, animals, and people. She influences the underground currents in earth energy, the mood swings of mind, body, behavior, and emotion. The moon is closer to the earth than any other heavenly body. The earth actually has two primary relationships in the universe: one with the moon who circles around her and one with the sun whom she circles around. Both are equal in her eyes. The phases of the moon reflect the dance of all three: the moon, the sun, and the earth, who together weave the web of light and dark into our lives. No wonder so much of our life on earth is intimately connected with the phases of the moon!

◻ *Musawa*

The Eight Lunar Phases

As above, so below. Look into the sky and observe which phase the moon is in. Then you will know where you are in the growth cycle of each lunar month. The phase that the moon was in when you were born reflects your purpose, personality, and preferences.

1. The **new moon** is like a SEED planted in the earth. We cannot see her but she is ready to grow, full of potential and energy for her new journey. We'moon born during the new moon are impulsive, passionate, and intuitive. They are risk takers and pioneers.

2. The **crescent moon** is the SPROUT. The seed has broken through the earth and reaches upward as she ventures from the dark, moist earth she has known. We'moon born during the crescent moon must break from the past, from the culture of their childhood, to create their own destiny. They represent the next generation, the new order that improves on the past.

3. The **first quarter moon** (waxing half moon) is the GROWTH phase. Roots go deeper, the stem shoots up, and leaves form as she creates a new strong body. We'moon born during the first quarter moon live a full life of much activity and excitement as old structures are cleared away to provide room for new developments.

4. The **gibbous moon** is the BUD of the plant, the pulse of life tightly wrapped, wanting to expand. For we'moon born during the gibbous moon, their talents lie in the ability to refine,

organize, and purify. They are seekers, utilizing spiritual tools as guides and allies on their journey to self-discovery.

5. She opens and blossoms during the **full moon** into the FLOWER, with the desire to share her beauty with others. We'moon born during the full moon enjoy companionship and partnership and have a desire to merge deeply. Fulfillment, abundance, and illumination are their goals.

6. As we go into the darkening phase of the **disseminating moon,** we get the FRUIT of the plant's life cycle, the fruits of wisdom and experience. For we'moon born during the disseminating moon, life must have meaning and purpose. They enjoy sharing their beliefs and ideas with others and are often teachers.

7. The **last quarter moon** (waning half moon) is the HARVEST phase, when the plant gives her life so that others may continue theirs. We'moon born during the last quarter have a powerful internal life of reflection and transformation. They can assume different roles and wear many masks while balancing their internal and external worlds.

8. The **balsamic moon** is the COMPOST phase, when the nutrients remain in the soil, providing nourishment for the next new seed. We'moon born during the balsamic moon possess the potential to be wise, insightful, understanding, and patient. They are prophetic and unique, and march to the beat of their own drummer.

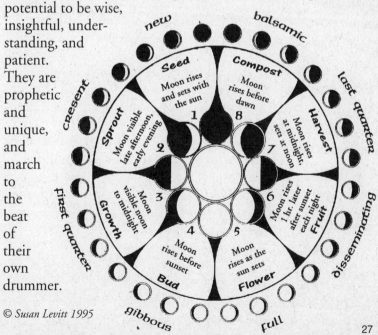

© Susan Levitt 1995

27

WHERE'S THAT MOON ?

Why is the moon sometimes visible during the day? And why does the moon sometimes rise very late at night? The answers lie in what phase the moon is in, which reflects the angle between the sun and moon as seen from earth. For each of the eight moon phases, the angle between the sun and moon progresses in 45° increments. Each phase lasts approximately 3–4 days of the moon's entire 29^1/$_5$ day cycle.

- The **new moon** (or dark moon) rises at sunrise and sets at sunset. Astrologically, the sun and the moon are in *conjunction*. Because the sun's light overpowers the nearby moon in the day, and the moon is on the other side of the earth with the sun at night, she is not visible in the sky at all.

- The **crescent moon** (or waxing crescent moon) rises midmorning and sets after sunset. She is the first visible sliver of moon, seen in the western sky in the late afternoon and early evening.

- The **first quarter moon** (or waxing half moon) rises around noon and sets around midnight. Astrologically, the moon is *square* to the sun. She is visible from the time she rises until she sets.

- The **gibbous moon** rises midafternoon and sets before dawn. She is the bulging moon getting ready to be full, visible soon after she rises until she sets.

- The **full moon** rises at sunset and sets at sunrise. Astrologically, the sun and moon are in *opposition* (ie., opposite each other in the sky and in opposite signs of the zodiac). She is visible all night long, from moonrise to moonset.

- The **disseminating moon** is the waning full moon getting visibly smaller. She rises midevening and sets midmorning. She is visible from the time she rises almost until she sets.

- The **last quarter moon** (or waning half moon) rises around midnight and sets around noon. Astrologically, the moon is *square* to the sun. She is visible from the time she rises until she sets.

- The **balsamic moon** (or waning crescent moon) rises before dawn and sets midafternoon. She is the last sliver of moon, seen in the eastern sky in the dawn and the very early morning.

WORLD TIME ZONES

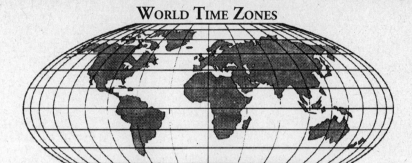

| ID | NT | CA | YST | PST | MST | CST | EST | AST | BST | AT | WAT | GMT | CET | EET | BT | USSR | USSR | USSR | SST | CCT | JST | GST | USSR | ID |
LW	BT	HT														Z3	Z4	Z5					Z10	LE
-12	-11	-10	-9	-8	-7	-6	-5	-4	-3	-2	-1	0	+1	+2	+3	+4	+5	+6	+7	+8	+9	+10	+11	+12
-4	-3	-2	-1	0	+1	+2	+3	+4	+5	+6	+7	+8	+9	+10	+11	+12	+13	+14	+15	+16	+17	+18	+19	+20

STANDARD TIME ZONES FROM WEST TO EAST CALCULATED FROM PST AS ZERO POINT:

IDLW:	International Date Line West	-4
NT/BT:	Nome Time/Bering Time	-3
CA/HT:	Central Alaska & Hawaiian Time	-2
YST:	Yukon Standard Time	-1
PST:	Pacific Standard Time	0
MST:	Mountain Standard Time	+1
CST:	Central Standard Time	+2
EST:	Eastern Standard Time	+3
AST:	Atlantic Standard Time	+4
NFT:	Newfoundland Time	+4 1/2
BST:	Brazil Standard Time	+5
AT:	Azores Time	+6
WAT:	West African Time	+7
GMT:	Greenwich Mean Time	+8
WET:	Western European Time (England)	+8
CET:	Central European Time	+9
EET:	Eastern European Time	+10
BT:	Bagdhad Time	+11
IT:	Iran Time	+11 1/2
USSR	Zone 3	+12
USSR	Zone 4	+13
IST:	Indian Standard Time	+13 1/2
USSR	Zone 5	+14
NST:	North Sumatra Time	+14 1/2
SST:	South Sumatra Time & USSR Zone 6	+15
JT:	Java Time	+15 1/2
CCT:	China Coast Time	+16
MT:	Moluccas Time	+16 1/2
JST:	Japanese Standard Time	+17
SAST:	South Australian Standard Time	+17 1/2
GST:	Guam Standard Time	+18
USSR	Zone 10	+19
IDLE:	International Date Line East	+20

HOW TO CALCULATE TIME ZONE CORRECTIONS IN YOUR AREA:

ADD if you are **east** of PST (Pacific Standard Time); **SUBTRACT** if you are **west** of PST on this map (see right-hand column of chart above).

All times in this calendar are calculated from the West Coast of North America where it is made. Pacific Standard Time (PST Zone 8) is zero point for this calendar except during Daylight Savings Time (April 6–October 26, 1997, during which times are given for PDT Zone 7). If your time zone does not use Daylight Savings Time, add one hour to the standard correction during this time. Time corrections for GMT are also given for major turning points in the moon and sun cycles. At the bottom of each page EST/EDT (Eastern Standard or Daylight Time) and GMT (Greenwich Mean Time) times are also given. For all other time zones, calculate your time zone correction(s) from this map and write it on the inside cover for easy reference.

THE WHEEL OF THE YEAR: HOLY DAYS

The seasonal cycle of the year is created by the tilt of the earth's axis as she leans toward the sun in the north or south at different points in her annual dance. *Solstices* are the extremes in the sun cycle (like new and full moon) when days and nights are either longest or shortest. At *equinoxes* days and nights are equal (like

©*Thela Brown 1994*

the waxing or waning half moons). The four *cross-quarter days* roughly mark the midpoints in between the solstices and equinoxes, giving eight seasonal "holy days" based on the natural cycles.

If you do not find your traditional holiday in the **We'Moon**, look for the nearest lunar or solar cycle turning point and it is bound to be very close. At the root of all people's cultures—if you dig far enough—is a reverence for Mother Earth and a celebration of the natural cycles throughout the seasons of earth's passage in relation to her closest relatives in the universe. Only the names, dates and specific events of the holidays have changed through the ages according to the prevailing culture. There are still cultures (such as Hindu, Jewish, Muslim and Buddhist) that honor the lunar cycles by celebrating holidays on new and full moons.

We use the fixed dates from the Gregorian calendar for the cross-quarter days, although traditionally they are lunar holidays. Traditionally Beltane (May Day) and Lammas (Lugnasadh) are full moon festivals at which fertile, abundant, creative energy is celebrated while Samhain (Hallowmas) and Imbolc (Candlemas) are dark moon festivals, when death and rebirth, the crone and the underworld journey are celebrated. The cross-quarter days are fire festivals celebrating the height of each season, when the subtle shifts in energy, initiated at the balance points of solstice and equinox, begin to be visible in nature. For example, the increasing amount of daylight that begins at Winter Solstice becomes noticeable by Imbolc.

◻ *Musawa*

O. OUTSIDE THE CIRCLE MOON

□ Shoshana Rothaizer 1977

Walking down the Path at Limesaddle

Living
in isolation
from
friends, family
i am
independent
self-
sufficient
sustaining
reliant
yet
lonely.

Longing
for community
with
values shared
earth cycles respected
diversity accepted
i dream
independence
self-
sufficiency
sustenance
reliance
and
interconnection.
□ Guida Veronda 1995

Window Shopper

peering through the pane of other women's lives
is safe

huddled in the shadows, I am free
to move on

always free
to move on

their lives captured in frames like photographs—
easy to romanticize
easy to imagine what they have
I don't

easy to move on

restless,
wrapped in ego
clinging to myself—
my lonesome self—
against the night

wide-open
gaping
in an emptiness that offers no resistance
or refuge

waiting for the face to turn
from cozy glow of quilted domesticity
and catch a glimpse of me

waiting for the handle of impenetrable doors
to turn as if by magic,
swing open, welcome—
welcome to your home!

and hear my startled self
shattering illusion
with the solid clatter of my boots
down these familiar empty streets—
again

□ *Carolyn Gage 1995*

© Cora Yee 1988

I am a winter woman
comforted by the quiet white quilt
a million tiny crystals
pieced together
by our Mother

◻ *Ann Marie Mitchell 1995*

♉ ♊	🌒	**Saturday** 21			*Solstice*

☽△☿ 12:19 am
☉→♑ 6:07 am
☽△♃ 7:56 am
☽△♂ 1:02 pm   ☽→♊ 9:18 pm
☽△♆ 2:43 pm   v/c   ☽⚹♄ 11:02 pm

♑

Sun in Capricorn 6:07 am PST, 14:07 GMT

♊	🌒	**Sunday** 22

☽△♅ 2:27 am
☉□♄ 4:10 am
☽☍♇ 4:53 am
☽☍♀ 10:14 am

December

ⅅⅅⅅ

♊ ○ **Monday**
23

♅sR 11:40 am
☽□♂ 11:30 pm v/c

© Cora Yee 1988

Dream Wanderer

♂♂♂

♊ ○ **Tuesday**
♋ ## 24

♂△♆ 3:12 am
☽→♋ 6:15 am
☽□♄ 8:13 am
☉☍☽ 12:42 pm

☿☿☿   Full Moon in ♋ Cancer 12:42 pm PST, 20:42 GMT

♋ ○ **Wednesday**
25

☽☍☿ 6:47 pm

♃♃♃

♋ ○ **Thursday**
♌ ## 26

☽☍♃ 5:03 am
☽☍♆ 10:28 am
☽✳︎♂ 12:03 pm v/c
☽→♌ 5:10 pm
☽△♄ 7:23 pm
☽☍♅ 11:11 pm

♀♀♀

♌ ☽ **Friday**
27

☽△♇ 1:37 am
☽△♀ 8:39 pm v/c

All aspects in Pacific Standard Time; add 3 hours for EST; add 8 hours for GMT

Futures

I was taught two possible futures.

A family, dusty and crusty in relics, congealed.
A house, dusty piano and husband
knee-deep in laundry, children's toys, like mire
feeling like I want to fly, but out
there I would have to learn to do things,
take the bus, walk alone, meet people.

Or: Alone, one adventure one place one lover
after another
always scrambling for a foothold for
a moment to take a breath but
never loved for very long, always
imagining how restful if someone asked me to stay.

There must be worlds
where I could love, trust,
be trusted enough to never forget
how to fly run walk.

I cannot yet imagine such a place.

© Josée Lafrenière 1995

ꙮ ꙮ ꙮ

♌ ◗ Saturday
         28

☽ApG   9:23 pm

◉◉◉

♌ ◗ Sunday
♍   29

♉→♏   4:10 am
☽→♍   5:46 am
☽□♇   2:33 pm
☉△☽ 11:53 pm

Dezember

♍ **Montag**
30

D△♀ 11:32 am
D□♀ 4:49 pm

© Cora Yee 1988

Conversations

♍ **Dienstag**
♎ **31**

D△♃ 8:42 am
D△♆ 12:10 pm
D♂♂ 5:03 pm v/c
D→♎ 6:33 pm
D☍♄ 9:14 pm

♎ **Mittwoch**
1

Januar 1997

D△♅ 1:07 am
D⚹♇ 3:20 am
☉♂♅ 5:23 pm
D□♅ 5:42 pm
☉□D 5:46 pm

Waning Half Moon in ♎ Libra 5:46 pm PST
1:46 GMT

♎ **Donnerstag**
2

☿PrG 9:13 am
D⚹♀ 11:18 am
D□♃ 8:51 pm
D□♆ 11:12 pm v/c

♎ **Freitag**
♏ **3**

♂→♎ 12:11 am
D→♏ 5:03 am
D□♅ 11:29 am
D⚹☿ 9:27 pm

All aspects in Pacific Standard Time; add 3 hours for EST; add 8 hours for GMT

Woven Too Tightly

A circle of women, weaving in and out of each other, moving pulsing growing stronger moving away, always in motion. Ties would glow with added strength, then quietly fade to ember's light, still holding, still tight, but unnoticed for a time. And then one day a tie with too much heat exploded, sending the circle into uncontrolled spinning, wild. The ties that were dimmest snapped in two while those that could hold were covered in soot and ash, dulling their shine to near extinction. Flailing, loose-ended, each woman tried to find what was right, to explain what had happened, to salvage what was left. But the wake from destruction, so powerful, had shifted all the ties.

Some that survived the initial blast were cut in the name of cleanliness. Others took months of digging debris to prove that they were strong. But always the truth remained bare to see: the circle had become a line.

© *Lyena Strelkoff 1995*

© *A. Kimberlin Blackburn 1986*
Cane Counsel

Community Ramble

For me, community is a journey. Concepts of community roll like a snowball, picking up ideas, growing with each revolution. First community, the one we grow up in, is where interactions that we recreate or avoid at all costs are codified in our psyches. Yoga principles extended my parents' teachings. The introspection and focus in yoga communities prepared me to fully experience the ribald camaraderie of New York dyke life; in turn the wimmin of Lesbian Feminist Liberation dispelled my shyness and reticence. My big old loft served as a wimmin's hostelry and gathering place. Clearly I was at heart a Lesbian Feminist innkeeper. The loft brought Amoja and me together, and we left it to work and live at what we were led to believe was a wimmin's community and conference center. There, after much angst and protracted drama, I learned what community is **not**. With credit cards and what remained of my life savings, we bought an escape vehicle, six gourds, beads, and string and launched the craft business we called Market Wimmin. None of the rules for starting a business were applicable. We survived because the larger wimmin's community provided opportunities to sell and to do work exchange for table fees. Wimmin from Mississippi to Minnesota, from New England to Iowa, put us up in their homes. Working hard 200 days a year selling at events, we paid off the truck and most of the credit cards. When our rented 160-year-old log cabin burned to the ground, destroying gourds, tools, history books, papers, notes, and everything else, it was the extended community, gathered over years of events and festivals, that came to our rescue. Donations of clothing, cash, books, and tools kept us afloat, kept us connected. Through all of this we continued to gather the insights, inspiration, and resources needed to pursue the vision of Maat Dompim, a project that would facilitate community-building from the theoretical to the practical: a nonprofit, ecologically based rural retreat and conference center, designed to foster intergroup understanding and skills. After ten years of struggle and synthesis of evolving definitions, we finally approach our destination and I am well on the way to actually becoming a Lesbian Feminist innkeeper.

□ *Blanche M. Jackson 1995*

I. VISIONS OF COMMUNITY MOON

Mujeres Unidas

© *Marsha Gómez 1995*

janvier

♐ 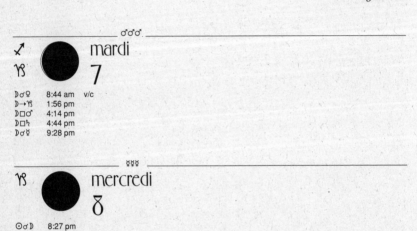 **lundi**
6

⟩⟩⟩

Creative
Chaos

Cohesive
Coexistence

☼ *Ní Aódagaín 1995*

σσσ

♐
♑ **mardi**
7

☽σ♀   8:44 am   v/c
☽→♑   1:56 pm
☽□σ   4:14 pm
☽□♄   4:44 pm
☽σ♅   9:28 pm

☿☿☿

♑ **mercredi**
8

☉σ☽   8:27 pm

♃♃♃

♑
♒ **jeudi**
9

New Moon in ♑ Capricorn 8:27 pm PST
4:27 GMT

σ☍♄   2:54 am
♃σ♇   3:41 am
☽σ♇   9:30 am   ☽△σ   5:09 pm
☽σ♃   9:34 am   v/c   ☽σ♅   8:01 pm
☽→♒   2:01 pm   ☽✶♇   9:26 pm
☽✶♄   4:57 pm   ♀→♑   9:33 pm

♀♀♀

♒ **vendredi**
10

☽PrG   12:46 am
♀✶♂   3:42 pm

All aspects in Pacific Standard Time; add 3 hours for EST; add 8 hours for GMT

Community Hope Chest

I am going to retire.
I am leaving the battleground.
I am not turning tail or giving up,
I am marching purposefully away
    from the enemy.

Community is the enemy:
Community which is planned,
Community which is walled,
Community which is uncom-
    municative and stagnant.

I see lonely old women in tiny apartments.
I see acres of similar houses, similar families, similar jobs.
I am dancing toward a new life.
I am dancing toward community:

Community which has a diverse and interactive population,
Community which is nurturing, not stifling,
Community which is based on reciprocity and responsibility,
Community which grows organically from deep passion.

I see two houses connected by a garden.
I see five strong womyn around an apple tree.
I see concentric circles of friends and family spreading
    across the planet.
I see many wise old womyn marking the seasons and
    years together.

Welcome to our community!   © *Suzannah Dalzell 1995*

♒
♓

samedi
11

♀□♄	11:17 am
☽→♓	1:51 pm
☽✳♀	5:33 pm
☽✳☿	6:43 pm
☽□♇	9:31 pm
♀□♂	10:36 pm

♓

dimanche
12

| ☿♂♀ | 6:31 am |
| ☿ ☽ | 12:41 pm |

enero

© Kathy Crabbe 1995

Aquarius

ⅮⅮⅮ

♓
♈   lunes
13

☉⚹☽	4:11 am
☽⚹♆	10:49 am
☽⚹♃	12:16 pm v/c
☽→♈	3:22 pm
☽☌♄	6:58 pm
☽☍♂	8:30 pm
☽□♅	8:37 pm

☽⚹♅	10:12 pm
☽△♇	11:32 pm

♂♂♂

♈   martes
14

☽□♀	12:07 am

☿☿☿

♈
♉   miércoles
15

☉□☽	12:02 pm
☽□♆	3:00 pm
☽□♃	5:19 pm v/c
☽→♉	7:40 pm

♃♃♃   Waxing Half Moon in ♈ Aries 12:02 pm PST, 20:02 GMT

♉   jueves
16

☽△☿	2:31 am
☽□♅	3:08 am
☽△♀	10:28 am

♀♀♀

♉ ◗ viernes
17

☉☌♆	4:34 am
♆ApG	7:47 am
♃ApG	9:54 am
☽△♆	10:08 pm
☉△☽	11:36 pm

All aspects in Pacific Standard Time; add 3 hours for EST; add 8 hours for GMT

Year at a glance for AQUARIUS ≈ (Jan. 19–Feb. 18)

Jupiter, planet of opportunity, is in your sign from late January 1997 until early February 1998. Take advantage of this to push your luck; take chances, the stars are on your side. Jupiter joins Uranus, planet of inspiration and sudden change, which has been in Aquarius for a year. This is a good time to be adventurous. Trust your intuition.

You need to deepen your outlook and bring a more universal, visionary quality into your life. You've felt this coming for a few years, in your restlessness and discontent. Through dreams or meditations, try to open to the collective mind. Go beyond the ordinary approaches of people around you. There's an unmet need out there and you are the person to fill it. New goals appear on your horizon, filling you with excitement and purpose. A friend may be the link to new ventures.

Doors open everywhere. It's important to make your connections in person whenever possible. Contacts made in 1997 will be helpful to you for years. Think of this as a time for seeding; it will be hard to stay focused on any one thing. Later you will have to thin the crop, but for now just plant seeds wherever opportunities present themselves.

Where are the pitfalls? Not everyone will be able to rise to your expectations and visions, or even understand what you are talking about. Petty problems and daily routines thwart your lofty ambitions—cars break down, computers malfunction, mail gets lost. What helps? Get philosophical about adversity. Don't beat yourself up, or isolate yourself. Take time and care in communications with others. You may return to school for new training or to learn how to get your ideas across more effectively.

◻ *Gretchen Lawlor 1996*

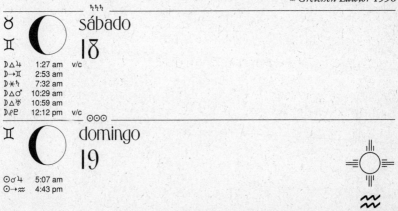

ħħħ

♉
Ⅱ **sábado**
18

☽△♃ 1:27 am v/c
☽→Ⅱ 2:53 am
☽⚹♄ 7:32 am
☽△♂ 10:29 am
☽△♅ 10:59 am
☽☍♇ 12:12 pm v/c

○○○

Ⅱ **domingo**
19

☉♂♃ 5:07 am
☉→≈ 4:43 pm

Sun in Aquarius 4:43 pm PST, 0:43 GMT (Jan. 20)

MOON I

January

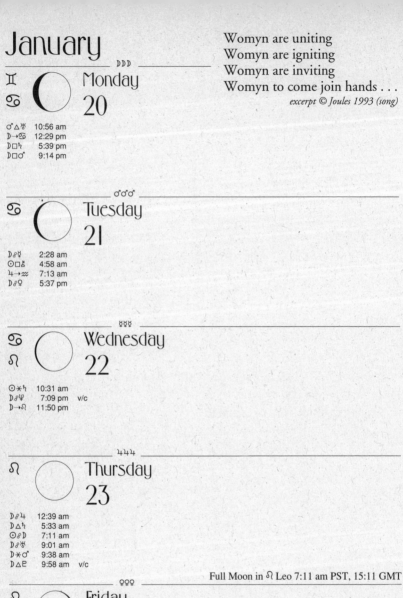

♊
♋

♍♍♍

Monday
20

♂△♅	10:56 am
☽→♋	12:29 pm
☽□♄	5:39 pm
☽□♂	9:14 pm

♋

♂♂♂

Tuesday
21

☽⚹♀	2:28 am
☉□♃	4:58 am
♃→♒	7:13 am
☽⚹♀	5:37 pm

♋
♌

☿☿☿

Wednesday
22

☉⚹♄	10:31 am	
☽⚹♆	7:09 pm	v/c
☽→♌	11:50 pm	

♌

♃♃♃

Thursday
23

☽⚹♃	12:39 am	
☽△♄	5:33 am	
☉⚹☽	7:11 am	
☽⚹♅	9:01 am	
☽⚹♂	9:38 am	
☽△♇	9:58 am	v/c

Full Moon in ♌ Leo 7:11 am PST, 15:11 GMT

♌

♀♀♀

Friday
24

☉♂♅	5:53 am
☉△♂	4:25 pm
☉⚹♇	4:38 pm
♂⚹♇	6:20 pm

All aspects in Pacific Standard Time; add 3 hours for EST; add 8 hours for GMT

Stronger Than Blood

Community is how I choose where I live. Community is the women who are there for me and who want me to be there for them, the women who are real and present. They are the women who respect me and know that they are worthy of the respect I accord them. They are the women who make me laugh, the women who make me cry, the women who confront me instead of walking away and complaining behind my back; and they are the women who ultimately appreciate me doing that for them. They are glorious, magnificent, gorgeous women. They are the women who are growing and looking at themselves, who dare to speak the truth and show what they feel. These are powerful women, women with strong tears and deep feelings, women who know themselves and know their fears, women who face the world with their heads held high, and refuse to carry the burden of society's idea of what a woman should be. They are passionate, intense, and bold. They listen to the music of their souls, and follow their heart's desires. They are women who walk with eyes wide open and meet your gaze without flinching. They are healed and healing. This is my community. These are the women who will drum and sing around my body when I die.   ¤ *Mikaya Heart 1995*

♌
♍   ◗   Saturday
25

ⱵApG   2:23 am
☽ApG   8:44 am
☽→♍   12:26 pm
☽□♇   10:50 pm

♍   ◗   Sunday
26

☽△♉   2:09 pm

Community
© *Sudie Rakusin 1993*

Januar

♍ ◗))) **Montag**
27

☽△♀ 8:56 am
☽△♆ 9:01 pm v/c

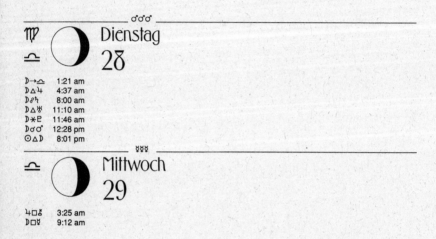

♍
♎ ◗ ♂♂♂ **Dienstag**
28

☽→♎ 1:21 am
☽△♃ 4:37 am
☽♂♄ 8:00 am
☽△♅ 11:10 am
☽✶♇ 11:46 am
☽♂♂ 12:28 pm
☉△☽ 8:01 pm

♎ ◗ ☿☿☿ **Mittwoch**
29

♃□♄ 3:25 am
☽□♅ 9:12 am

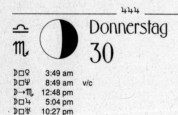

♎
♏ ◖ ♃♃♃ **Donnerstag**
30

☽□♀ 3:49 am
☽□♆ 8:49 am v/c
☽→♏ 12:48 pm
☽□♃ 5:04 pm
☽□♅ 10:27 pm

♏ ◖ ♀♀♀ **Freitag**
31

☉□☽ 11:40 am

Waning Half Moon in ♏ Scorpio 11:40 am PST, 19:40 GMT

All aspects in Pacific Standard Time; add 3 hours for EST; add 8 hours for GMT

Living an Island Vision

I was born on an island in the middle of the Pacific. My community of mostly Hawaiians was the only thing I knew for many years. I live on land that my great-grandparents, grandparents, and parents lived on.

An island woman, indigenous and proud. Songs, rituals, native foods, traditions, respect for the land, for the elders and their sacred stories. I didn't know there was any other way to be.

When I'm driving down the street, greetings come from nearly every car that passes. It's my cousin, my dad, my neighbor, my classmate. All of them familiar. There's a safety in knowing nearly everyone on the island. People ask, "How can you live in a place where everyone knows your business?" The thought comes that something might be wrong with that. A white concept I suppose. So everyone knows me. I like that.

These familiar people watched me grow up. They saw me get married, get divorced. They watched me grieve when my baby died, they saw me through my triumphs and my losses.

As a singer and keeper of traditional songs I am very visible. I am well-known, well-liked, and respected.

The latest thing my community witnessed was me coming home after a year in San Francisco with a new lover. A woman. A white woman. Victoria. Will they accept me? Will they accept her? What will happen to my place in the community?

It was frightening to think of being an outcast. Well, my questions got answered as I began to weave myself back into the community. I have been greeted with opened arms, smiles, and kisses. Victoria, too, has been welcomed.

People are a lot more relaxed here. Not so much in their heads. It's a body kind of place, Hawaii.

I'm so glad to have been raised by my grandparents. Hearing the ways of old and learning them firsthand was an experience I'll always treasure. So, we sit on the lanai and watch the whales. My sister drops by to "talk story" and we watch her children play.

Ah . . . my home . . . Moloka'i.

□ *Zelie Kūliaikanu'u Duvauchelle 1995*

Imbolc: February 2   New Moon in Aquarius

Imbolc, also known as Brigid (later renamed Candlemas by the Christians), is a cross-quarter fire festival, halfway between Winter Solstice and Spring Equinox. The newborn moon of Winter becomes the infant crescent moon of early Spring. Under the waxing light of the Aquarian sun, we honor Februa, Goddess of Purification, and Brigid, Irish Triple Goddess of Poetry, Healing, and Smithcraft.

This is the time of individuation, when we dare to become our own person. The time of the unpossessed virgin Goddess, expressed through the essential, anarchistic feminine principle of Inner Power. Take time to be alone. Purify a sacred space for yourself. Take courage from the words of Susan B. Anthony, born February 14, truly a daughter of Brigid:

Cautious, careful people, always casting about to preserve their reputation and social standing, never can bring about a reform. Those who are really in earnest must be willing to be Anything and Nothing in the world's estimation, and publicly and privately in season and out avow their sympathies with despised and persecuted ideas and their advocates and bear the consequences. Blessed be!

excerpt ©
Dánahy Sharonrose 1996

© *Suzanne Benton 1994*
The Signing

When the Ship Sets Sail

When the ship sets sail will you be on board?
Our three-masted carrack will take us toward
northern shores. Even in the smallest winds
we'll maneuver as if we had whale fins
to swish us through channels and along leeward

coasts where the chinook salmon go, into fjords
and around ice floes. You are the breeze, untethered.
You're the discovery. It's you, you will find
when the ship sets sail.

This ocean-going vessel has a song that's been heard
echoing 'round the rim. All voices are honored;
we work as one crew yet we're each one of a kind.
If you don't come this day, we'll catch you next time.
We'll keep you posted. We'll put out the word
when the ship sets sail.

© Shirley Kishiyama 1995

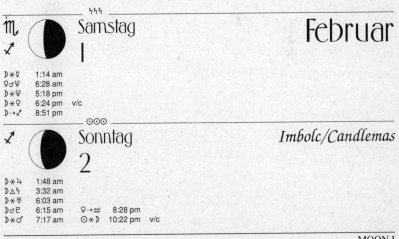

♏︎
♐︎
ᚻᚻᚻ
Samstag
1

Februar

☽✶♅	1:14 am	
♀☌♆	6:28 am	
☽✶♆	5:18 pm	
☽✶♀	6:24 pm	v/c
☽→♐︎	8:51 pm	

♐︎
◎◎◎
Sonntag
2

Imbolc/Candlemas

☽✶♃	1:48 am		
☽△♄	3:32 am		
☽✶♅	6:03 am		
☽☌♇	6:15 am	♀→♒︎	8:28 pm
☽✶♂	7:17 am	☉✶☽	10:22 pm	v/c

MOON I

février

♐ lundi
3

♂♂♂

♐
♑ mardi
4

D→♑	12:44 am
D□♄	7:17 am
D□♂	10:32 am
♀□♃	10:47 am

☿☿☿

♑ mercredi
5

♅⚹♇	2:48 am	
♂ R	4:37 pm	
♀♂♃	5:48 pm	
D♂♅	6:17 pm	
D♂♆	10:29 pm	v/c

♃♃♃

♑
♒ jeudi
6

D→♒	1:21 am			
♀⚹♄	3:34 am			
D♂♃	7:17 am			
D⚹♄	7:55 am			
D♂♀	8:16 am	D♂♅	9:53 am	
D⚹♇	9:48 am	D△♂	10:43 am	

♀♀♀

♒ vendredi
7

♀⚹♇	3:06 am	
♀♂♅	4:44 am	
☉♂D	7:06 am	v/c
DPrG	12:51 pm	
♀△♂	1:33 pm	
♅♂♆	4:31 pm	

Lunar Imbolc
New Moon in ♒ Aquarius 7:06 am PST, 15:06 GMT

All aspects in Pacific Standard Time; add 3 hours for EST; add 8 hours for GMT

Africa: Pounding Millet, Sharing Dreams

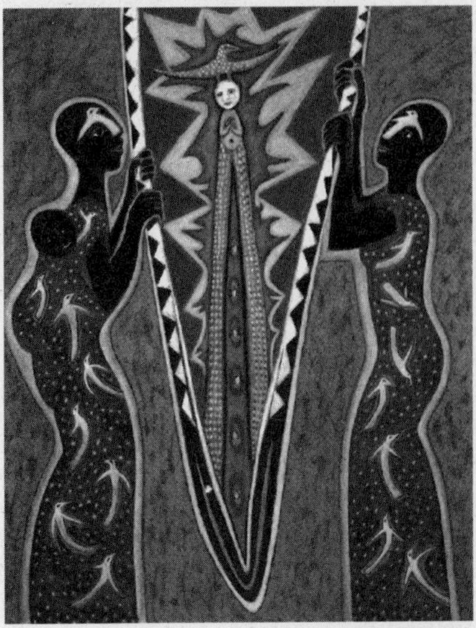

© *Betty La Duke 1993*

Birch *Betula* spp.

Birch is synonymous with beginnings; in some cultures its name literally means "birth." Its beautiful snowy-white bark and twigs are the parts used medicinally. The tea is used as a cleanser and tonic in birch beer and root beer. Tea taken internally or added to the bath has a mild anti-inflammatory effect on swollen and stiff joints. Place images or writing expressing your visions in a birch basket to protect and birth your dreams.

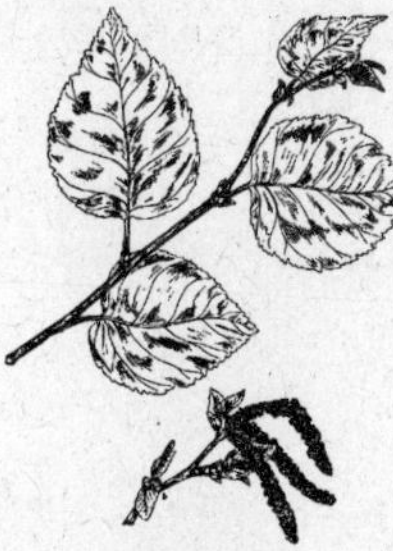

© *Colette Gardiner 1996*

♄♄♄

♒ ♓

samedi

8

☽→♓ 12:34 am
☽□♇ 9:02 am
☿→♒ 9:53 pm

☉☉☉

♓

dimanche

9

♃✱♄ 7:32 am
☽✱♆ 9:46 pm v/c

A Decade of Homesteading on Open Womyn's Land

Ten years ago, my goal in coming to Oregon Womyn's Land (OWL) was to learn how to put seed in the ground and grow my own food; to learn how to chop wood, cook on a woodstove, and take care of a two-year-old in diapers without running water or electricity. As well, I had begun the enormous task of taking OWL back from years of misuse and lack of care. *(1985)*

Many changes occurred at OWL, as new interest in womyn's land took hold in the Lesbian Nation. What had been, up to this time, a mostly solitary work of maintaining the buildings, welcoming visitors, and tending the small garden, would, in this year and a half, become the work of two, then three, then six. By winter of 1990 twelve womyn made their home at OWL, and the work of building community began. *(1988–1990)*

I have come to understand that there are skills we must gain to create true community, the first being to respect each other for the unique individuals we are. Inherent in that is the recognition of our differences. Our diversity is the source of our strength. *(1991)*

By June, only five of the twelve womyn remained. The difficult work of living in community was the catalyst for several womyn to return to the city. New womyn came, and the continuity that living on land provides gave structure and order to this transition time. *(1992)*

The wimmin of OWL are still in the throes of birthing, creating a new way of living on the earth as womyn. To step away from the mainstream culture, to relinquish old conditioning, to envision new forms of family, tribe, community, and to live this vision out in a daily way is very hard work. No birthing is without labor and pain. May our minds and hearts be open enough to allow for all the internal and external changes we must each make. Womyn's land is womyn's home. Blessed be. ▫ *Ní Aódagaín 1996, excerpted and reprinted from* A Decade of Homesteading on Open Women's Land *1995 and* OWL Trust Newsletter *(April 1989, December 1991, April 1992)*

II. WOMYN'S LAND MOON

STOP
TRIDENT

febrero

⟨ DDD ⟩ ——————————

♓   ◑   lunes
♈   10

D→♈	12:29 am		
D⚹♉	3:24 am		
D♂♂	7:57 am		
D⚹♃	8:10 am	D⚹♅	9:43 am
♉□♃	8:13 am	D☍♂	9:58 am
D△♇	9:21 am	D⚹♀	4:39 pm

First Quarter Moon

© Sandra Calvo 1993

⟨ ♂♂♂ ⟩ ——————————

♈   ◑   martes
        11

| ☉⚹D | 3:22 pm |
| ♂△♅ | 4:06 pm |

⟨ ☿☿☿ ⟩ ——————————

♈   ◑   miércoles
♉   12

D□♆	12:10 am	v/c	
D→♉	2:56 am		
☿⚹♄	3:33 am		
☿♂♃	10:22 am		
D□♃	11:59 am	☿⚹♇	2:47 pm
D□☿	12:10 pm	☿△♂	5:29 pm
D□♅	12:59 pm	☿♂♅	7:57 pm

⟨ ♃♃♃ ⟩ ——————————

♉   ◐   jueves
        13

D□♀	1:29 am
♃⚹♇	4:41 pm
♂△♃	9:07 pm

⟨ ♀♀♀ ⟩ ——————————

♉   ◐   viernes
♊   14

☉□D	12:58 am		
♄ R	2:39 am		
♂⚹♇	5:05 am		
D△♆	6:04 am	v/c	
D→♊	8:53 am	D☍♇	7:06 pm
D⚹♄	6:16 pm	D△♃	7:34 pm
D△♂	6:58 pm	D△♅	7:52 pm

Waxing Half Moon in ♉ Taurus 12:58 am PST, 8:58 GMT

——————————————————————

All aspects in Pacific Standard Time; add 3 hours for EST; add 8 hours for GMT

¤ Rashani 1995

Earthsong (Na Mele O Ka Aina) is a women's community/retreat center on the Big Island, also known as Hawai'i. It is a healing sanctuary where the many, everchanging aspects and archetypes of the Divine Feminine are invited, without exception . . . It is a place where women from all ethnic, racial, social, and spiritual backgrounds come together to explore and celebrate diversity and interconnectedness while redefining *power* and *sacredness* and co-creating a feminine-based paradigm.

excerpt ¤ Rashani 1995

♊ ⬕ sábado
15

☽△♅	2:07 am
☽△♀	3:05 pm
♃♂♅	6:22 pm

♊ ⬕ domingo
♋ 16

♂⚻♄	9:14 am	
☉△☽	2:56 pm	v/c
☽→♋	6:13 pm	

February

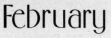

♋

Monday
17

☽□♂ 4:11 am
☽□♄ 4:35 am

Under the Blanket

© Nancy Ann Jones 1995

♂♂♂

♋

Tuesday
18

☉→♓ 6:52 am

♓

Sun in Pisces 6:52 am PST, 14:52 GMT

☿☿☿

♋
♌

Wednesday
19

☽☍♆ 3:09 am v/c
☽→♌ 5:52 am
♄△♇ 8:43 am
☽⚹♂ 3:18 pm
☽△♇ 5:01 pm   ☽☍♅ 6:16 pm
☽△♄ 5:05 pm   ☽☍♃ 7:41 pm

♃♃♃

♌ ◯

Thursday
20

☉△♅ 7:33 am
☽☍♀ 6:36 pm

♀♀♀

♌
♍

Friday
21

☽☍♀ 4:17 am v/c
☽ApG 9:06 am
☽→♍ 6:38 pm

All aspects in Pacific Standard Time; add 3 hours for EST; add 8 hours for GMT

Year at a glance for PISCES ♓ (Feb. 18–Mar. 20)

Pisces has been unbelievably serious and focused in the last three years, as Saturn moved slowly through your sign. You have become more real, more substantial, hopefully better qualified. Now you need to use your skills in a responsible manner, to support yourself.

Since early 1996 you have been assessing your net worth. Evaluation and approval are more useful here than self-criticism. You'll have to tighten your belt this year if you're truly committed to pursuing a specialized field. Don't spread yourself thinly across many obligations; focus on an area you are passionate about. Issues of power continue to arise in your professional life. Examine your own goals and convictions to find a compromise without losing your integrity.

With the Jupiter/Uranus conjunction in your solar 12th house, faith will become a much larger part of your life. Your life is ready for a fresh infusion of spirituality. Someone will come forward as teacher or guardian angel, or you may become that wise guide for someone else.

An opportunity will arise, probably early in the year, to work with institutions or with disadvantaged people. It may be volunteer work. Take it on; there is joy in it. Besides, there will be contacts made for future professional advancement.

1998 will be a significant year for you, full of opportunities and new horizons. Lay the groundwork by being open to healing and inspiration from spiritual realms. Take time to daydream and to meditate. There are surprises welling up from your past, or your unconscious, which need contemplating. People or situations from other lives return for resolution, or to become a part of this life.

ħħħ   ¤ *Gretchen Lawlor 1996*

♍ ◯ **Saturday**
22

⊙☌☾   2:27 am
☾□♇   5:54 am
⊙☍♂   9:21 am

¤ *zana 1984*

Outdoor Tub at Adobeland
Full Moon in ♍ Virgo 2:27 am PST, 10:27 GMT

♍ ◯ **Sunday**
23

⊙□♇   7:17 pm

Februar

♍
♎ ◐ ### Montag
24

☽△♆	5:00 am	v/c
☽→♎	7:23 am	
☽♂♂	2:40 pm	
☽⚹♇	6:33 pm	
☽☍♄	7:42 pm	
☽△♅	8:16 pm	
☽△♃	11:25 pm	

♎ ◑ ### Dienstag
25

♎
♏ ◑ ### Mittwoch
26

☽△♅	2:52 pm	
☽□♆	4:47 pm	
☽△♀	6:49 pm	v/c
☽→♏	6:57 pm	
♀→♓	8:01 pm	

♏ ◑ ### Donnerstag
27

☽□♅	7:39 am	
☽□♃	11:30 am	
☉△☽	12:59 pm	
☿→♓	7:54 pm	

♏ ◑ ### Freitag
28

♀△♇	8:12 am	
♀⚻♂	8:07 pm	
☿△♇	9:34 pm	

All aspects in Pacific Standard Time; add 3 hours for EST; add 8 hours for GMT

Apple Pie

My stomach is full of apple pie. My own homemade pie, with a rye and barley flour and cornmeal crust, and filled with apples from our orchard. Today we finished the apple harvest, begun yesterday morning through the generosity of stalwart dykes who stayed overnight from the legal issues workshop we had here. The five of them filled the buckets with this year's abundance as they continued to discuss the topic of how we all manage our Lesbian lands, especially how we see the legal disposition of our lands in the present and future.

The legal issues workshop has me thinking about my origins and endings, about who will tend this land when I am no longer able, or just not willing, to climb trees or carry heavy buckets up the hill. My land partner and I, and many other Lesbians in this rural community, are finding ourselves pondering the future of our homes in ways that take us into questions of wills and life-estates, nonprofit organizations and trusts. We know we are making herstory here, and we want this story to continue beyond our individual lives and collectives. We will have more daylong meetings wrapped around delicious potlucks. We'll discuss, and perhaps argue about, the pros and cons of various landholding alternatives, and in the end give each other support as we all listen to our experience and our visions to figure out what works best for each of us. And in the process I'll make sure we eat lots of apple pies.

© Hawk Madrone 1994, reprinted and excerpted from MAIZE *(Fall 9995)*

♏ ☽ **Samstag**
♐   **1**

☽✳Ψ	2:06 am	v/c		
☽→♐	4:01 am		☽□♀	9:57 am
♀⊼♂	4:48 am		☽☌♇	2:17 pm
♄✳♅	5:24 am		☽✳♅	4:15 pm
☽✳♂	8:21 am		☽△♄	4:18 pm
☽□☿	9:00 am		☽✳♃	8:36 pm

♐ ☽ **Sonntag**
       2

| ☉□☽ | 1:37 am | v/c |
| ☿☌♀ | 6:32 am | |

Waning Half Moon in ♐ Sagittarius 1:37 am PST, 9:37 GMT

März

mars

♐   **lundi**
♑   **3**

☿□♇	12:00 am
♀□♇	7:31 am
☽→♑	9:38 am
☽□♂	12:33 pm
☽✳♀	8:23 pm
☽□♄	9:34 pm
☽✳♅	10:04 pm

Raven's Cabin at ARF
◻ *zana 1985*

♑   **mardi**
                         4

| ☉✳☽ | 9:48 am |
| ☿ApG | 12:37 pm |

♑   **mercredi**
♒   **5**

☽☌♆	10:26 am	v/c
☽→♒	11:54 am	
☽△♂	1:34 pm	
☽✳♇	9:00 pm	
☽☌♅	11:04 pm	
☽✳♄	11:36 pm	

♒   **jeudi**
                         6

| ☽☌♃ | 4:04 am | v/c |

♒ **vendredi**
♓   **7**

| ☽→♓ | 11:57 am |
| ☽□♇ | 8:49 pm |

All aspects in Pacific Standard Time; add 3 hours for EST; add 8 hours for GMT

Cefnfoelallt Uchaf, Women's Land, Wales

□ *Tracy Litterick 1988*

Basil *Ocimum basilicum*

Basil is a warming, stimulating herb. Cooking with basil assists digestion, relieves gas, and promotes menstrual flow (mild emmenagogue). It also promotes happiness and a sense of abundance in those who share the meal together. Hang a wreath or bundle of basil in a new home or community to bring abundance and to banish past negative influences.

© *Colette Gardiner 1996*

ℏℏℏ

♓ **samedi**

☿

8

☽PrG	12:56 am
♀ R	4:53 am
☽☌♀	6:36 am
♂→♏	11:50 am
☽☌☿	12:56 pm
☉☌☽	5:15 pm

New Moon in ♓ Pisces 5:15 pm PST, 1:15 GMT (Mar. 9)
Total Solar Eclipse (2 min., 50 sec.) 5:24 pm PST

☉☉☉

♓ **dimanche**

♈

9

☽✶♆	10:16 am
☽☍♂	10:59 am v/c
☽→♈	11:33 am
☽△♇	8:32 pm
☽✶♅	10:55 pm
☽☌♄	11:55 pm

Sister, Fear Has No Place Here

What Brenda and Wanda Henson are doing at Camp Sister Spirit, a 120-acre feminist education retreat in Ovett, Mississippi, is important. The Hensons have not dropped out—nor have they sold out.

When the Hensons decided to buy land, with the help of a grant from Lesbian Natural Resources, they sought to establish a place of refuge, not of confrontation. Harassment, however, has been persistent. By mid-February 1994, Attorney General Janet Reno directed the Department of Justice to mediate the situation. It was likely the first time federal mediators were called in to deal with violence directed at homosexuals.

Combating violence, visible hate, and racism is part of what Camp Sister Spirit is about.

Camp Sister Spirit was created as a feminist and progressive education retreat. The women are security conscious—they have to be. Camp Sister Spirit has been forced, very much against its will, to build a fence around the property. ("We could have fed ten families for ten years with the money the fence is costing us," Wanda Henson says.) The Hensons' version of feminism is essentially one of service; they run food banks and clothes closets, they counsel battered women and incest and rape victims.

Some ask: Why is the Camp courting such danger? Why not retreat to some "safer" place? That would be nice, but women are always in danger.

As Wanda told me: "A woman at the farmer's market put her hands on me and stood real close to me and said, 'Honey, what's your name?' I told her my name was Wanda Henson. She said, 'I thought so. This doesn't have anything to do with the fact that you're different.' I asked her what she meant. She said, 'What's happening to you has to do with the fact that you're a woman . . . Keep doing what you're doing because you're doing it for all of us.'"

© *Phyllis Chesler 1994, excerpted and reprinted from* On the Issues *(Fall 1994) and* Patriarchy: Notes of an Expert Witness, *published by Common Courage Press*

III. WOMYN IN ACTION MOON

*well, no, so far the neighbors haven't been
what you call friendly*

Camp Sister Spirit

For the past nineteen months our presence in Ovett, Mississippi, has been a target of the Religious Right. Mississippi for Family Values is trying to cultivate and sustain a culture of hate against us because we are feminists, lesbians, and gays.

We at Camp Sister Spirit have escalated our efforts to maintain our right to stay and thrive in Mississippi. We continue to expand our programs and facilities. Camp Sister Spirit is part of Sister Spirit Incorporated, a 501(c)(3), nonprofit corporation established in 1989, primarily to serve the needs of poor working people like ourselves in Mississippi. Over the past four years the Sister Spirit food pantry has distributed over 100,000 pounds of food. We offer information, education, referrals, advocacy, and meeting space regarding social issues; and intervene in crisis situations.

Camp Sister Spirit was founded in 1993 as a haven for lesbians and other womyn—a womyn's land. Because of the militant Religious Right's intimidation, harassment, and violence, we must work even harder to meet the challenge of feminist education, teaching and learning non-oppressive lifeways in the Deep South.

© *Camp Sister Spirit 1995*

marzo

♈ lunes
10

☽✶♃ 5:01 am
♂△♆ 1:58 pm

© *Muriel's Graffiti Gang! 1995*

♈
♉ martes
11

☉♂♉ 7:34 am
☽□♆ 11:23 am v/c
☽→♉ 12:37 pm

♉ miércoles
12

☽□♅ 12:46 am
☽□♃ 7:49 am
☽✶♀ 6:25 pm

♉
♊ jueves
13

☉✶☽ 4:14 am
☽✶☿ 7:54 am
☽△♂ 1:24 pm
☽△♆ 3:34 pm v/c
☽→♊ 4:48 pm

♊ viernes
14

☽⚹♇ 2:58 am
☽△♅ 6:02 am
☽✶♄ 7:47 am
☽△♃ 2:17 pm
☿☍♂ 4:06 pm

All aspects in Pacific Standard Time; add 3 hours for EST; add 8 hours for GMT

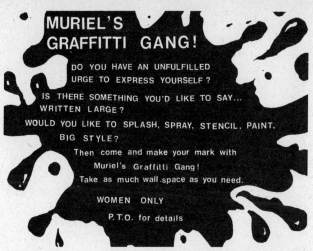

MURIEL'S GRAFFITTI GANG!

DO YOU HAVE AN UNFULFILLED
URGE TO EXPRESS YOURSELF?

IS THERE SOMETHING YOU'D LIKE TO SAY...
WRITTEN LARGE?

WOULD YOU LIKE TO SPLASH, SPRAY, STENCIL, PAINT,
BIG STYLE?

Then come and make your mark with
Muriel's Graffiti Gang!
Take as much wall space as you need.

WOMEN ONLY

P.T.O. for details

The Power of Women Is Here

♊ sábado

15

☽□♀	6:44 am	
♀⚹♆	12:30 pm	
☉□☽	4:06 pm	
☽□♂	7:31 pm	v/c
♀→♈	8:13 pm	

Waxing Half Moon in ♊ Gemini 4:06 pm PST
0:06 GMT

♊
♋ domingo

16

☽→♋	12:51 am
☽□☿	1:44 am
☿⊼♄	10:56 am
☽□♄	5:24 pm
☉☍♂	11:55 pm

MOON III

Blue Butterfly Theatre

Blue Butterfly Theatre is a women's theatre group performing in street theatre and open air community venues.

Waiting to Go On

Suffice to Make Her Glad

The group was formed in 1993 and consists of professional and semi-professional performers from a wide age range who experiment with different formats and styles of dance, music, and costume. Blue Butterfly Theatre uses dance, sound, and improvisation to communicate issues of human estrangement from the environment. It aims to inspire people to reconnect with nature. It takes patterns, symbols, and personae from the native British tradition (Keltic, Saxon, and Pictish influences), and reweaves these elements into new forms which stir the memory and touch the heart.   *photos and writing © Sheila Broun 1994*

Spring Equinox: March 20

Spring is here. Time to wake up. Break the chains of Winter. Animals come out of caves, shedding their winter coats. Under a first quarter moon, life bursts forth; flowers smile. The Aries sun shines upon the young child Goddess playing hide and seek with the balance of light and dark. It is the time of the Goddess Eostara, the hare and egg her symbols of fertility. Persephone returns from the underworld to be reunited with her mother, Demeter. Joy abounds.

As the wheel turns let us remember our childhood and heal the mother-daughter connection and strengthen the bond of sisterhood. Honor the children; teach them new stories of creation, revering all the peoples of the planet. Become a child yourself. Blessed be!

excerpt © Dánahy Sharonrose 1996

Greenham Women's Peace Encampment

¤ *Tracy Litterick 1985, all photos*

March

♋ ## Monday
17

D△♀   11:54 pm

♂♂♂

♋
♌ ## Tuesday
18

D⚹♂   4:42 am
☉△D   8:20 am
D☍♆   11:00 am   v/c
D→♌   12:08 pm
☿△♇   3:17 pm
D△♇   11:22 pm

☿☿☿

♌ ## Wednesday
19

D△☿   1:01 am
D☍♅   3:14 am
D△♄   5:59 am
♀☍♂   12:08 pm
D☍♃   1:54 pm   v/c
☿⚹♅   2:30 pm
☉⚹♆   4:52 pm

♃♃♃

♌ ## Thursday
20

☉→♈   5:55 am
☿♂♄   8:15 am
♂PrG   8:50 am
DApG   3:43 pm

Equinox

♈

Sun in Aries 5:55 am PST, 13:55 GMT

♀♀♀

♌
♍ ## Friday
21

D→♍   12:59 am
☉⚻⚷   4:54 am
D□♇   12:16 pm

All aspects in Pacific Standard Time; add 3 hours for EST; add 8 hours for GMT

Year at a glance for ARIES ♈ (Mar. 20–Apr. 19)

As Saturn joins your Aries sun, the theme for 1997 emerges: aggressively pursue increased stature and self-esteem through disciplined efforts. Demands will be made on your energy, finances, and patience. You benefit from taking on responsibilities; it is not a year for drifting or taking the easy route. In this way you satisfy the requirements of the times and avoid delays and frustrations. Don't expect your reputation to carry you; beware of shortcuts. You do not have to think big—this is a time for small projects and simple beginnings. You will be working towards something that won't mature for a few years.

You inspire others through a willingness to break from tradition in law, politics, or religion. Because you dare to consider what may seem unusual or mysterious to most people, new ambitions and opportunities materialize. Friends or groups involved in humanitarian or political change have a magnetic appeal for you with their fresh, exciting optimism.

In 1996, you may have sustained damage to your self-esteem, or experienced a significant change in your looks, tastes, or lifestyle. It will take time to regain your momentum; you may experience occasional energy crises until mid-1997. This is not a time for you to hold onto old habits or positions of power. In late 1997 you will feel more confident as you witness the results of your steady efforts to create a new image.

As Mars joins Jupiter and Uranus in Aquarius in December, you feel a new burst of enthusiasm. Don't expect your goals to stay focused in one direction; new input could alter things by Winter Solstice.

¤ *Gretchen Lawlor 1996*

♍ ○ Saturday
    22

♀✶♆ 12:12 pm
☿✶♃ 1:23 pm
♀→♈ 9:26 pm

♍ ○ Sunday
♎   **23**

☽♂♂ 2:21 am
☽△♆ 12:40 pm   v/c
♀⊼♄ 1:01 pm
☽→♎ 1:35 pm
☽☍♀ 3:27 pm
☉☍☽ 8:45 pm

It's Written
All Over Her

© *Sierra Lonepine Briano 1992*

Partial Lunar Eclipse 8:40 pm PST (.920 mag.)
Full Moon in ♎ Libra 8:45 pm PST, 4:45 GMT (Mar. 24)

März

A Woman Parade
¤ *Tamara Thiebaux 1994*

DDD

♎ ◯ **Montag**
24

☽⚹♇	12:37 am
☽△♅	4:54 am
☽☍♄	8:26 am
☽△♃	4:52 pm

♂♂♂

♎ ◖ **Dienstag**
25

☽☍♅	1:28 am	
☉△♇	7:24 pm	
☽□♆	11:55 pm	v/c

☿☿☿

♎
♏ ◖ **Mittwoch**
26

☽→♏	12:42 am
☽□♅	3:41 pm

♃♃♃

♏ ◖ **Donnerstag**
27

☽□♃	3:56 am
♀△♇	7:35 am
☿⊼♂	2:51 pm
☽⚹♂	7:54 pm

♀♀♀

♏
♐ ◖ **Freitag**
28

☉⚹♅	3:30 am	
☽⚹♆	8:59 am	v/c
☽→♐	9:40 am	
☽♂♇	7:49 pm	
☽△♀	11:39 pm	

Breaking the Tabu: Doing the Unthinkable

On May 9 at 10 a.m., a group of women taking part in a conference, "Breaking the Silence/Ama Mawu," did an action in a Bristol cathedral. My dream had been to walk into a church during a service and confront the priest and the church with their "blasphemes against the Mother." I made a placard out of a poster of my painting *God Giving Birth*, adding the words: "Return of the Goddess" and "The Beginning of the End of Patriarchy." By 10 a.m. some fifteen women had arrived. We walked into the cathedral virtually unnoticed. No one realized what was happening until we were lined up in front of the altar facing the astonished congregation. It was significant to me that I confronted the bishop with my painting, which I consider sacred and of the Goddess. He attempted to take it from me and told me that he was holding a service and that the cathedral is his, at which I answered that the cathedrals are built on sacred sites of the Goddess and that we were holding a service of our own. When he asked me how long we would be there, I told him we wanted to sing a song. So there we were, candles burning, singing all the verses of "Burning Times"!

Liberating Our Minds: Cathedral Action
© *Monica Sjöö 1993*

© *Monica Sjöö 1993, excerpted and reprinted from* From the Flames *(1993)*

ꙮꙮꙮ

♐	🌓	Samstag
		29

☽✶♅	12:11 am
☉△☽	1:48 am
☽△♄	4:14 am
♀✶♅	5:17 am
☽✶♃	12:32 pm

◯◯◯

♐	🌓	Sonntag
♑		**30**

☽□♂	1:35 am	
☽△♅	11:31 am	v/c
☉♂♄	2:20 pm	
♄ApG	2:52 pm	
☽→♑	4:07 pm	

mars

ⅮⅮⅮ

♑ ◐ ## lundi
31

♀♂♄	4:48 am
☽□♄	10:18 am
☽□♀	10:47 am
☉□☽	11:38 am

Ozone
Waning Half Moon in ♑ Capricorn 11:38 am PST, 19:38 GMT

♂♂♂

♑
♒ ◐ ## mardi
1

avril

♉□♆	12:39 am	
☽△♂	4:55 am	
☿→♉	5:45 am	
♉♂♄	9:26 am	
☽♂♆	7:30 pm	v/c
☽→♒	7:59 pm	
☽□♉	9:30 pm	

☿☿☿

♒ ◑ ## mercredi
2

☽✶♇	5:07 am	
☉♂♀	5:45 am	
☽♂♅	9:25 am	
☽✶♄	1:47 pm	
☉✶☽	6:22 pm	
☽✶♀	6:36 pm	
☽♂♃	9:44 pm	v/c

♃♃♃

♒
♓ ● ## jeudi
3

☽→♓	9:42 pm

♀♀♀

♓ ● ## vendredi
4

☽✶♉	3:42 am
☽□♇	6:30 am
♄→♎	8:23 am
♀✶♃	12:29 pm

All aspects except Apr. 6 in Pacific Standard Time; add 3 hours for EST; add 8 hours for GMT

Women in Black

Editor's note: Women in Black is an international peace action all women are invited to participate in; every Thursday at noon join the global web, wear black, and devote an hour of silence and positive thought, either alone or in a group, to those caught in armed conflict.

Dandelion *Taraxacum officinale*

Prolific everywhere, dandelion is one of the most useful allies in contemporary culture for healing the physical stresses of urban life. All parts are useful. The root and leaf help to remove pollutants from our bodies; aid liver, spleen, and gallbladder function; help to balance blood sugar; stimulate bladder and kidney function; aid digestion and absorption; and contain incredible amounts of vitamins A and C, as well as high amounts of calcium, iron, and other vital nutrients. Tap-rooted weeds like dandelion are especially at home in depleted soils because they pull up and store nutrients from deeper levels. Use as tea, tincture, or food. © *Colette Gardiner 1996*

♓
♈   samedi
                5

☉✳♄	5:40 am	
☽⚹♂	6:00 am	
☽PrG	8:55 am	
☿☌♇	6:32 pm	
☽✳♆	9:57 pm	v/c
☽→♈	10:19 pm	

♈   dimanche
                6

♀ApG	12:32 am
☽△♇	8:01 am
☽✳♅	12:30 pm
☽☌♄	5:23 pm

Daylight Savings Time begins 2:00 am PST

MOON III

We are three womyn who have loved each other in a variety of dynamic combinations. Valerie and Annie, lovers from 1979 to 1983, bought Rainbow's Other End in 1980 and live there still, in separate dwellings. They are land mates, work mates and best friends who share a deep spiritual bond through their love of the earth and the land they live on. Shortly after Katherine moved to Roseburg in 1984, Valerie, who had been "calling" for a teacher in her heart path of midwifery, approached Katherine after hearing her speak. The two women recognized each other as kindred spirits and have shared work, hearth, and best friendship in the ensuing twelve years. In 1985, captivated by sky-blue eyes and Amazon potential, Katherine and Annie began a five-year relationship. When Annie left, Valerie nursed Katherine through her grief, and in that healing, they too became lovers. In those same months it became apparent that the heart connection between Katherine and Annie remained strong. That relationship was rekindled twenty-three months after its ending. Three and a half years later, they are lovers, life partners, and best friends of heart and spirit.

We are family, not only with each other, but in the rituals of our families of origin. We have held each other through the deaths of parents. We have celebrated the births of Annie's nephews and Katherine's grandchildren and the reunion of Valerie with her sons. We are medical and legal powers of attorney for each other.

Though we have talked of buying land together over the years, the vision took new form when the land adjacent to Rainbow's Other End came up for sale. Our intense desire to secure this land for lesbians resulted in the formation of a nonprofit corporation called RavenSong. We raised over $70,000 in thirteen months and bought the land.

We have made a commitment to the land and to each other. What holds us together is our conscious desire to love each other inclusively, regardless of differences. We treat our friendships with high regard. We get angry and frustrated and disheartened with each other at times, but the commitment, the love, the respect stand strong. We trust that *we* will last our lifetimes.

◻ *Annie Ocean, Katherine, and Valerie 1996*

IV. LOVING WOMYN MOON

*Sunwise from top left: **Annie, Katherine, and Valerie** © Lava 1988; **Untitled** © Marita Holdaway/Benham Studio Gallery 1995; **Merlovers** © Megaera 1995 **Three Wise Women** © Reeva 1995; **Transforming White Supremacy** ¤ Rashani 1995*

abril

♈ **lunes**
7

☽✳♃ 1:29 am
☉☌☽ 4:02 am
♆□♄ 4:16 am
☽☌♀ 6:16 am
♀⚼♂ 11:45 am

New Moon in ♈ Aries 4:02 am PDT, 11:02 GMT

♈
♉ **martes**
8

☽□♆ 12:01 am v/c
☽→♉ 12:20 am
☽☌♅ 1:02 pm
☉⚼♂ 1:41 pm
☽□♅ 2:01 pm

♉ **miércoles**
9

☽□♃ 4:02 am
☽△♂ 8:09 am
♉□♅ 12:49 pm

♉
♊ **jueves**
10

☽△♆ 3:10 am v/c
☽→♊ 3:28 am
☽☍♇ 12:50 pm
☽△♅ 6:05 pm

♊ **viernes**
11

☽✳♄ 12:15 am
☽△♃ 9:36 am
☽□♂ 12:27 pm
☉✳☽ 7:33 pm

All aspects in Pacific Daylight Time; add 3 hours for EDT; add 7 hours for GMT

A Call to Arms

Womyn,
this is a Call to Arms.
A call to the arms
of womyn.
All these arms going to waste
arms too often empty
when so many womyn
need holding.
Lovers leave,
children grow up
and where
will your arms
be then?
Womyn,
I call you to arms:
the arms of your mothers,
your best friends,
your sisters . . .
Don't deprive yourself
of womon-love.
Reach out your arms,
your souls to those

© Benjie Lasseau 1992

who can love,
and hold womyn.
Hold womyn
close to your heart.
Womyn,
this is a Call to Arms.

© Erin Dragonsong 1995

♊
♋   ☽   **sábado**
              12

☽⚹♀   12:34 am   v/c
☽→♋   10:03 am

♋   ☽   **domingo**
              13

☽⚹♅   4:13 am
☽□♄   8:54 am
☽⚹♂   8:31 pm

April

□ Linda Sweatt 1987

♋
♌

▷▷▷ Monday
14

☉□☽	10:00 am	
☽□♀	4:53 pm	
☿ R	5:01 pm	
☽☌Ψ	8:07 pm	v/c
☽→♌	8:22 pm	

Martha & Polly at Home

Waxing Half Moon in ♋ Cancer 10:00 am PDT, 17:00 GMT

♌

♂♂♂ Tuesday
15

☽△♇	6:48 am
♀☌♄	10:25 am
☽☌♅	1:08 pm
☽□☿	3:39 pm
☽△♄	9:01 pm

♌

☿☿☿ Wednesday
16

♀□Ψ	12:35 am
♀→♉	2:43 am
♂⚻♃	4:13 am
☽☌♃	7:46 am

♌
♍

♃♃♃ Thursday
17

☉△☽	3:51 am	v/c
☽ApG	8:28 am	
♄PrG	8:34 am	
☽→♍	9:00 am	
☽△♀	12:33 pm	
☽□♇	7:30 pm	

♍

♀♀♀ Friday
18

☽△☿	3:27 am
☉☌♄	3:17 pm
☽☌♂	7:56 pm

All aspects in Pacific Daylight Time; add 3 hours for EDT; add 7 hours for GMT

Year at a glance for TAURUS ♉ (Apr. 19–May 20)

Taurus is an unquenchable beacon of light this year. The public and those in power will see you as someone special and unusual. Take advantage of the doors that open. Don't try to be steady or conservative. Revel in your eccentricities.

Watch out for a career opportunity, especially in February 1997. Don't expect the chance to come around again. Choose areas to excel in which do not require long and steady growth. This is a year of rollercoaster ups and downs. To truly live the moment, have your bags packed and your eyes peeled for opportunities. Collective efforts, especially associations with other like-minded individuals, are advantageous. No one will have a lukewarm reaction to you.

Neptune's position (in the last degrees of Capricorn approaching your solar midheaven) suggests a tug towards idealistic, mystical, or spiritual causes. This may be a challenge for your pragmatic Taurus self to accept. It may materialize through dedicated work on a project that benefits an underprivileged group. Both Saturn and Neptune suggest this year is not a time to make permanent decisions about career or long-term directions. It may be difficult to see the direction in which you are moving. Through your efforts there is completion, the paying off of old debts or redressing of an imbalance.

Occasional retreats are necessary for study or for critical assessment of your progress. Meditation, dreamwork, or journaling helps you bring to consciousness both hidden assets and unconscious self-destructive habits. It is a good time to take up studies which develop latent talents.

¤ *Gretchen Lawlor 1996*

♍ ⏾ **Saturday**
♎ **19**

☉□♆	4:02 pm	
♂□♅	5:48 pm	
☉→♉	6:03 pm	
☽△♆	9:27 pm	v/c
☽→♎	9:36 pm	

♉

♎ ⏾ **Sunday**
20

♀⊼♇	5:56 am
☽✶♇	7:46 am
☽△♅	2:25 pm
☽☍♄	11:08 pm

Sun in Taurus 6:03 pm PDT
1:03 GMT

April

♎ ○ Montag
21

☽△♃ 9:44 am
☿☌♀ 11:55 pm

Festies
© Lin Karmon 1994

♂♂♂

♎ ○ Dienstag
♏ **22**

☽□♆ 8:11 am v/c
☽→♏ 8:19 am
☉☍☽ 1:34 pm
☽☍☿ 9:09 pm
♀□♅ 11:56 pm

Lunar Beltane
Full Moon in ♏ Scorpio 1:34 pm PDT, 20:34 GMT

☿☿☿

♏ ○ Mittwoch
23

☽□♅ 12:31 am
☽☍♀ 12:34 am
☽✶♂ 4:09 pm
☽□♃ 7:32 pm

♃♃♃

♏ ☽ Donnerstag
♐ **24**

☽✶♆ 4:26 pm v/c
☽→♐ 4:32 pm
☉⚼♇ 9:27 pm

♀♀♀

♐ ☽ Freitag
25

☽☌♇ 1:41 am
☉☌♉ 3:32 am
☽✶♅ 8:07 am
☿⚼♇ 12:50 pm
☽△♄ 5:01 pm
☽□♂ 10:56 pm

All aspects in Pacific Daylight Time; add 3 hours for EDT; add 7 hours for GMT

Untitled

What a precious scene
Two girls in their early teens
Discovering for the first time
Insights of a woman's mind
Giggling silly at the wonder
Of communicating in ways nonverbal
Pinked cheeks and eyes downcast
Each girl is compelled to ask
Did you feel that?
High-pitched tones reply in answer
Confirming what had just happened
Four arms flailing, hands a flutter
Coming to rest intertwined with another
Smiling lips and sparkling eyes
Marveling in their secret surprise.

© Wendy Olson 1995

♐
♑ ☽ Samstag
26

☽⚹♃   2:51 am   v/c
☽→♑   10:32 pm

♑ ☽ Sonntag
27

☽△☿   5:21 am
☉△☽   11:50 am
♂ D   12:09 pm
☽□♄   10:40 pm

avril

ⅅⅅⅅ

♑ **lundi**
28

☽△♀	12:21 am
☿PrG	1:00 am
☽△♂	3:54 am
☉□♅	1:44 pm

♂♂♂

♑ ♒ **mardi**
29

☽☌♆	2:46 am	v/c
☽→♒	2:50 am	
☽□♉	7:11 am	
☽⚹♇	11:15 am	
♀△♂	4:32 pm	
☽☌♅	5:35 pm	
☉□☽	7:37 pm	

☿☿☿

Waning Half Moon in ♒ Aquarius 7:37 pm PDT
2:37 GMT

♒ **mercredi**
30

☽⚹♄	2:45 am	
☽□♀	8:54 am	
☽☌♃	12:04 pm	v/c

♃♃♃

♒ ♓ **jeudi**
1

☽→♓	5:50 am
☽⚹♉	8:10 am
☽□♇	1:59 pm
♆R	4:20 pm

mai

Beltane

♀♀♀

♓ **vendredi**
2

♀□♃	12:43 am
☉⚹☽	1:57 am
☽☍♂	10:08 am
☽⚹♀	4:04 pm

All aspects in Pacific Daylight Time; add 3 hours for EDT; add 7 hours for GMT

©*Sue DuMonde 1993*

Beltane: May 1 Full Moon in Scorpio

The wheel turns again and we come to the cross-quarter fire festival of Beltane. It is halfway between Spring Equinox and Summer Solstice. Buds open, flowers color the green fields as the sun enters Taurus and the gibbous moon shines on young love.

We join the Queen of May for a sexual dance around the maypole as lovers enact the fertility of Mother Earth. The maiden Goddess fertilizes Earth with her blood for the first time. Sexuality is experienced in all innocence without ownership or judgment. We honor our individual sexuality as source of life and creativity. We recognize the different parts of ourselves and unite them in "conjunctio," sacred marriage.

Rejoice. Leap the fire with friends and lovers, releasing past hurts. Allow the warmth of the fire to open your heart. Party in celebration of the erotic as sacred source of life. "All acts of love and pleasure are the Goddess' rituals." Blessed be! *excerpt © Dánahy Sharonrose 1996*

Beltane on the Land

naked women
make mud
like children
but on a grander scale
the pit is wide and deep
at the north end of the garden

they dig
with pitchforks and shovels
dig in hard soil
add cold, cold water
make mud
dark as chocolate
rough as sandpaper
thick worms head for shore
fat drops of warm rain
plop down from no clouds
pieces of sky for mud stew

some women
wear broad-brimmed hats
sit on tidy blanket islands
in the meadow grass
they worry their skin might be
torn by thorns

the fearless yell
and jump in
grab and slide
take one another down
and down again
full weight against full weight
against slippery skin

the solid woman
one dark earth color
even her eyes
call to those still wearing
pristine skin

virgin, virgin
come in, come in
let this earth between your toes
between your legs
into your ears

slide down my strong back
over my head
my body will be your bridge
your bridge
into this good mud

taste it
rub your hands in your hair
lean against me
let my hands sand your skin

we are buried
in this wet earth
then held by sun and wind
until we are gray
skin taut and dry
cracked and open

© Beth Freewomon 1995
Ila and Judith

© Beth Freewomon 1995
Shannon and Alea

Rose   *Rosa* spp.

Roses are strongly aligned with both womyn and love. In fact, the rose family is ruled astrologically by Venus. Rose fragrance opens the

heart and soothes the mind. Roses can be placed on the altar or strewn on the ground during commitment ceremonies, infused in oil for a loving massage, placed on a mirror for a self-blessing ritual, or added to the bath to welcome a new we'moon to the community.

© *Colette Gardiner 1996*

♓
♈

ƕƕƕ

samedi

3

☽PrG	4:14 am	
☽⚹♆	7:55 am	v/c
☽→♈	7:59 am	
☽△♇	3:59 pm	
☽⚹♅	10:22 pm	

♈

☉☉☉

dimanche

4

☽♂♄	8:06 am
☽⚹♃	5:14 pm
♅→♈	6:47 pm
♅□♆	10:40 pm

The Dream of the Saguaro Sisters

For most of our early days we were hardly aware of the human presence. To stand tall, our sister saguaros all around us, this was our joy in being alive. Everything in perfect harmony. Within us, the awareness of our infinite connection to our surroundings and to each other. Yet we delighted in our individual expression.

Then my sister and I dreamed of our human sisters. In the near future wimmin would seek out havens away from men, to heal their connection to the earth, to each other, and especially to themselves. This dream gave us inspiration for new growth. In all directions we sprouted arms to support this dream of sisterhood. Our work was to be steadfast in supporting them. "Trust what is" was our tenet.

Deep in the earth we began to feel the movement of the wimmin, ever nearer, ever more restless and searching. A sense of freedom and possibility began to attract wimmin to the land. Certain ones would walk by, recognizing us as sisters. Some acknowledged us as overseers, reverence in their hearts. We knew they shared our dream of oneness. The sense of being separate disappeared!

The earth felt deeply the constancy of joyous movement on her surface. She was being touched in places long denied, awakening her passion; her joy making possible a path to wholeness. The land became a place of safety, not only to share the joys of community and sisterhood, but also to speak boldly of the hurt places.

Conflict arose. The patience needed to move through habits of fighting and resistance seemed unattainable. Lurking around every corner was the temptation to think in terms of separation, to look for differences and to use them as a lever. The painful locking of oneself into a definition, of seeing things as better or worse, richer or poorer—unlearning habits of hierarchy and seeing through the illusion of separateness would take longer than most could endure. Many grew discouraged. "Wimmin's land is just a dream", "It's not working," they would say. Peace and harmony seemed elusive.

But the aching desire for community, in an uncanny way, turned any obstacle into a challenge to keep on dreaming. All of nature called out with her beauty, "SEE THE BEAUTY IN EACH OTHER."

excerpt © Oldfeather 1995

V. COMMUNING WITH
NATURE MOON

Amazon Cactus

mayo

♈
♉

lunes
5

☽♂♉   9:48 am
☽□♇   10:00 am   v/c
☽→♉   10:04 am

□ Sandra Spicer 1993

Goddess Tree

♂♂♂

♉

martes
6

☽□♅   12:41 am
☉♂☽   1:47 pm
☽△♂   3:18 pm
☽□♃   8:20 pm

New Moon in ♉ Taurus 1:47 pm PDT, 20:47 GMT

☿☿☿

♉
♊

miércoles
7

☽♂♀   6:35 am
☽△♇   1:15 pm   v/c
☽→♊   1:21 pm
☉△♂   2:30 pm
☽☍♇   9:34 pm

♃♃♃

♊

jueves
8

☽△♅   4:35 am
♀⊼♄   8:19 am
☿ D   11:05 am
☽⚹♄   3:49 pm
☽□♂   8:22 pm

♀♀♀

♊
♋

viernes
9

☽△♃   1:36 am
☽⚹♉   6:22 pm   v/c
☽→♋   7:13 pm

All aspects in Pacific Daylight Time; add 3 hours for EDT; add 7 hours for GMT

We are descended from trees
It is easy to tell
Looking at fingers
As they emerge from crevices
Gnarled with oil
And spread toes
Horny with hard skin
Sisters to roots
Beneath mossy bowls
Straining both to hold on
As they spread and stretch
And wrap like vines
We are related to the trees
I can tell
As you bend over me
Supple. Weathered
By waiting
Sweet sap singing
As our branches
Tangle storms

¤ Emma 1994   *© Berta Freistadt 1992*

sábado
10

♀△Ψ	9:07 am
♀→♊	10:20 am
☉□♃	10:16 pm
☽□♄	11:52 pm

domingo
11

☽⚹♂	4:53 am
☉⚹☽	11:08 am
☿□Ψ	9:14 pm

May

♋︎
♌︎

Monday
12

♉︎→♉	3:25 am	
☽☌♆	4:24 am	v/c
☽→♌	4:33 am	
☽□♀	4:34 am	
☽⚹♀	9:18 am	
☽△♇	1:34 pm	
♅ R	9:05 pm	
☽☌♅	9:44 pm	

♌︎

Tuesday
13

| ☽△♄ | 11:24 am |
| ☽☍♃ | 10:07 pm |

♌︎
♍︎

Wednesday
14

♀☍♇	2:45 am	
☉□☽	3:55 am	v/c
☽→♍	4:43 pm	
☽△♉	6:46 pm	

Waxing Half Moon in ♌︎ Leo 3:55 am PDT, 10:55 GMT

♍︎

Thursday
15

☽□♇	1:53 am
☽ApG	3:09 am
☽□♀	4:37 am

♍︎

Friday
16

| ☽☌♂ | 6:49 am |
| ☉△☽ | 10:07 pm |

All aspects in Pacific Daylight Time; add 3 hours for EDT; add 7 hours for GMT

Tribute

Soft little mouse, dying observed in the night
Warmed by the bodies of your two little friends.
Soft fur turned coarse,
    tiny feet blue.
What an ungainly death for such a gentle creature.

Your little friends miss you,
    won't sleep where you died.
They huddle together, burrow a bit,
    circle their hutch looking for you.

I wrap you carefully in white paper,
    with a blessing
Crying for all my friends who've died silently,
    alone in the night.

© Luna Dancing Waters 1991

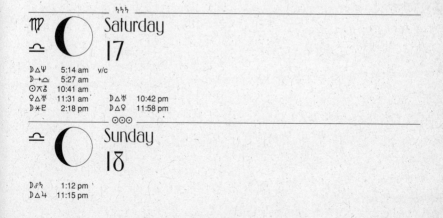

♍
♎
    ħħħ

Saturday 17

☽△♆	5:14 am	v/c
☽→♎	5:27 am	
☉⊼♄	10:41 am	
♀△♅	11:31 am	☽△♅ 10:42 pm
☽⚹♇	2:18 pm	☽△♀ 11:58 pm

⊙⊙⊙

♎

Sunday 18

| ☽⚯♄ | 1:12 pm |
| ☽△♃ | 11:15 pm |

Mai

〰 ⧖〰

☍ ☾ **Montag**
♏ **19**

☽□♇ 3:57 pm v/c
☽→♏ 4:12 pm

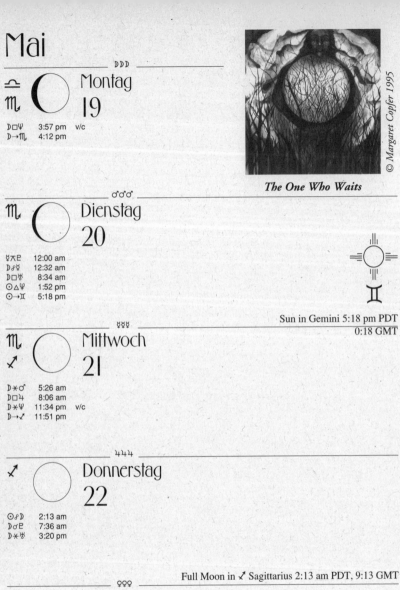

The One Who Waits

♂♂♂

♏ ☾ **Dienstag**
20

☿⊼♇ 12:00 am
☽☌☿ 12:32 am
☽□♅ 8:34 am
☉△♀ 1:52 pm
☉→♊ 5:18 pm

Sun in Gemini 5:18 pm PDT
0:18 GMT

♀♀♀

♏ ☾ **Mittwoch**
♐ **21**

☽✶♂ 5:26 am
☽□♃ 8:06 am
☽✶♇ 11:34 am v/c
☽→♐ 11:51 pm

♃♃♃

♐ ○ **Donnerstag**
22

☉☍☽ 2:13 am
☽☌♇ 7:36 am
☽✶♅ 3:20 pm

Full Moon in ♐ Sagittarius 2:13 am PDT, 9:13 GMT

♀♀♀

♐ ○ **Freitag**
23

☽☍♀ 3:43 am
☽△♄ 5:17 am
☽□♂ 12:16 pm
☽✶♃ 2:00 pm v/c
♀✶♄ 10:23 pm

All aspects in Pacific Daylight Time; add 3 hours for EDT; add 7 hours for GMT

Year at a glance for GEMINI ♊ (May 20–June 21)

Naturally inquisitive Gemini will be even more so in 1997—with a burning enthusiasm to explore uncharted territory. Gemini is usually happiest pursuing several goals simultaneously. Watch out for impatience, irritability, and scattering of efforts in January, February, and December. Ground yourself by focusing on a long-range plan or clearly defined goal.

There will be sudden opportunities for travel and contacts with other cultures or religions. Travel is exceptionally stimulating this year. New interests are awakened and you feel freer to live out parts of yourself that don't "fit" back at home. You return changed, more vital, unwilling to veil yourself.

A new philosophy or faith attracts you with its optimistic view of the future. It will be characterized by its eclectic roots. You may suddenly decide to return to school to pursue a new interest, or use electronic media to convey your unique perspective to a broader audience.

A significant encounter with someone who is willful and opinionated will ultimately make you stronger, though your life will change significantly through the contact. A battle of wills leads you to redefine the entire nature of your relationship. The first few months of the year contain influences that support you in overcoming compulsive responses, particularly when confronted by difficult people in positions of power. You are more relaxed, less fearful and suspicious of others. Remember this later in the year, especially during October when you are more inclined to be headstrong and opinionated. You'll meet resistance, and will need to compromise. ¤ *Gretchen Lawlor 1996*

♐ ◗ Samstag
♑   24

D→♑   4:51 am
♂□♅   12:60 pm
D△♀   8:18 pm
ⒺPrG   11:41 pm

♑ ◗ Sonntag
        25

☉☍♇   2:57 am
D□♄   9:40 am
D△♂   5:09 pm

Wild Women of the Forest Series
© *Amarah K. Gabriel 1994*

mai

♑
♒
lundi
26

☽☌♆   8:00 am   v/c
☽→♒   8:20 am
☽⚹♇   3:28 pm
☉△☽   6:12 pm
☽☌♅   10:57 pm

♒
mardi
27

☽□♅   4:01 am
☽⚹♄   1:07 pm
♂⚻♃   4:17 pm
☽△♀   8:42 pm
☽☌♃   9:10 pm   v/c

♒
♓
mercredi
28

♀△♃   2:20 am
♀□♂   5:10 am
☽→♓   11:18 am
☽□♇   6:19 pm

♓
jeudi
29

☽PrG   12:01 am
☉□☽   12:51 am
☽⚹☿   11:51 am
☉△♅   3:16 pm

Waning Half Moon in ♓ Pisces 12:51 am PDT, 7:51 GMT

♓
♈
vendredi
30

☽☍♂   1:22 am
☽□♀   4:30 am
☽⚹♆   1:51 pm   v/c
☽→♈   2:18 pm
☽△♇   9:14 pm

All aspects in Pacific Daylight Time; add 3 hours for EDT; add 7 hours for GMT

© *Cilla Ericson 1994*

Usnea *Usnea* spp.

Usnea is a lichen that grows on older branches in rainy forests without harming the trees. It has strong antifungal and lung healing properties. German research has found it effective in treating serious lung ailments. Best used when a cold or flu is moving into the lungs, it can help us to heal faster. Use as a tea, tincture, or cough syrup. Heat seems to extract its abilities best. Since it is fairly sensitive

to air pollution and prefers older trees, you need to be careful not to overharvest. Take only what is blown down by storms. Have an experienced herbalist point out the correct lichen since there are others that look similar.

© *Colette Gardiner 199*

♈	samedi 31	

ↄↄↄ

☽⚹♅ 4:51 am
☉⚹☽ 7:39 am
♀△♂ 5:30 pm
☽♂♄ 7:54 pm

♈ ♉	dimanche 1	juin

☉☉☉

☽⚹♃ 3:35 am
☽⚹♀ 12:41 pm
☽□♆ 5:09 pm v/c
☽→♉ 5:39 pm

Breaking The Cycle:
The Power Of Community-Based Projects

This beautiful beadwear (opposite) is created by the women of the Humla Bead Cooperative in Kathmandu, Nepal, as part of the Barouti Beadwear Alternative Income Producing Project.

Some of the goals of these women are to return income to their families and community, and speak to the world of their lives, through the distribution of their traditional barouti beadwear.

By working together and generating independent income, the women of the Cooperative have created choice in their lives. And by preparing their daughters for lives like their own, they will teach their children and their community that, as individuals, they can make a difference. *This* is women thinking positively: leading the way in a male-dominated society, one by one realizing the power they have to change the world for their children.

It is hoped that the Barouti Beadwear Project will help to break the cycle of neglect and exploitation of women and girls which is mercilessly widespread in developing countries.

It is all too easy to forget that these women in far-away Nepal are women like you and me, with feelings, loves, hopes, dreams, and their own goals in life. The only difference is that we have had the fortune to be part of a society which allows us to nurture those hopes and dreams.

Please remember, if we wish to embrace it, there is always the Power of One by One.

© Sally-Ann Gray 1995

VI. WORKING TOGETHER MOON

When women visit women
they stop in an old place together,
the place called Work.

Work requires thought
        emptiness
        talk
        silence
        speaking
        listening

song
dance
food
and
some
form
of
silver
light.

When the women Work
    they are moving earth
    they are leaving Her in peace.

© Sally-Ann Gray 1995

Barouti Beadwear

□ Mary Sojourner 1995

junio

Yurt Building
© *Sue DuMonde 1993*

〜 ⟩⟩⟩ ———————————

♉ 　 **lunes**

　　　2

☽□♅　8:20 am

♂♂♂ ———————————

♉　 **martes**
♊　 **3**

☽♂♉　6:23 am
☽□♃　7:37 am
☽△♂　11:07 am
♀⚹♆　2:58 pm
♉□♃　5:39 pm
♀→♋　9:18 pm
☽△♆　9:20 pm　v/c
☽→♊　9:55 pm

☿☿☿ ———————————

♊　 **miércoles**
　　 4

☽☍♇　4:55 am
☽△♅　12:57 pm

♃♃♃ ———————————

♊　 **jueves**

　　 5

☉♂☽　12:04 am
☽⚹♄　5:36 am
☿△♂　10:42 am
☽△♃　1:12 pm
☽□♂　6:15 pm　v/c

New Moon in ♊ Gemini 12:04 am PDT, 7:04 GMT

♀♀♀ ———————————

♊　 **viernes**
♋　 **6**

☽→♋　4:02 am
☿⚹♂　6:57 am
☽♂♀　9:44 am

All aspects in Pacific Daylight Time; add 3 hours for EDT; add 7 hours for GMT

Women in Community: A Personal Reflection

How kind they were, the Sisters of Mercy. This is a powerful remembrance for me. A little child from a large family, eleven children, a widowed mother. Life was very tough. Basic necessities were scarce and violence had invaded our family. This community of women with their love and concern was a window into a different life. Catholic women religious have been living in community since biblical times. Religious congregations of women practicing the works of mercy have flourished since the fifth century. Shelter, food, education and nursing are part of their mission.

Since the Second Vatican Council in the sixties, religious congregations and orders have been in serious decline. New communities, more reflective of our societal and cultural changes, have begun. Such a community is ours.

H.O.M.E., Inc., and St. Francis community have five shelters for the homeless, a food bank, a craft village with weaving, pottery, stitchery, and woodworking, a sawmill, a shingle mill, land trusts, house construction, farming, education and daycare.

I remember, once, a Marxist and a Baptist Evangelical came to help us on the first house we built. They got along fine as long as they nailed the trusses on the new roof. By working together they developed an emotional openness to each other. They could speak, they helped someone in greater need, and a homeless family now has a home. Ours is a diverse community of believers and nonbelievers working together, with women in leadership roles.

¤ *Lucy Poulin 1996*

♋ ● sábado
7

♀⊼♇ 1:24 am
☽□♄ 1:41 pm

♋ ● domingo
♌ 8

☽⚹♂ 4:23 am   ☽⚹♅ 12:24 pm v/c
♅△♆ 10:49 am ☽→♌ 12:58 pm
☉⚹♄ 11:51 am ♅→♊ 4:25 pm
☽☍♆ 12:10 pm ☽△♇ 8:27 pm

June

ℌ 〉〉〉 Monday
9

☽☍♅ 5:24 am
♃ R 5:24 pm

□ Becky Bee 1995

Mother Holding All

♂♂♂

ℌ Tuesday
10

☽△♄ 12:48 am
☉⚹☽ 3:44 am
☽☍♃ 8:27 am v/c
♀⚺♅ 5:07 pm
☿☍♇ 7:04 pm

☿☿☿

ℌ
♍ Wednesday
11

☽→♍ 12:43 am
☽□♇ 8:21 am
☽□☿ 10:51 am
☽⚹♀ 8:29 pm
☽ApG 9:59 pm

♃♃♃

♍ Thursday
12

☉△♃ 2:22 pm
☉□☽ 9:52 pm

Waxing Half Moon in ♍ Virgo 9:52 pm PDT
4:52 GMT

♀♀♀

♍
♎ Friday
13

☿△♅ 4:30 am
☽♂♂ 8:45 am
☽△♆ 12:34 pm v/c
☽→♎ 1:35 pm
☽⚹♇ 9:02 pm

All aspects in Pacific Daylight Time; add 3 hours for EDT; add 7 hours for GMT

The Farm

The Farm is a self-supporting colony for women artists. We grow both Christmas and landscape trees, and our crop supports the colony's expenses. In return for housing, all residents contribute five hours of work each weekday morning. We spend the seven hours from one till dinner doing our art.

Women come for a whole summer, sometimes less. We alternate between building and farming, and learn a lot from both. The Farm is a kind of school, giving us skills, know-how, empowerment, courage. We have done all the restoration and conversion of our barns ourselves and built one large barn from scratch. From early June to mid-July we devote ourselves to our trees and working in the fields.

The Farm is about the paintings and prose you do here, mornings in the fields, afternoons in the studios, reading in the evening, the experience of living with women in freedom, in friendship, the comradeship in nature and at the dinner table, good talk, the sun on our flesh by the pond—everywhere around us flowers and woods, a world we have invented here, are perfecting and enjoying, creating a new way to live.

excerpt ▢ Kate Millet 1995

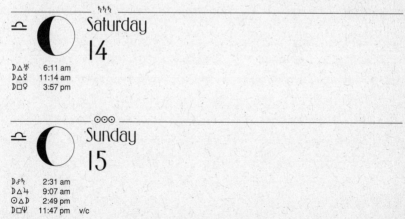

♎ ☽ **Saturday** ᕁᕁᕁ
14

☽△♅ 6:11 am
☽△♀ 11:14 am
☽□♀ 3:57 pm

♎ ☽ **Sunday** ☉☉☉
15

☽☍♄ 2:31 am
☽△♃ 9:07 am
☉△☽ 2:49 pm
☽□♆ 11:47 pm v/c

© *Sue DuMonde 1993*

Summer Solstice: June 21

This is the longest day and shortest night of the year. Emotions rule under a full moon and a Cancer sun. The Goddess as mother is at the culmination of her fertility, sexuality, and power. The promise of possibility conceived at Winter Solstice is manifest.

This is the time of committed lovers. A magical time to make a commitment to love ourselves as well as the partner of our choice. A time to honor our sisterhood and women loving women.

In the midst of brightness we take our first steps into the darkness as the wheel turns and we begin the waning half of the cycle. In the light there is the dark, both having value and bringing completeness to the wheel of the year. Blessed be!   *excerpt © Dánahy Sharonrose 1996*

To My Other Bodies

It's strange, this relationship/relationships.
You are each my hands, my feet,
   sometimes my eyes and mouth to interpret unclear speech.

I spend more time with you than with my lover.
Our boundaries blur with painful necessity
   as I know when you are hungry, but saying you are not,
   or constipated, or doubting yourself,
and you suffer my medical abuses as if they were your own,
   just as you know my everything
from my love of chocolate, my bank balance,
   and what brand of tuna I buy
   to how my twisted body must be placed at night so that
we both get a good night's sleep,
   and how I need you to wash my labia, my hair, my teeth
   but need you to be invisible,
so I can feel alone
   at dinner with my lover while you feed me.

I pay you, but it's never enough to compete with
   Burger King or MacDonalds,
but it's all I have.
It's all THEY will give
   a person with a disability to pay a personal assistant.

Why do you do it?
   I know your friends think this job is weird.
   People at Woolworth's think you're all my daughters,
as a way to rationalize your attentiveness to my every move,
   or normalize the closeness they see between us.

You personal assistants are a crazy bunch
   with precious humor and the insight to know
that crips are far more interesting than Big Macs,
and that sometimes
   we must cross a boundary or risk climbing over a fence
to realize our fullest sense of self
as it is reflected in those around us.

□ *Connie Panzarino 1995*

Juni

☌ ♎ / ♏ ☽ Montag 16

D→♏ 12:51 am
☉△♄ 1:41 pm
D□♅ 4:29 pm

Indigo Art Studio & Gallery:
Womyn Building with Earth
▫ *Linda Meagaen 1995*

♏ / ♍ ☽ Dienstag 17

D△♀ 7:51 am
♂△♆ 4:33 pm
D□♃ 5:50 pm

♏ / ♐ ☽ Mittwoch 18

D⚹♆ 7:34 am
D⚹♂ 8:05 am v/c
☿⚹♄ 8:35 am
D→♐ 8:39 am
D☌♇ 3:04 pm
D⚹♅ 11:10 pm

♐ ◯ Donnerstag 19

♂→♎ 1:30 am
♀□♄ 7:12 am
D△♄ 5:54 pm
☿△♃ 6:46 pm
D⚹♃ 10:57 pm
D☍♀ 11:43 pm

♐ / ♑ ◯ Freitag 20

☉⚻♆ 8:58 am
☉☍D 12:09 pm v/c
D→♑ 1:02 pm
D□♂ 2:11 pm

Full Moon in ♐ Sagittarius 12:09 pm PDT, 19:09 GMT

All aspects in Pacific Daylight Time; add 3 hours for EDT; add 7 hours for GMT

Year at a glance for CANCER ♋ (June 21–July 22)

1996 ended a challenging seven-year phase of upset and disturbance in partnerships (perhaps you've met all the weird people you need to for a while?). Relationships that survived are likely to stabilize. Don't forget all you've learned about the need for space and independence in your close unions. A change in business partners will be lucrative.

In 1997, patience and perseverance further your professional efforts. In the last couple of years you have put your abilities on trial by trying out in a new field, or a new medium. You should be well received, seen as competent and responsible. Make sure you live up to your promises, but be realistic about how much you can handle.

You will need to reevaluate your position and ambitions; remain open to new opportunities. Don't allow yourself to be straitjacketed by obligations; "shoulds" can be suffocating to you. Your body may signal this through a crisis that requires you to pause. This is a reminder that your body is your most significant tool and needs daily regeneration. This is best done through a discipline like yoga, that attends to both body and spirit. Detoxifying helps clear residues from past indulgence.

There will be the occasional pang of regret at leaving behind an old, more easygoing life. Just remember your chances for success are maximized during 1997 and 1998. Make the most of this time. People will look to you for leadership, whether you want it or not. In February 1997, you will be offered an opportunity to break from an old style of doing things. Take an original step. It's a year of beneficial change. If there is a choice, take the option with gradual development. Don't miss the chance entirely; there will be no retakes.

¤ *Gretchen Lawlor 1996*

♑ ○ Samstag
21

☉→♋ 1:20 am
♂△♇ 2:10 pm
♀⊼♃ 4:11 pm
☽□♄ 9:01 pm

Solstice

♋

Sun in Cancer 1:20 am PDT, 8:20 GMT

♑ ○ Sonntag
≈ **22**

☽☌♀ 2:26 am
☽☌♆ 2:11 pm v/c
☽→≈ 3:20 pm
☽△♂ 6:03 pm   ☽✶♇ 9:07 pm
☉□♂ 6:49 pm   ♄ D 10:34 pm

juin

☽☽☽

♒ lundi 23

☽☌♅ 4:39 am
☿⊼♆ 5:49 am
☿→♋ 1:41 pm
☽PrG 9:55 pm
☽✶♄ 11:04 pm

♂♂♂

♒ ♓ mardi 24

☽☌♃ 3:12 am v/c
☉⊼♇ 3:55 pm
☽→♓ 5:09 pm
☿□♂ 5:26 pm
☽△☿ 10:05 pm
♀□⚷ 10:23 pm
☽□♇ 10:53 pm
☉△☽ 11:23 pm

☿☿☿

♓ mercredi 25

☿⊼♇ 3:16 am
☉☌☿ 12:14 pm

♃♃♃

♓ ♈ jeudi 26

♂✶♇ 2:09 pm
☿ApG 2:36 pm
☽△♀ 3:52 pm
☽✶♆ 6:17 pm v/c
☽→♈ 7:38 pm

♀♀♀

♈ vendredi 27

☽△♇ 1:25 am
☽☍♂ 1:49 am
☿⊼♅ 4:23 am
☉□☽ 5:42 am
☽✶♅ 9:07 am
☽□☿ 10:00 am
♀☍♆ 7:21 pm

Waning Half Moon in ♈ Aries 5:42 am PDT, 12:42 GMT

All aspects in Pacific Daylight Time; add 3 hours for EDT; add 7 hours for GMT

Summer

Ishtar in the laundromat
the full moon in our
backyard
laughter in our tent.

¤ *Pesha Gertler 1993*

Denman Island Craft Shop

We are a group of ten craftswomen who have many talents and skills: candlemaking, honey and jam production, glassworking, jewelrymaking, knitting, sewing, weaving, quilting, spinning, photography, pottery, and painting.

Since the beginning of 1993 we have promoted our own artistry, as well as the consigned work of over fifty Denman artists, through our small craft shop on Denman Island.

We take turns (shifts) at running the shop, divide up tasks, and have monthly meetings. We come to group decisions using a form of consensus; disagreements are usually resolved by the use of "rounds"—discussions which go 'round the circle, maybe two or three times until a decision is reached. Our enthusiasm and support for each other, coupled with the variety and beauty of our handcrafted creations, are sources of encouragement and joy for us all.

© *Lynn Thompson 1995*

Denman Island Craft Shop Crew

¤ *Denman Island Craft Shop Crew 1995*

♈ ♉ samedi
28

☽☌♄	4:54 am	
☽✶♃	8:24 am	
♀→♌	11:38 am	
☽□♆	9:54 pm	v/c
☽→♉	11:23 pm	

♉ dimanche
29

☽□♀	12:32 am
☉⊼♅	6:26 am
☽□♅	1:07 pm
☉✶☽	1:38 pm
☽✶♉	11:57 pm

junio

ↃↃↃ
—————————————————————

♉  ## lunes
30

☽□♃   12:56 pm

Womyn Work

© *Laura Irene Wayne 1995*

julio

♂♂♂
—————————————————————

♉
♊ ## martes
1

☽△♆   2:57 am   v/c
☽→♊   4:35 am
♀△♇   4:47 am
☽☍♇   10:32 am
☽⚹♀   11:07 am
☽△♂   3:04 pm
☽△♅   6:36 pm

☿☿☿
—————————————————————

♊ ## miércoles
2

☽⚹♄   4:17 pm
♉□♄   4:46 pm
☽△♃   7:02 pm   v/c

♃♃♃
—————————————————————

♊
♋ ## jueves
3

♉⚼♃   9:44 am
☽→♋   11:33 am

♀♀♀
—————————————————————

♋ ## viernes
4

☽□♂   12:39 am
♀⚹♂   9:11 am
☉☌☽   11:40 am
♀☍♅   6:40 pm

New Moon in ♋ Cancer 11:40 am PDT, 18:40 GMT

All aspects in Pacific Daylight Time; add 3 hours for EDT; add 7 hours for GMT

□ *Shoshana Rothaizer 1977*

Arnica   *Arnica* spp.

Arnica is a wonderful healing balm for stressed muscles. It works best (as do all herbal oils) when we "rub it in" for each other. Arnica can also be taken internally in a one-time dose as a trauma relief following injuries. 10–15 drops of tincture is the recommended dose. Arnica is not an instant pain reliever. Instead, it works to support and enhance the body's own mechanisms for healing muscle and tissue damage. Pregnant women and young children need to consult a practitioner before using arnica internally. Arnica should not be used on broken skin.

© *Colette Gardiner 1996*

♑ ☽☽☽

♌

sábado
5

☽□♄	12:53 am	
♂△♅	7:18 am	
☽♂♅	11:29 am	
♅□♃	6:39 pm	
☽☍♆	6:45 pm	v/c
☽→♌	8:45 pm	

♌ ☉☉☉

domingo
6

☽△♇	3:00 am
☽☍♅	11:36 am
☽✶♂	12:55 pm
☽♂♀	4:16 pm

Journal Entry: Michigan Womyn's Music Festival
(At last, my family, you are here!)

i want a photograph of your faces
each and every one
i need a picture of you
i need to gaze   and stare   and take in
slowly
the indescribable beauty
endless precious miracle
of each of you
so different
i would put them in my wallet
and carry them with me
all 8,748
in a folding plastic accordion
that i
would unflip
and your faces would pour out
spilling forth
fold after fold   like a river
stretching a mile or more
and i would say,
"here,
let me show you my children . . ."

¤ *Christine Pierce 1995*

© Marsha Gómez 1995

Native Women at Michigan Womyn's Music Festival:
2 Spirit Thunder People Dance Troupe & Ulali Music Group

VII. GATHERING TOGETHER MOON

Glimpses of the NGO Forum from the UN Conference on Women, Beijing '95
all photos © Marita Holdaway/Benham Studio Gallery 1996

Letter From Beijing

At the World Conference on Women in Beijing, we were all energized by our power as women. I was in awe of the diversity represented, both in age and ethnicity. The thousands of workshops, panels, discussions, tribunals, and gatherings offered us the space and time to share, learn, explore, exchange. We realized our common desire to have power together, not power over. The work of the conference has only begun. It is through the advocacy of each and every one of us for the rights of women and children, the elderly, the earth and all her species, that it all may come into balance.

© Alea Brage 1995, reprinted and excerpted from Blue Stocking *(Fall 1995)*

July

♌

⟫⟫⟫

Monday
7

♅☌♆	9:04 am	
☽△♄	11:55 am	
☽☍♃	1:44 pm	v/c
♅→♌	10:28 pm	

Umoja: Unity
© *Laura Irene Wayne 1992*

♌
♍

♂♂♂

Tuesday
8

| ☽→♍ | 8:22 am |
| ☽□♇ | 2:45 pm |

♍

☿☿☿

Wednesday
9

♅△♇	2:39 pm
☽ApG	3:56 pm
☉⚹☽	8:48 pm

♍
♎

♃♃♃

Thursday
10

| ☽△♆ | 7:00 pm | v/c |
| ☽→♎ | 9:21 pm | |

♎

♀♀♀

Friday
11

☽⚹♇	3:40 am
☽⚹♅	10:26 am
☽△♅	12:20 pm
☽☌♂	7:32 pm
♅☍♅	10:55 pm

All aspects in Pacific Daylight Time; add 3 hours for EDT; add 7 hours for GMT

Suddenly she discovered that there was a place to be safe amongst the wimmin,

With A-mazingness she joined them in the battle, with wondrous, glorious fear.

They spiraled through myth and cut into deception, touching hands,

They were larger than life, reaching for each other, finally in unison, moving. Seeing no danger anymore, she rested and gently breathed.

© *Tracy Litterick 1986, scene from* The Wandergound, *a Celtic-Amazon film*

♎ Saturday

12

☉□♄	12:48 am
☽⚹♀	7:09 am
☉⚻♃	8:23 am
☽☍♄	1:40 pm
☽△♃	2:11 pm
☉□☽	2:44 pm

Waxing Half Moon in ♎ Libra 2:44 pm PDT, 21:44 GMT

♎
♏ Sunday

13

☽□♆	6:57 am	v/c
☽→♏	9:20 am
☽□♅	11:31 pm

Juli

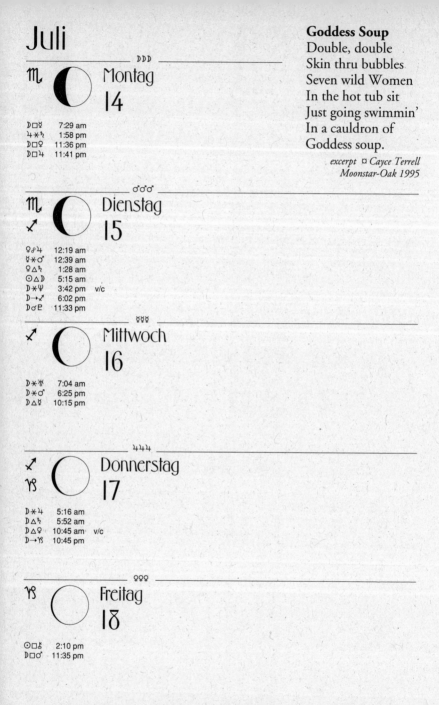

♏ Montag
14

DDD

♏ | ☽ |
D□♂ 7:29 am
♃⚹♄ 1:58 pm
D□♀ 11:36 pm
D□♃ 11:41 pm

♏ Dienstag
♐ 15

♂♂♂

♀☍♃ 12:19 am
☿⚹♂ 12:39 am
♀△♄ 1:28 am
☉△☽ 5:15 am
D⚹♆ 3:42 pm v/c
D→♐ 6:02 pm
D♂♇ 11:33 pm

♐ Mittwoch
16

☿☿☿

D⚹♅ 7:04 am
D⚹♂ 6:25 pm
D△♄ 10:15 pm

♐ Donnerstag
♑ 17

♃♃♃

D⚹♃ 5:16 am
D△♄ 5:52 am
D△♀ 10:45 am v/c
D→♑ 10:45 pm

♑ Freitag
18

♀♀♀

☉□♄ 2:10 pm
D□♂ 11:35 pm

Goddess Soup
Double, double
Skin thru bubbles
Seven wild Women
In the hot tub sit
Just going swimmin'
In a cauldron of
Goddess soup.

excerpt ¤ Cayce Terrell
Moonstar-Oak 1995

All aspects in Pacific Daylight Time; add 3 hours for EDT; add 7 hours for GMT

© Laura Irene Wayne 1994

Womyn Circle

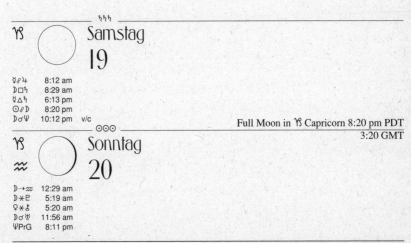

♄♄♄

♑ ◯ Samstag
19

♂☌♃   8:12 am
☽□♄   8:29 am
♂△♄   6:13 pm
☉☍☽   8:20 pm
☽☌♆   10:12 pm   v/c

Full Moon in ♑ Capricorn 8:20 pm PDT
3:20 GMT

◉◉◉

♑ ◯ Sonntag
♒ 20

☽→♒   12:29 am
☽⚹♇   5:19 am
♀⚹♄   5:20 am
☽☌♅   11:56 am
♆PrG   8:11 pm

juillet

Passing It On

© *Lena Bartula 1994*

ⅅⅅⅅ

♒ **lundi**
21

☉⚻♆	12:15 am	
☽△♂	2:21 am	
☽♂♃	7:49 am	
☽✳♄	9:15 am	
☽⚻♅	1:32 pm	
☽PrG	4:13 pm	
☽⚻♀	10:24 pm	v/c

♂♂♂

♒
♓ **mardi**
22

☽→♓	1:00 am
♀⚼♆	1:12 am
☽□♇	5:47 am
☉→♌	12:15 pm

Sun in Leo 12:15 pm PDT, 19:15 GMT

♌

☿☿☿

♓ **mercredi**
23

| ♀→♍ | 6:16 am | |
| ☽✳♆ | 11:32 pm | v/c |

♃♃♃

♓
♈ **jeudi**
24

☽→♈	2:03 am
☿✳♄	3:03 am
☉△☽	4:43 am
☽△♇	6:56 am
☽✳♅	1:33 pm

♀♀♀

♈ **vendredi**
25

☽⚻♂	8:55 am
☽✳♃	9:48 am
☽♂♄	12:14 pm
☿⚼♆	1:02 pm
☉△♇	1:40 pm
♀□♇	4:28 pm

All aspects in Pacific Daylight Time; add 3 hours for EDT; add 7 hours for GMT

Year at a glance for LEO ♌ (July 22–Aug. 22)

There's lots of drama in store for Leo in 1997. As Jupiter, "luck-bringer," joins Uranus, "lightning-force changemaker," in your house of relationships, a mate or close associate has some big surprises for you. Someone close to you is in a very unsettled state. You are less interested in being stable or dependable yourself. Rewrite your agreements to accommodate more spontaneity and freedom to explore, for both of you. If you are not already involved with somebody, your status could change very quickly. Someone very different from yourself is ready to enter your life and change it.

1996 was an unsettling year. It was a good year to lighten your load and clear away old obligations or commitments. You may have explored an assortment of new interests. In the process, you have realized you aren't happy with just dabbling. Something you have done up to this point purely for fun, or as a sideline, could become a passion in 1997. You are hungry for something to throw yourself into. Whatever it is has got to challenge you, to call upon all your resources.

Saturn in your solar 9th house suggests your work may involve travel or politics. This is a time for significant progress in work; take advantage of the impression you make on others at this time.

Leos need to be vigilant about taking up too much of center stage. Do what you can to let everyone shine—that's how you elicit cooperation. Take opportunities that arise for further training. The more you accomplish now, the easier it will be to live up to the demands that will be made upon you a few years from now.   ◻ *Gretchen Lawlor 1996*

♈ ◐ samedi
♉   26

☽□♆	2:10 am	
♂△♃	3:16 am	☽△♀ 11:38 am
☽△♉	3:34 am v/c	☽□♅ 4:45 pm
☽→♉	4:53 am	☿→♍ 5:42 pm
☉□☽	11:28 am	

Waning Half Moon in ♉ Taurus 11:28 am PDT, 18:28 GMT

♉ ◑ dimanche
        27

☽□♃   1:37 pm

---

julio

♉
♊ **lunes**
28

☽△Ψ	7:07 am	v/c	
☽→♊	10:04 am		
☽□♉	2:16 pm		
☽⚹♇	3:20 pm		
♅PrG	4:58 pm	☉⚹☽	9:09 pm
♀⚼♅	8:22 pm	☽△♅	10:19 pm
♂⚹♄	8:25 pm	☽□♀	10:31 pm

Michigan 20
¤ *Kia 1995*

♂♂♂

♊ **martes**
29

♉□♇	1:47 am
☉⚼♅	12:29 pm
☽△♃	7:47 pm
☽⚹♄	11:31 pm

☿☿☿

♊
♋ **miércoles**
30

☽△♂	12:47 am	v/c
☽→♋	5:38 pm	

♃♃♃

♋ **jueves**
31

☽⚹♉	3:39 am
☽⚹♀	12:33 pm

♀♀♀

♋ **viernes**
1

agosto

♉⚼♅	8:33 am
☽□♄	8:38 am
♄ R	9:56 am
☽□♂	12:46 pm

All aspects in Pacific Daylight Time; add 3 hours for EDT; add 7 hours for GMT

Fire Dancing ♀

Witch Camp

At Lammas time
our small circle of four
swells to one hundred and four strong
holding hands and hearts around the big circle.

Thank Habondia, abundance,
for the richness of harmonies and the power
that blossom bursts in the fullness
of community.

Through the dark time
we journey solo or in tight clusters
doing piecework, invisible
and potent.

But here, in the lushness of summer
we are many, and we are seen
in each other's eyes and felt
in the sparks which leap and fly

from our connection.
Bigger and wilder and pregnant with splendid fruit
to nourish us in our parting
until we meet again.

□ *Shoshana Rothaizer 1982*

Campfire, New Mexico

Lammas: August 2   Full Moon in Aquarius

Lammas honors the turning of the wheel once again as we reach the midpoint between summer and fall. The mother Goddess becomes the matron. Under the disseminating moon, the days continue to slowly grow shorter and the heat of the Leo sun intensifies. We may feel excited, anxious, and impatient as we enter the time of waiting. The grain is ripe but not yet harvested.

Lammas (Old English "loaf Mass") in the Wiccan tradition is a cross-quarter holiday acknowledging the miracle of rebirth. We celebrate the Grain Goddess (Corn Mother, Demeter, the Morrigan, Mawb) as source of life and offer her the first ear of corn.

For all of us it is a time to thank and honor Mother Earth. A time to recognize the fruits of our growth and labors. A time to release fears into the fire and state our hopes for the harvest to come. Perhaps simply a time to slow down, listen to the wind, and tune into the rhythm of the earth and sky. Blessed be!

excerpt © Dánahy Sharonrose 1996

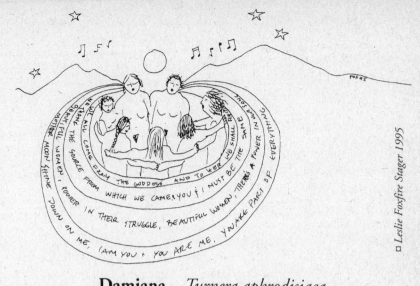

BE MY COME FROM THE GODDESS, AND TO HER WE SHALL RETURN, YOU BE MY GENTLE WOMEN, TOWER IN THEIR STRUGGLE, BEAUTIFUL WOMEN, THERE'S A POWER IN YOUR SOUL MOON SHINING DOWN ON ME, I AM YOU + YOU ARE ME, YOU ARE PART OF EVERYTHING SOURCE FROM WHICH WE CAME, YOU & I MUST BE THE SAME

□ *Leslie Foxfire Stager 1995*

Damiana   *Turnera aphrodisiaca*

The leaf of damiana can be a powerful ally if used wisely. Used internally, it has a calming effect, and will raise the strength of any group work. Tincture is probably a better choice than tea since damiana has a fairly bitter taste. Damiana also brings blood to the genital areas, giving it a mild aphrodisiac quality. It can help make you more psychically aware. Consult a practitioner before using regularly.

© *Colette Gardiner 1996*

♋ ♄♄♄
∞   **sábado**
      2

☽ ♆	12:01 am	v/c
☽→∞	3:27 am	
☽△♇	9:04 am	
☽ °	4:19 pm	

Lughnasadh/Lammas

      ☉☉☉
∞   **domingo**
      3

☉♂☽	1:14 am
☽ ♃	2:36 pm
☽△♄	7:50 pm

New Moon in ∞ Leo 1:14 am PDT, 8:14 GMT

Southern Oregon Women Writers Group, Gourmet Eating Society, and Chorus

These are the women I write for.

When something enormous happens in my life, I write about it. I read what I have written to these women, and the writing and the reading become enormous.

I care to craft what I write because I want to delight these women with my curls of phrase. I want to hear their deep sighs when I have finished reading. Their attention is exquisite. I am known, heard.

We are audience for one another. Every three weeks, regular as a woman who bleeds, some combination of us gathers to read and to listen, to share visual and performing art—photographs as well as poems, songs as well as short stories. Some of us are regular attenders, some occasional. There is structure: a meeting time of 11a.m.–4 p.m., a check-in to announce our offerings for the day and how long each will take, a grand potluck around 1 p.m., a decision each meeting about who will host us next. We drive one, two, three hours to attend; we are scattered over a radius of 150 miles. We travel freeways and dirt roads to reach one another.

There are rules: No wrangles over content. When time is short, fresh material takes priority over older writing that is not being reworked. Be on time, and be present for the entire session. Announcements not pertinent to Writers Group happen over lunch. Any woman who comes with serious intent is welcome.

We laugh a lot. We cry, moved by each other's presentations. We tussle freely over grammar and word choice. We give each other praise, criticism, suggestions.

These women are full of opinions about how something might be said differently.

These women are full of wonder at the power and beauty of their work.

These women encourage one another toward publication, toward daring.

These women make community based on creation.

I write, of course, to please my very own self, to pour my imagination out onto the page and marvel. But to have these women/ this community available in my life as listeners, as editors, as excuse for crafting something sooner rather than later, as fans—ah, this is living among the Muses!

◻ *Bethroot Gwynn 1995*

VIII. CREATING CULTURE MOON

Dyke/Warrior-
Prayers
featuring Sonja Parks
© the root wy'mn theatre
company 1996,
photo by Rita DeBellis

root wy'mn

the root wy'mn theatre company is an ensemble of Afrikan American wy'mn formed to present a herstory of Afrikan-American wy'mn's stories through performances, workshops, and presentations.

root wy'mn's primary objectives are to present a portion of the lives of various coloured wy'mn and to chronicle the herstory of Afrikan-American wy'mn, honoring the Indigenous People of Turtle Island, acknowledging the mixing of the Souls/the Surviving-Spirits/the diverse and brave wy'mn of dark blood/those still to come.

root wy'mn uses words/performance/visual art/dance/music to reach the Ancient/the universal in us, to awaken Spirits, to connect and inspire.

it is our hope that the power of combining art forms will incite
healing/bridging/reclaiming/movement towards
   self-lovve and unification
and that the result of
like-vision lacing
will be a tribute to
COLOURED WY'MNS
of all times
and places.

© the root wy'mn theatre company 1996

August

© Cookie Andrews-Hunt 1992

Paris Muses

♌ ♍ ◅◅◅ **Monday**
4

☽✳♂ 3:11 am v/c
☽→♍ 3:15 pm
☽□♇ 9:00 pm

♍ ♂♂♂ **Tuesday**
5

☽♂♅ 12:44 pm

♍ ☿☿☿ **Wednesday**
6

☽♂♀ 12:51 am
☽ApG 6:33 am
♀☌♃ 4:43 pm

♍ ♎ ♃♃♃ **Thursday**
7

☽△♆ 12:26 am v/c
☽→♎ 4:17 am
☽✳♇ 10:04 am
☽△♅ 5:10 pm

♎ ♀♀♀ **Friday**
8

☉✳☽ 1:24 pm
☽△♃ 2:58 pm
☽☍♄ 9:28 pm

All aspects in Pacific Daylight Time; add 3 hours for EDT; add 7 hours for GMT

Dance Brigade:
Cinderella . . . A Tale of Survival

Dance Brigade has created a magical production—with humor, storytelling, and uplifting choreography. In *Cinderella*, we explore the cycle of abuse and the issues that contemporary women face, revealing the lie behind the standard fairy tale plot of abuse and rescue, which permeates our culture. In the Dance Brigade production, we do not rescue Cinderella, but provide her with choices and insights along her path of self discovery. We sprinkle lightness, laughter, and craziness along the way.   ¤ *Dance Brigade 1993*

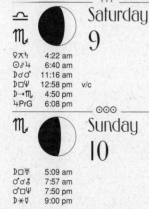

≏
♏   **Saturday**
           9

♀⚷♄   4:22 am
☉☍♃   6:40 am
☽☌♂   11:16 am
☽□♆   12:58 pm   v/c
☽→♏   4:50 pm
♃PrG   6:08 pm

♏   **Sunday**
           10

☽□♅   5:09 am
♂☌♀   7:57 am
♂□♆   7:50 pm
☽⚹♅   9:00 pm

August

 DDD

♏ Montag
11

☽□♃	1:39 am	
☉□☽	5:42 am	
☽✶♀	1:53 pm	
☽✶♆	10:59 pm	v/c

♂♂♂ Waxing Half Moon in ♏ Scorpio 5:42 am PDT, 12:42 GMT

♏ Dienstag
♐
12

☽→♐	2:45 am
☽☌♇	8:01 am
☽✶♅	2:08 pm
☉△♄	4:00 pm

♀♀♀

♐ Mittwoch
13

♇ D	1:30 am
♆□♊	5:05 am
☽□☿	7:03 am
☽✶♃	8:52 am
☽△♄	3:35 pm
☉△☽	5:25 pm

♃♃♃

♐ Donnerstag
♑
14

♂→♏	1:42 am	
☽□♀	2:01 am	v/c
☽→♑	8:42 am	
☽✶♂	9:02 am	

♀♀♀

♑ Freitag
15

☽△☿	11:58 am
♀△♆	1:13 pm
☽□♄	6:51 pm

All aspects in Pacific Daylight Time; add 3 hours for EDT; add 7 hours for GMT

Grrllapalooza

Tough grrl bands
all-wimmin bands
thrashing powerful music
forth from angry, courageous bellies
showing how different we can be
how colorful in our creative
methods of survival

Communities of wimmin onstage
communities of wimmin dancing below

wearing big boots and no shirts
moshing together feeling power surging
       releasing
wimmin/grrls weaving together
expression, desire and deep satisfaction

Grrrowl!!

□ Raggy 1995

ϫϫϫ

♑
♒ ◗ Samstag
16

♀⊼♃	12:08 am	
☽☌♆	7:31 am	
☽△♀	9:10 am	v/c
☽→♒	10:58 am	
☽□♂	1:28 pm	
☽⚹♇	3:34 pm	
☽☌♅	8:40 pm	

☉☉☉

♒ ◗ Sonntag
17

♀→♎	7:31 am
☽☌♃	12:38 pm
♀ R	12:49 pm
☽⚹♄	7:20 pm

août

ᗡᗡᗡ

≈
♓

lundi

18

☉☍☽ 3:55 am v/c
☽→♓ 11:01 am
☽△♂ 3:30 pm
☽□♇ 3:30 pm
☽PrG 9:53 pm

Lunar Lammas
Full Moon in ≈ Aquarius 3:55 am PDT, 10:55 GMT

᚛ ♂♂♂

♓

mardi

19

☽☍♅ 12:28 pm
♀⚹♇ 4:54 pm

☿☿☿

♓
♈

mercredi

20

☽⚹♆ 7:12 am v/c
☽→♈ 10:45 am
☉⚻♆ 12:13 pm
☽△♇ 3:19 pm
☽☍♀ 5:15 pm
☽⚹♅ 8:09 pm

♄♄♄

♈

jeudi

21

☉⚹♃ 11:17 am
☽⚹♃ 11:47 am
♅⚻♃ 5:03 pm
☽♂♄ 7:18 pm

♀♀♀

♈
♉

vendredi

22

♀△♅ 4:34 am
☽□♆ 8:11 am
☉△☽ 11:25 am v/c
☽→♉ 11:57 am
☉→♍ 7:19 pm
☽☍♂ 9:14 pm
☽□♅ 9:42 pm

Sun in Virgo 7:19 pm PDT, 2:19 GMT (Aug. 23)

All aspects in Pacific Daylight Time; add 3 hours for EDT; add 7 hours for GMT

Year at a glance for VIRGO ♍ (Aug. 22–Sept. 22)

Since 1996 Pluto has been sitting in a powerful location at the base of your chart. Though most obvious to the August-born of your sign, all Virgos are experiencing crises and dramatic changes. A significant element of your personal life is due for an overhaul. This could result in members of your family coming and going, a new residence, or extensive house repairs or remodeling. Psychologically, watch out for the reemergence of old childhood issues. It's time to get rid of irrational compulsions and inappropriate childish behaviors that you indulge in now and then. Therapy or body work accelerates the clearing.

You will experience tremendous stimulation through your work. You have a flair for innovation and manage to make the experience enjoyable to coworkers. Saturn's placement suggests a challenge to the realization of your goals in 1997, from a social group which you are a part of. There is some middle ground to be found between totally conforming to external dictates and utterly disregarding convention. Remain true to yourself while continuing to collaborate with others for common gain.

Your rebellion manifests in an eclectic use of tools and techniques, which others may consider too avant-garde. The horizons of your work expand in directions you had not previously dreamed of. Enlist the help of others who are respected in your field. Progress requires collaboration.

¤ Gretchen Lawlor 1996

Africa: Celebrating
© *Betty La Duke 1994*

♉ 　　　♄♄♄

◗ samedi
23

♂□♅ 6:53 am
☽△♉ 12:44 pm
☽□♃ 1:52 pm

♉ 　　　☉☉☉
♊

◗ dimanche
24

☽△♆ 11:50 am v/c
☽→♊ 3:56 pm
☉□☽ 7:24 pm
☽☍♇ 9:04 pm

Waning Half Moon in ♊ Gemini 7:24 pm PDT, 2:24 GMT (Aug. 25)

agosto

♊))) lunes
25

☽△♅	2:09 am
☽△♀	9:12 am
☽□♅	3:43 pm
☉□♇	6:48 pm
☽△♃	7:00 pm

♊ ♂♂♂ martes
♋ ## 26

| ☽⚹♄ | 4:07 am | v/c |
| ☽→♋ | 11:10 pm | |

♋ ☿☿☿ miércoles
27

☉⚹☽	7:26 am
☽△♂	3:26 pm
☽⚹☿	8:50 pm
☽□♀	11:19 pm

♋ ♃♃♃ jueves
28

☿PrG	7:20 am
☽□♄	1:09 pm
☉⚻♅	1:48 pm

♋ ♀♀♀ viernes
♌ ## 29

☽☍♆	4:35 am	v/c
☽→♌	9:19 am	
♀△♃	1:16 pm	
☿⚹♂	1:59 pm	
☽△♇	3:04 pm	
☽☍♅	8:16 pm	

All aspects in Pacific Daylight Time; add 3 hours for EDT; add 7 hours for GMT

Laurie York 1993

Birthplace

Horehound *Marrubium vulgare*

Horehound leaf has the unique ability to remove internal blocks to creativity and inspiration, a useful ally when you are creating culture. Carry it with you, burn it as an incense, or put a few drops of tincture in water. Medicinally, it is used in larger amounts to clear stubborn mucous from the lungs following a cold. Its bitter quality has a stimulating effect on digestion.

© *Colette Gardiner 1996*

♌ ♄♄♄

sábado
30

☽□♂ 5:34 am
☽☍♃ 1:56 pm
☽⚹♀ 4:53 pm

♌ ◉◉◉
♍

domingo
31

☽△♄ 12:30 am v/c
☉♂♉ 6:43 am
☽→♍ 9:27 pm

An Open Letter to My Sisters on the Land

Yes, meetings are difficult. Yes, coming together as wimmin outside the dominant male-ruled culture is difficult. Why?

I believe it is because we carry into our meetings a lot more than agenda items. We carry our family-of-origin material. Who do you remind me of? What buttons do I push for you?

We carry our conditioning, including definitions learned in a male-dominated society: definitions for words such as *power*. What is power, what is power over, what is powerlessness, who's got the power, how do we take it away from who's got it? Is there enough to go around? If I am powerful, then who is not? What is empowerment? (If you want, replace *power* with *control, in control, out of control*.)

We also carry into our meetings class issues, cultural issues, able-bodiedism, internalized homophobia, racism, just to name a few. So, it isn't surprising that meetings are difficult. In fact, what is surprising is that we think they shouldn't be.

I hear my sisters talk of the revolution, of creating new paradigms, of bringing down the patriarchy. How do we do that if we can't figure out how to sit in a "meeting" together for two hours without huge pain?

Traditionally, our wimmin's way has been oral, sitting around a task such as weaving, quilting, cooking, shelling peas, or cleaning herbs, talking about ourselves, our families, our work. *His*torically, we wimmin have been silenced. I ask you to search with me for a way to return to what is truly a wimmin's world—gentle communication; honest communication; loving communication; loud, boisterous, exhilarating communication; difficult communication; painful communication; but, in all, communication.

Communicate, commune, common, commonality, community.

□ *NiAódagaín 1990*

IX. TOOLS OF COMMUNITY MOON

© Marita Holdaway/Benham Studio Gallery 1996

◻ Jan Van Pelt 1995

Consensus Haiku
We choose to decide
each one has a piece of truth
life's divine purpose.

◻ Diana Aleyn Cohen 1994

September

DDD

♍ Monday

1

Having people walk in on me
while I'm going
to the bathroom
is not my idea of community.
excerpt ▢ Juana Maria Gonzalez Paz 1995

☽□♇	3:23 am
☽♂♅	11:48 am
☉♂☽	4:52 pm
☽⚹♂	9:41 pm

New Moon in ♍ Virgo 4:52 pm PDT, 23:52 GMT
Partial Solar Eclipse 5:04 pm PDT (.899 mag.)

♂♂♂

♍ Tuesday

2

☽ApG	2:13 pm
♀☌♄	7:26 pm
⚷→♏	8:00 pm

☿☿☿

♍ Wednesday
♎

3

☽△♆	5:25 am	v/c
☽→♎	10:30 am	
☿△♅	11:43 am	
☽⚹♇	4:31 pm	
☽△♅	9:25 pm	

♃♃♃

♎ Thursday

4

☽△♃	2:37 pm
♂□♃	7:05 pm

♀♀♀

♎ Friday
♏

5

☽⚹♄	1:48 am	
☽☌♀	8:00 am	
☽□♆	6:05 pm	v/c
☽→♏	11:10 pm	
☉△♃	11:33 pm	

All aspects in Pacific Daylight Time; add 3 hours for EDT; add 7 hours for GMT

GIVE WINGS TO THE HEART ♥ ONGOING STAY CONNECTED TO EACH OTHER ♥ PROCESS ♥ CENTER ♥ DON'T DISCARD EACH OTHER ♥ STAY CONNECTED TO YOUR SOURCE ♥ COMFORT ♥ HOLD ONE ANOTHER ♥ EQUALITY ♥ SHARE AND PASS POWER ♥ MAKE CONTRACTS ♥ GENTLE TOUCH ♥ LOVE ALLOWING FREEDOM ♥ MEDIATE ♥ PASSION IS SACRED ♥ LOVE REMAINS COMMUNITY SUPPORT ♥ HEALING IS POSSIBLE ♥ TAKE SOME ACCOUNTABILITY FOR EACH OTHER'S WELL-BEING ♥ TALK ♥ DANCE ♥ ASK FOR HELP ♥ LISTEN ♥ RESPECT ♥ OPENNESS ♥ APPRECIATE THE GIFT OF ATTRACTION ♥ NOURISHMENT ♥ BREATHE ♥ HUG ♥ SILENCE ♥ RESPECT ♥ TIMING ♥ SLOWNESS ♥ WAIT ♥ VALUE RELATIONSHIP ♥ HONOR YOURSELF ♥ WE NEED EACH OF US ♥

© *Kathy Randel 1995*

♏   ☊☊☊

Saturday
6

☽⚹♉ 6:20 am
☽□♅ 9:43 am

♏   ☉☉☉

Sunday
7

☽□♃ 2:08 am
☉⚹☽ 4:39 am
☽☌♂ 5:44 am
☿□♇ 5:34 pm

September

♏
♐   **Montag**
   8

☽✶♆	4:59 am	v/c
☽→♐	9:54 am	
☽□♉	3:14 pm	
☽☌♇	3:40 pm	
☽✶♅	7:51 pm	
☉✶♂	9:27 pm	

♐   **Dienstag**
   9

☽✶♃	11:08 am
♀□♆	1:52 pm
☉□☽	6:31 pm
☿ D	6:43 pm
☽△♄	9:38 pm

Waxing Half Moon in ♐ Sagittarius 6:31 pm PDT
1:31 GMT

♐
♑   **Mittwoch**
   10

☽✶♀	2:56 pm	v/c
☽→♑	5:23 pm	
☽△♉	10:22 pm	

♑   **Donnerstag**
   11

☉✷♄	10:09 am
♀→♏	7:17 pm
☿□♇	11:54 pm

♑
♒   **Freitag**
   12

☽✶♂	2:01 am	
☽□♄	2:30 am	
☉△☽	3:48 am	
♂✷♄	11:22 am	
☽☌♆	4:45 pm	v/c
♀☌♴	7:06 pm	
☽→♒	9:10 pm	
☽□♀	11:26 pm	

All aspects in Pacific Daylight Time; add 3 hours for EDT; add 7 hours for GMT

Spiraling*

Living in community is an opening process, almost like opening to a lover. I trust that even the wimmin I'm most angry with have the group's best interests at heart. I love these wimmin who have abandoned personal gain in order to create something new and unknown with me, with each other. Because we love each other, we can open layer after layer of the truths in our hearts. Because we love each other, we take the time to listen to what each womyn is really saying. In meetings, this is not efficient. But it is the best way we've found to make decisions that reflect each of us, that might possibly satisfy all. Even when we seriously disagree, we listen, and wait for consensus to appear.

It sounds idealistic, and it is. It sounds impractical, and sometimes we have to force a decision when events won't wait. Yet, at our core, we know we are rediscovering ancient ways wimmin must have had to share and govern. This inspiring and sometimes awkward present is the direction we've taken out of patriarchy and into a female future.

¤ Kate Ellison 1995

SPIRAL is womyn-only land in Kentucky, 250 acres of woods with some cleared fields. The land has been in wimmin's hands since 9980, but really started growing as a community after 9987. There have been up to ten wimmin here; now there are only three.

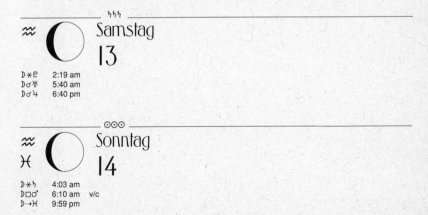

≋ ⟨moon⟩ Samstag
13

☽⚹♇	2:19 am
☽☌♅	5:40 am
☽☌♃	6:40 pm

≋ ⟨moon⟩ Sonntag
ℋ 14

☽⚹♄	4:03 am	
☽□♂	6:10 am	v/c
☽→ℋ	9:59 pm	

septembre

ᗁᗁᗁ

♓ **lundi**

15

☾□♇	2:58 am
☾△♀	4:13 am
☾☍♅	5:51 am
☿⚹♆	9:33 am

As a national parks ranger, isolated from wimmin, I find community in correspondence with friends scattered all over the world.

¤ Guida Veronda 1996

♂♂♂

♓
♈ **mardi**

16

♀□♅	3:50 am	
☾△♂	8:04 am	
☾PrG	8:27 am	
☉☍☾	11:51 am	
☾⚹♆	5:10 pm	v/c
☾→♈	9:25 pm	

Total Lunar Eclipse 11:47 am PDT (1.191 mag.)
Full Moon in ♓ Pisces 11:51 am PDT, 18:51 GMT

☿☿☿

♈ **mercredi**

17

☾△♇	2:25 am
☾⚹♅	5:22 am
☾⚹♃	5:37 pm

♃♃♃

♈
♉ **jeudi**

18

☾♂♄	2:53 am	
☾□♆	4:57 pm	v/c
☾→♉	9:21 pm	

♀♀♀

♉ **vendredi**

19

☾□♅	5:31 am
☾☍♀	11:58 am
☾△♉	1:02 pm
☾□♃	6:09 pm
☉△♆	10:06 pm

All aspects in Pacific Daylight Time; add 3 hours for EDT; add 7 hours for GMT

© *Megaera 1992*

Sage   *Salvia officinalis*

Sage has long been a symbol of wisdom and clarity. The word *sage* has been used to designate a wise person. The leaf of sage stimulates the mental processes and has been used as a brain tonic to keep the brain functioning properly. Years of living and working in community have convinced me that

wise communication and clarity are essential. Taking the time to pass a cup of sage tea or a sage sprig at the beginning of a meeting can start the process with intent and clarity. Sage is generally used as a dried herb and should not be used by nursing womyn.

© *Colette Gardiner 1996*

ϟϟϟ

♉   samedi
♊   **20**

☽ ☍ ♂	2:04 pm	
☽ △ ♆	6:56 pm	
☉ △ ☽	8:31 pm	v/c
☽ → ♊	11:39 pm	

◎◎◎

♊   dimanche
      21

☽ ☍ ♇	5:18 am
☽ △ ♅	8:16 am
☿ ⊼ ♃	4:10 pm
☽ △ ♃	9:39 pm
☽ ☐ ☿	10:22 pm

*Africa:
Brief
Flowering*

© Betty La Duke 1993

Fall Equinox: September 22

Fall Equinox is also known as Mabon, for Queen Maeve of the Faery people. The promise of Solstice and Lammas is fulfilled as we reap the harvest. It is the Witches' Thanksgiving, and the wheel turns once more, bringing a balance of light and dark, with sun in Libra and waning moon at last quarter. The Goddess enters menopause as Earth no longer bears fruit, and Persephone silently enters the underworld. We give thanks as we gather the fruits and grains that will sustain us through the winter and increasing darkness.

This is also the time of the Greater Eleusinian Mysteries. A single stalk of wheat is presented, symbol of Demeter and Persephone—life gone into death until the miracle of rebirth.

At this time of balance and justice, let us not forget that it is just over five hundred years since European settlers first came to Turtle Island. May we honor indigenous people by crying out against the oppression that followed and continues, and by preserving Mother Earth and all her sacred relations. Blessed be!

excerpt © Dánahy Sharonrose 1996

Weaving the Web: ♀♀♀ _Land Networking_

MAIZE*

Landyke community is alive and growing. Lesbians are creating communities on the land, reaching out to country Dyke neighbors, and connecting with Landykes across the country and world. We are moving, together, to live as we are meant to live, in touch with the earth, with each other. Communication creates our community.

MAIZE: A Lesbian Country Magazine is one networking tool which allows us to find each other, to share our words, our images, ourselves. Through _MAIZE_, we put our lives out there, our hopes and disappointments, as we figure out how best to live this life.

When we describe a sunrise, explain how we build our outhouses, lament a recent loss, or offer our skills to one another, we get to know each other. We are nourished by each story, strengthened by each life. This sense of being a community of land-loving Lesbians is essential—knowing we are not alone, knowing we are creating something larger than ourselves.

© _Lee Lanning 1995_

Shewolf's Directory*

Contains current information (descriptions, locations, contacts, philosophies) on over fifty different settlements in the United States and Canada, where wimmin have gathered for community building, enterprises, activities, and/or non-patriarchal living, and for developing cottage industries, retirement communities, and/or wimmin's campgrounds.

© _Shewolf 1996,_ Shewolf's Directory of Wimmin's Lands and Lesbian Communities: 1997–1998

LNR*

Lesbian Natural Resources (LNR) was established to create a network within which Lesbians who are living on land or wishing to live on land could share resources such as skills, information about land purchase and structure, and financial support.

In prioritizing Lesbian-focused space and an environment in which to interact naturally with the earth, many land communities serve as an oasis in patriarchy and almost universally offer retreat and respite to Lesbians in need of them. And in inventing and living sustainable lifestyles, Lesbians on land offer a vision and reality of a future for Lesbians.

◻ _Nett Hart 1995_

*See by-lines for further information

septiembre

〉〉〉

♊ **lunes**
22

☽⚹♄	7:59 am	v/c
♀□♃	2:29 pm	
☉→♎	4:56 pm	

Equinox

♎

♂♂♂

Sun in Libra 4:56 pm PDT, 23:56 GMT

♊
♋ **martes**
23

| ☽→♋ | 5:33 am |
| ☉□☽ | 6:35 am |

☿☿☿

Waning Half Moon in ♋ Cancer 6:35 am PDT, 13:35 GMT

♋ **miércoles**
24

☽△♀	9:01 am
☽⚹☿	2:01 pm
♂⚹♆	3:52 pm
☽□♄	3:55 pm

♃♃♃

♋
♌ **jueves**
25

☿☌♄	3:35 am	
☽☍♆	9:45 am	
☽△♂	10:50 am	v/c
☽→♌	3:12 pm	
☉⚹☽	9:23 pm	
☽△♇	9:51 pm	

♀♀♀

♌ **viernes**
26

☽☍♅	12:52 am
☉⚹♇	3:12 am
☽☍♃	3:42 pm

All aspects in Pacific Daylight Time; add 3 hours for EDT; add 7 hours for GMT

Year at a glance for LIBRA ♎ (Sept. 22–Oct. 23)

Responsibilities and hard work figured prominently in September-born Librans' lives during 1996. The early-October-born Librans will most feel this Saturnian influence in 1997. Partnerships demand time and attention. You benefit from making clear agreements and having good personal boundaries. All Librans are likely to experience challenges in getting along with others. Identifying common goals will help.

You may feel acutely sensitive to other people's hidden agendas. Your willingness to communicate profoundly helps you to achieve a satisfying degree of honesty. Therapy or journaling provides you with a safe setting for getting in touch with your feelings.

You have begun a fourteen-year cycle of greater visibility. People will be more aware of your efforts. Your reputation grows through a willingness to participate in creative partnerships. Cooperate to move forward. Producing goods or services valued in the marketplace helps you get organized and set long-range goals.

Jump at the opportunities presented to you to explore your creative, playful self. In 1997 it is to your advantage to appear as a bit of a character, to display your eccentricities (watch out for excessive pride or arrogance). Take up a new hobby or sport; experiment with music or art. You are in touch with a rare creativity; give it a chance to develop.

Uranus and Jupiter bring surprises, upsets, and opportunities through love affairs and children. Take care if you don't want to get pregnant, especially during February. A fling could break you out of old relating ruts but may not be enduring. Children could be rebellious or inspiring as they uncover their own sparkling genius.

¤ *Gretchen Lawlor 1996*

♌ sábado
27

☽□♀ 2:24 am
☽△♄ 2:58 am
♀⊼♄ 7:57 am
☉△♅ 3:40 pm

♌
♍ domingo
28

☽□♂ 2:43 am v/c
☽→♍ 3:27 am
☽□♇ 10:24 am
♂→♐ 3:22 pm

what a meeting
we had last night!
we all argued—
or was it a fight?
we strove for
            consensus
it sure did tense us
but today (i think)
things are all right.
¤ *zana 1991*

Laura Light

Mirror of My Future, Reflection of My Past

Ancestor Mothers

X. GENERATIONS MOON

© Betty La Duke 1994

Africa: Women Coming Together

Free Speech

When women talked together
In my mother's generation,
They were called "hens."

When they talk together, now,
In my generation,
They're called "revolutionary feminists."

When they talk together
In my daughter's generation,
I dream that they'll be called women. © *Magie Dominic 1993*

September

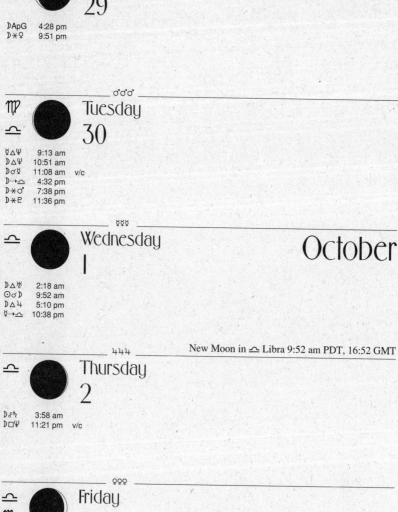

♍ 🌑 ☽☽☽ **Monday**
29

☽ApG 4:28 pm
☽✶♀ 9:51 pm

♍
♎ ♂♂♂ **Tuesday**
30

☿△♆ 9:13 am
☽△♆ 10:51 am
☽♂♅ 11:08 am v/c
☽→♎ 4:32 pm
☽✶♂ 7:38 pm
☽✶♇ 11:36 pm

♎ ☿☿☿ **Wednesday**
1

October

☽△♅ 2:18 am
☉♂☽ 9:52 am
☽△♃ 5:10 pm
☿→♎ 10:38 pm

♈ ♃♃♃ New Moon in ♎ Libra 9:52 am PDT, 16:52 GMT

♎ **Thursday**
2

☽☍♄ 3:58 am
☽□♆ 11:21 pm v/c

♎
♏ ♀♀♀ **Friday**
3

☽→♏ 4:57 am
☽□♅ 2:27 pm
♂♂♇ 4:44 pm
☿✶♇ 10:03 pm

All aspects in Pacific Daylight Time; add 3 hours for EDT; add 7 hours for GMT

© *Marcia Diane 1994*

Graduating Granddaughters

We seek our roots not so we can remain with them, reliving our grandmothers' lives, but so we can choose our own existences more clearly, with full knowledge of their source.

© *Anndee Hochman 1994, reprinted and excerpted from "Acquired Ancestors and Borrowed Kin," in* Everyday Acts & Small Subversions, *with permission from The Eighth Mountain Press*

ħħħ

♏ Saturday
4

♉⚹♂	1:22 am
☽□♃	4:56 am
♉△♅	2:21 pm

○○○

♏ Sunday
♐ 5

☉△♃	12:42 am			
☽☌♀	10:01 am			
♂⚹♅	10:08 am			
☽⚹♆	10:17 am	v/c	☽→♐	3:43 pm
♀⚹♆	1:06 pm		☽☌♇	10:38 pm

Oktober

  Montag
6

♐

☽✶♅	12:50 am
☽♂♂	1:44 am
☽✶♉	6:34 am
☽✶♃	2:45 pm
☉✶☽	5:59 pm

♂♂♂

  Dienstag
7

♐

| ☽△♄ | 12:14 am | v/c |
| ♃ D | 9:37 pm | |

☿☿☿

  Mittwoch
8

♐
♑

☽→♑	12:04 am
♀→♐	1:25 am
☿△♃	5:01 pm
♆ D	6:29 pm
☽□♉	10:43 pm

♃♃♃

  Donnerstag
9

♑

☉□☽	5:22 am
☽□♄	6:38 am
♄PrG	8:22 pm
☉☍♄	9:26 pm

Waxing Half Moon in ♑ Capricorn 5:22 am PDT, 12:22 GMT

♀♀♀

 Freitag
10

♑
♒

☽♂♆	12:35 am	v/c
☽→♒	5:29 am	
♅□♅	8:56 am	
☽✶♀	10:01 am	
☽✶♇	11:56 am	
☽♂♅	1:39 pm	
☽✶♂	8:17 pm	

All aspects in Pacific Daylight Time; add 3 hours for EDT; add 7 hours for GMT

Babymoon

We gaze into each other's eyes,
I grow excited.
You smile,
My heart beats faster.
While others slumber,
We dance under moonlit skies.
Your warm gentle breath caresses my neck,
Reminding me of a spring breeze.
Oblivious to the time,
I draw you closer.
We embrace,
Attempting to shut out the rest of the world.
I want to wrap us in our own cocoon,
Hoping to hold on to each glorious moment
    for eternity.
I dream of the future,
Knowing there will be many more precious moments ahead.
Our souls now already intertwined.
While others sleep,
We shall continue our dance,
As only mothers and their babes can do.

¤ *Mary Rowe 1990*

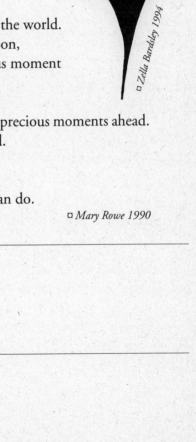

¤ *Zella Bardsley 1994*

♒   **Samstag**

11

☽☌♃	2:11 am	
♀☍♄	9:28 am	
☽⚹♄	10:04 am	
☽△♅	10:09 am	
♀☌♇	10:41 am	
☉△☽	1:00 pm	v/c

♒   **Sonntag**

12

♀⚹♅	7:40 am
☽→♓	7:59 am
☽☐♇	2:13 pm
☽☐♀	4:24 pm

---

octobre

ⅮⅮⅮ

♓ ☽ **lundi**
13

☽□♂ 12:37 am
☉♂☿ 2:02 pm

♂♂♂

♓ ☽ **mardi**
♈   **14**

♅ D   3:48 am
☽⚹♆   3:56 am   v/c
☽→♈   8:25 am
☽△♇   2:34 pm
☽⚹♅   3:58 pm
☽PrG   6:49 pm
☽△♀   8:24 pm

☿☿☿

♈ ○ **mercredi**
15

☽△♂   3:03 am
☽⚹♃   3:48 am
☽♂♄   10:38 am
♂⚹♃   7:16 pm
☉☍☽   8:46 pm
☽☍☿   11:39 pm

♃♃♃   Full Moon in ♈ Aries 8:46 pm PDT
                                              3:46 GMT

♈ ○ **jeudi**
♉   **16**

☽□♆   3:46 am   v/c
☽→♉   8:16 am
☽□♅   3:54 pm

♀♀♀

♉ ○ **vendredi**
17

☽□♃   4:03 am
☿□♆   12:34 pm

All aspects in Pacific Daylight Time; add 3 hours for EDT; add 7 hours for GMT

Cedar
Thuja spp.

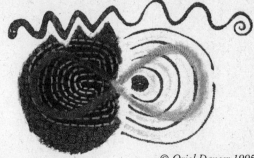

© Oriol Dancer 1995

Trees are the elders of the forest. Trees shelter many generations of plants and animals. In European tradition, evergreens symbolized immortality since they remained green year-round. On a magical level, cedar helps us to connect with our ancestors and can provide support and protection when we work on old issues from this life or from previous lives. The wood of cedar is strong and enduring. It resists rot and insect damage longer than many other types of wood. It was used extensively by the West Coast indigenous peoples of the American continent for shelter, healing, and cleansing. The volatile oils present in cedar leaf can be too strong for some people, so start slowly with this powerful ally. Baby trees and other plants can often be seen growing on old stumps or nurse logs of cedar.

© Colette Gardiner 1996

♉
♊ ☽ samedi
18

☽△♆	4:45 am	v/c
☽→♊	9:26 am	
☽☍♇	4:12 pm	
☽△♅	5:28 pm	

♊ ☽ dimanche
19

♉→♏	5:08 am
♀⚹♃	5:24 am
☽△♃	6:26 am
☽☍♀	6:31 am
☽☍♂	10:50 am
☽⚹♄	1:07 pm

octubre

♊ ☽☽☽
♋) **lunes**
20

☉□♆	7:07 am	
☉△☽	8:52 am	v/c
☽→♋	1:45 pm	
☽△♅	6:22 pm	
☿ApG	6:47 pm	

Acorn & A Young Friend
□ Shoshana Rothaizer 1977

♋ ♂♂♂
) **martes**
21

♂△♄	2:09 am
☽□♄	7:17 pm

♋ ☿☿☿
♌) **miércoles**
22

♅□♇	3:14 am	
♀△♄	1:51 pm	
☽☍♆	4:48 pm	
☉□☽	9:48 pm	v/c
☽→♌	10:10 pm	

♌ ♃♃♃
) **jueves**
23

☉→♏	2:15 am	
♅♂♇	5:37 am	
☽△♇	6:16 am	
☽☍♅	7:30 am	
☽□♅	11:46 am	
☽☍♃	10:49 pm	

Waning Half Moon in ♋ Cancer 9:48 pm PDT
4:48 GMT

♏

Sun in Scorpio 2:15 am PDT, 9:15 GMT

♌ ♀♀♀
) **viernes**
24

☽△♄	5:21 am	
☽△♀	9:30 am	
☽△♂	10:45 am	v/c

All aspects except Oct. 26 in Pacific Daylight Time; add 3 hours for EDT; add 7 hours for GMT

Year at a glance for SCORPIO ♏ (Oct. 23–Nov. 21)

Bolts of lightning illuminate your inner sky. This is not a year to deny your personal needs for the sake of keeping the peace. The changes you make in your home environment allow a new self to emerge. Redecorate; move; expect domestic disruptions, people coming and going. This unsettling Uranian influence, which has been in the air since early 1995, is exaggerated in 1997 when Jupiter also enters Aquarius. Fortunately, this combination also brings flashes of intuitive understanding and resourcefulness. You should be able to pick up the pieces of your personal life and create something new with speed and imagination.

You are contacting an inner independence. You are acutely sensitive to childhood patterns that still influence you, and find the means to quit repeating them in 1997. This occurs easily because you are able to handle truths about yourself that you are normally reluctant to face.

Challenges? Saturn in your solar 6th house indicates a tempering of emotional self-indulgence. You become more aware of the impact your emotional outbursts have upon others. If they bring pain and suffering, learn to discipline yourself. With Chiron transiting your sign, emotions can be focused in more constructive directions or discharged through regular exercise. It's not that you will become less emotional or intense, only that you can direct your passions more positively.

You have less energy and time—a challenge to become more efficient. Your health requires time and attention to maintain it. You may be preoccupied with a lot of small details or in a position where you are working hard without acknowledgment. It is a time of preparation for a debut in 1998.

¤ *Gretchen Lawlor 1996*

♌
♍

sábado
25

☽→♍ 9:59 am
☉✳☽ 3:07 pm
☽☐♇ 6:36 pm

♍

domingo
26

♀☌♂ 3:34 am
☽✳☿ 8:32 am

Dixie Peach
© *Laura Irene Wayne 1991*

Daylight Savings Time ends 2:00 am PDT

MOON X

October

♍︎
♎︎ ## Monday
27

☽ApG	1:02 am
♉︎□♃	1:46 am
☽□♂	2:42 am
☽□♀	3:24 am
☽△♆	4:33 pm v/c
☉□♅	9:11 pm
☽→♎︎	10:05 pm

♎︎ ## Tuesday
28

☽⚹♇	6:51 am
☽△♅	7:52 am
♉︎☌♄	8:07 pm

♎︎ ## Wednesday
29

☽△♃	12:00 am
☽☍♄	5:15 am
☽⚹♂	7:19 pm
☽⚹♀	9:48 pm

♎︎
♏︎ ## Thursday
30

☽□♆	4:56 am v/c
☽→♏︎	10:15 am
☉☌⚴	3:42 pm
☽□♅	7:49 pm

♏︎ ## Friday
31

Samhain/Hallowmas

☉☌☽	2:01 am
☽□♃	11:45 am

Lunar Samhain
New Moon in ♏︎ Scorpio 2:01 am PST, 10:01 GMT

All aspects in Pacific Standard Time; add 3 hours for EST; add 8 hours for GMT

© *Stephanie Gaydos 1989*

Samhain: October 31   New Moon in Scorpio

This cross-quarter holiday (midway between Fall Equinox and Winter Solstice) is the most powerful night of the year, the time when the veil between the worlds is the thinnest. The waning moon reaches her darkest in this balsamic phase. The sun sets deep in watery Scorpio. The Goddess turns crone as we encounter Death in order to be reborn. The ending is the beginning as the wheel turns and Hallowmas becomes the Witches' New Year. Triple Goddess Hecate stands at the gates of death and gives life through midwifery in a never-ending circle.

By donning our Halloween costumes we prepare to face the underworld. Purify with fire. Sit in silence; listen to the ancient ones, our ancestors and foremothers. We grieve the nine million healers burned as witches, the World War II Holocaust in Europe, the recent epidemics of AIDS and breast cancer. We grieve our loved ones who have died and the parts of ourselves which we must let die. We honor those gone before us as we realize what's gone is not lost, what dies is reborn. Blessed be!   *excerpt © Dánahy Sharonrose 1996*

Of Boiling Water

(Dedicated to the community of
Floyd County, Virginia)

In the sitcoms
when the hysterical is in labor
someone always yells
in a TV panic
"I'll go boil some water!"
but the why of boiling water
has been lost
to the voices
of fetal monitors
in some sterile white maternity ward.

When women boiled water at my labortime
their voices filled cups
of nettles and raspberry leaf tea.
Linda came to join Melody
on laborwatch
and boiled water for coffee
when my first pains woke us
and my breaking water
prompted a hasty search
in my new bedroom
for pads, a nose syringe, plastic sheets
for motherwort, black cohosh and fennel.

Melody calmly lit candles and sage
and Linda paced with incense
welcoming me to the sisterhood.

Kaylinda came and boiled water
for Pat's midwife tools
and Pat told me to begin pushing
while Kaylinda held my hand
and told me to moan deeply
connecting myself
with the tides of pain
as my body pushed my daughter
into a cool August dawn.

Later, when someone boiled water
calmly and knowingly
for the comfrey leaves
that healed the tiny tears
on my womanparts
boiling water
seemed to me
a collective
and redeemed
magic.

□ *Sekayi 1995*

XI. RITES OF PASSAGE MOON

Birthing Goddess and Midwives

Good-bye

They come to the river to say their good-bye.
They meet at Rooster Rock, sit and recall
the smoky all-nighters, the time they saw high
kites at the beach, the hike at Silver Creek Falls.

They skip stones on the water surface and talk
until the evening breeze kicks up and chills
them into final embrace. They part and walk
different ways, following different wills.

Widening circles ripple and pulse as they go,
reverberations not from the breeze or the tossed
pebbles but from the sudden void left to show
them what they could not see but by its loss.

They meet, a good-bye to commemorate,
never closer than as they separate.

© *Shirley Kishiyama 1995*

© Joey Garcia 1994

The Day of the Dead (November 1 or 2)

Each year, I organize a feast for the Day of the Dead. I invite friends and relatives. Everyone brings a dish that is the favorite of a dead person they love and admire. Everyone also brings a symbol of something or someone they have lost in the past year, or something they wish to !et go of in the coming year. We name these things, talk about the dead, have a moment of silence when people can pray. Then we eat.

© Josée Lafrenière 1995

		Saturday	November
♏ ♐		**1**	

☽♂♀	2:13 am
☽⚹♆	3:22 pm v/c
☽→♐	8:27 pm

♐ **Sunday 2**

☽♂♇	4:59 am
☽⚹♅	5:44 am
⚵ApG	8:12 am
☽⚹♃	9:21 pm

November

)))

Montag
3

☽△♄   12:55 am
☽☌♂   9:38 pm

♂♂♂

Dienstag
4

☽☌♀   2:49 am   v/c
☽→♑   4:31 am

☿☿☿

Mittwoch
5

♀→♑   12:50 am
☉⚹☽   4:24 am
☽□♄   7:42 am
☉□♃   11:27 am
☿⚹♆   3:49 pm

♃♃♃

Donnerstag
6

☽☌♆   5:58 am
☽⚹♅   7:42 am   v/c
☽→♒   10:33 am
☽⚹♇   6:47 pm
☽☌♅   7:19 pm
☉∠♄   9:37 pm

♀♀♀

Freitag
7

☿→♐   9:42 am
☽☌♃   10:24 am
☽⚹♄   12:29 pm
☉□☽   1:43 pm

Waxing Half Moon in ♒ Aquarius 1:43 pm PST, 21:43 GMT

All aspects in Pacific Standard Time; add 3 hours for EST; add 8 hours for GMT

When I die, give my body to the wimmin
They'll Know what to do.

They'll Know how to hold it
And lovingly wash it
And bless it with herbs & oil.

They'll Know how to wrap it
In a simple woven cloth
And lay it to rest.

They'll Know how to drum out a beat
And chant low & throaty and let
It grow and growl and keen.

They'll Know how to dance me &
Sing me & laugh me into Her arms
And how to celebrate who I was.

They'll Know how to lay me in a
Shallow grave & cover me with leaves
And trace an ochre spiral on my brow.

They'll Know how to call the slugs
And worms to feast on my flesh
And return this which was only borrowed.

Give my body to the wimmin.
They'll Know what to do.
                                    ¤ *Rose Johnson 1993*

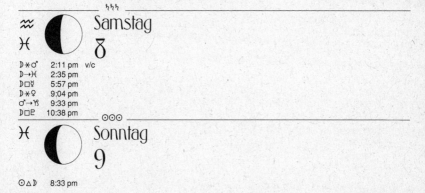

♒
♓   Samstag
            ♉

☽⚹♂   2:11 pm   v/c
☽→♓   2:35 pm
☽□♉   5:57 pm
☽⚹♀   9:04 pm
♂→♑   9:33 pm
☽□♇   10:38 pm

♓   Sonntag
            9

☉△☽   8:33 pm

novembre

♓
♈ 🌑 **lundi**
        10

☽✳Ψ	12:34 pm	v/c
☿☌♇	4:17 pm	
☽→♈	4:44 pm	
☽☌♂	7:04 pm	
☿✳♅	8:18 pm	

Women in Ritual Dance
© *Nancy Blair 1995*

♂♂♂

♈ 🌑 **mardi**
        11

☽△♇	12:40 am	
☽✳♅	1:03 am	
☽△♀	1:34 am	
☽☐♀	2:35 am	
☽✳♃	3:44 pm	
☽☌♄	4:35 pm	
☽PrG	11:49 pm	

☿☿☿

♈
♉ 🌑 **mercredi**
        12

☽☐Ψ	1:42 pm	v/c
☽→♉	5:45 pm	
☽△♂	10:43 pm	

♃♃♃

♉ 🌕 **jeudi**
        13

☽☐♅	2:06 am	
☽△♀	6:57 am	
☽☐♃	5:03 pm	

♀♀♀

♉
♊ 🌕 **vendredi**
        14

☉☍☽	6:12 am	
☽△Ψ	3:00 pm	v/c
☽→♊	7:05 pm	
♃✳♄	7:53 pm	

Full Moon in ♉ Taurus 6:12 am PST, 14:12 GMT

All aspects in Pacific Standard Time; add 3 hours for EST; add 8 hours for GMT

Always We Are Surrounded by the Circle

Circles of Women, Circles of Lesbians
Circles of Amazons
singing, witching, inventing ritual.
Sometimes at New Moon, sometimes at Full Moon
or Beltane or Candlemas
Always at Hallowmas.
These past few years,
Solstices and Equinoxes
Women gather at Fly Away Home
over and over again
repeatedly the same, sometimes not the same.
Lesbians circle, sing from their hearts,
honor the Seasons
raise power
nourish spirits together
enact family, the certainty of ritual, the certainty.
WE HAVE NEVER BEEN JUST THE TWO OF US.
There has always been The Land. The Animals. The Trees.
There has always been The Circle.
THERE IS, ALWAYS, THE CIRCLE,
NO MATTER WHAT HAPPENS TO PARTNERSHIPS.

◻ *Bethroot Gwynn 1989, excerpted from* Making Lesbian Family: The Hearth and the Circle, *a workshop/performance guided by Hawk Madrone and Bethroot Gwynn.*

♓♓♓

Ⅱ ◯ samedi
15

♀✱♄	1:18 am
☽♂♇	3:27 am
☽△⛢	3:45 am
☽♂♅	3:10 pm
☽✱♄	7:18 pm
☽△♃	7:35 pm v/c

☉☉☉

Ⅱ ◯ dimanche
♋ 16

☽→♋ 10:32 pm

---

noviembre

♢♢♢

♋  **lunes**
17

☿△♄	7:29 am
☽♂♂	10:01 am
☿⚹♃	3:35 pm
☽♂♀	8:41 pm

Journey to Isa
© *Uma Thunder Bear 1993*

♂♂♂

♋ **martes**
18

☽□♄	12:10 am
☉△☽	11:59 pm

☿☿☿

♋
♌ **miércoles**
19

☽♂♆	1:10 am	v/c
☽→♌	5:38 am	
☉⚹♆	3:14 pm	
☽△♇	3:32 pm	
☽♂♅	3:47 pm	
♀□♄	9:22 pm	

♃♃♃

♌ **jueves**
20

☽△♄	8:57 am
☽♂♃	10:51 am
☽△☿	6:27 pm

♀♀♀

♌
♍ **viernes**
21

☉□☽	3:58 pm	v/c
☽→♍	4:33 pm	
☉→♐	10:48 pm	

Waning Half Moon in ♌ Leo 3:58 pm PST, 23:58 GMT
Sun in Sagittarius 10:48 pm PST, 6:48 GMT (Nov. 22)

All aspects in Pacific Standard Time; add 3 hours for EST; add 8 hours for GMT

Year at a glance for SAGITTARIUS ✗ (Nov. 21– Dec. 21)

Sagittarians stretch to embrace Pluto, which has been in your sign since the end of 1996. Your life cannot help but be intense right now. Pluto relieves you of anything you no longer need so you can focus on the essential. November-born Sagittarians are the most likely to experience closure on an old life in 1997.

You inspire others in the way you go beyond the confines of the familiar and set your sights on new, previously unimagined futures. What will be the new frontiers? Likely they will be found while traveling, or in new religions or revolutionary political experiments.

Uranus and Jupiter conjoin in your solar 3rd house. Your mind is sharp, your optimism and outlook well received. Studies you embark upon whimsically this year inspire you for years and may be the source of future success. You may be involved in creating a new educational model—there's a future in it for you.

Challenges? If nervousness and restlessness crop up, you are probably trying too hard to impose the new on the old. Don't be attached to seeing through to completion every new idea. Some are purely meant to unsettle your thought processes. Sagittarius is an incurable optimist. Squash tendencies to create glib philosophical justifications for foolhardy mistakes. It is not a good year for gambling or speculation.

Discipline and hard work will be required in order to tap into your creativity in 1997. You should be able to advance in your field because you can work harder and more effectively. Others are impressed by your focus. Be aware of a tendency towards an obsessiveness that can be misread as ruthlessness or insensitivity.

◻ *Gretchen Lawlor 1996*

ጓጓጓ

♍ ◗ sábado
22

☽□♇ 3:10 am
☽△♂ 1:30 pm

◎◎◎

♍ ◖ domingo
23

☽△♀ 2:54 am
♂⚹♄ 5:25 am
☽□♅ 2:21 pm
☽ApG 6:20 pm

Speak Your Heart
© *Uma Thunder Bear 1990*

November

♍︎
♎︎

ⅅⅅⅅ

Monday
24

☽△♆	12:57 am	v/c
☽→♎︎	5:29 am	
☉⚹☽	10:37 am	
☽⚹♇	4:23 pm	
☽△♅	4:35 pm	

♎︎

♂♂♂

Tuesday
25

☽□♂	6:41 am	
☽☍♄	9:40 am	
☽△♃	1:26 pm	
☽□♀	8:17 pm	

♎︎
♏︎

☿☿☿

Wednesday
26

☽⚹♅	9:36 am	
☽□♆	1:26 pm	v/c
☽→♏︎	5:43 pm	

♏︎

♃♃♃

Thursday
27

♂□♄	3:05 am	
☽□♅	4:36 am	
☉☌♇	8:34 am	
☉⚹♅	10:34 am	
♇ApG	2:35 pm	
☽⚹♂	9:54 pm	

♏︎

♀♀♀

Friday
28

☽□♃	1:10 am	
☽⚹♀	10:58 am	
☽⚹♆	11:30 pm	v/c

All aspects in Pacific Standard Time; add 3 hours for EST; add 8 hours for GMT

Thyme *Thymus* spp.

On an esoteric level, thyme helps our bodies suspend their sense of time so that we can heal more quickly. Thyme used in food or as incense brings out the "child" in us and lets us play. A good herb to use in a ritual of transition, such as from childhood to adult life, or at a

© *Monica Sjöö 1993*

funeral when we send our wishes on with those who have passed to the other side. There are many flavors and varieties of thyme. Medicinally, it is a mild disinfectant and expectorant for the lungs.

© *Colette Gardiner 1996*

♏︎
♐︎
Saturday
29

ħ♄ħ

☽→♐︎ 3:28 am
☽☌♇ 1:52 pm
☽⚹♅ 2:01 pm
☉☌☽ 6:14 pm

New Moon in ♐︎ Sagittarius 6:14 pm PST
2:14 GMT

♐︎
Sunday
30

☽△♄ 5:04 am
☽⚹♃ 10:07 am v/c
☿→♑︎ 11:12 am

Full Circle Temple: *Sanctuary, Universe-ity, and Place of Worship for Womyn of All Ages*

Calling forth: all womyn pregnant with faith, that our combined resources can create holy Temple.

Calling forth: midwives whose skills are vast and are ready to catch this Temple.

Calling forth: tenders of the Fire.

Calling forth: priestesses from all walks of life, teachers and students of the healing crafts, facilitators of sacred time and space.

Calling forth: scribes, to maintain our archives.

Calling forth: web weavers, the ones who bring the circle tight and intricate.

Calling forth: womyn who know how to receive, and can teach others.

Calling forth: prayer, residents, visitors, offerings in all forms.

It is time to light the Sacred Flame once again.

We worship, honoring womyn as priestesses of traditions from all faiths. The gates open for womyn of all ages to receive and offer healings such as counseling, teaching, ritual, and support. Studying with sister priestesses, we draw upon our own wealth of knowledge and wisdom. Together, we create new forms, while also passing down traditions to our daughters.

□ Thsia for the Full Circle Temple 1995

© *Monica Sjöö 1993*

The Goddess of Malta and Gozo

XII. TEMPLE MOON

Big Time
wisdom women of many nations
gather whispering
beneath sun
stars
the shade of tents
the shade of arbors
the gentle slant
of round house roof

maidu
oswego
seminole
chugash
hoopa
cherokee
chippewa
apache
washo
we share

the tiny bits of wisdom
each of us
have been gifted

in the sharing
we grow
strong

◻ *Harvest McCampbell 1992*

Women's Totem
◻ *Nancy Bareis 1990*

Dezember

♐ ☽☽☽
♑

Montag
1

☽→♑ 10:38 am
☽☌♅ 12:11 pm

Pagoda
¤ *Rainbow Williams 1995*

♑ ♂♂♂

Dienstag
2

☽□♄ 11:10 am
☽☌♂ 7:12 pm

♑ ☿☿☿
♒

Mittwoch
3

☽☌♀ 6:52 am
☽☌♆ 12:29 pm v/c
☽→♒ 3:58 pm

♒ ♃♃♃

Donnerstag
4

☽⚹♇ 2:01 am
☽☌♅ 2:08 am
☉⚹☽ 2:21 am
☽⚹♄ 3:49 pm
☽☌♃ 10:02 pm v/c

♒ ♀♀♀
♓

Freitag
5

☉△♄ 9:53 am
☽→♓ 8:07 pm

All aspects in Pacific Standard Time; add 3 hours for EST; add 8 hours for GMT

Pagoda

Pagoda is a Lesbian residential community in St. Augustine, Florida, just over the sand dunes from the Atlantic Ocean. At present, twenty-one Lesbians live, more or less compatibly, in its fourteen small, fifty-year-old Lesbian-owned cottages. Pagoda is also the "Pagoda Temple of Love," a two-and-a-half story beach house that is incorporated as a tax-exempt temple of woman-centered worship and culture. We call it the Center. The Center houses a meeting space/lounge, five bedrooms, two bathrooms and kitchens; a small theater, and an adjacent, nudity-optional swimming pool. Each year, hundreds of women, mostly Lesbians, come from all over the USA, and from Canada, Australia, and Europe. They participate in Pagoda's ceremonies, celebrations, and parties;

splash in the pool, and attend concerts, plays, readings, workshops, and art exhibits in Pagoda's women-only space. Most residents, supporters, and guests think of the Center as a healing space, a place where we can renew our spirits, exhausted from the daily struggle of living in the patriarchy.

◻ *Rainbow Williams 1995*

Pagoda

excerpt © Marilyn Murphy 1995

ↄↄↄ

♓  Samstag

6

☽✶☿	1:41 am
☽□♇	6:08 am
☉□☽	10:09 pm

ʘʘʘ

Waxing Half Moon in ♓ Pisces 10:09 pm PST
6:09 GMT

♓
♈

Sonntag

7

☿ R	8:56 am	
☽✶♂	9:26 am	
☽✶♀	7:37 pm	
☽✶♆	8:15 pm	v/c
☽→♈	11:24 pm	

décembre

♈ ☽ **lundi**
♉ **8**

☽□☿	5:00 am
☽△♇	9:24 am
☽✳♅	9:32 am
♀♂♆	11:31 am
☽♂♄	10:22 pm

♂♂♂

♈ ☽ **mardi**
9

☉△☽	4:57 am
☽✳♃	5:44 am
☽PrG	8:55 am
☽□♂	3:06 pm
☉✳♃	6:00 pm
☽□♆	10:59 pm

☿☿☿

♈ ☽ **mercredi**
♉ **10**

☽□♀	12:22 am	v/c
☽→♉	2:00 am	
☽△☿	6:23 am	
☽□♅	12:13 pm	

♃♃♃

♉ ☽ **jeudi**
11

☽□♃	8:50 am
☽△♂	8:32 pm
♀→♒	8:39 pm

♀♀♀

♉ ☽ **vendredi**
♊ **12**

☽△♆	1:39 am	v/c
☽→♊	4:35 am	
☽△♀	4:52 am	
☽☍♇	2:55 pm	
☽△♅	3:06 pm	

All aspects in Pacific Standard Time; add 3 hours for EST; add 8 hours for GMT

Woman Gathering #2

¤ _Tamara Thiebaux 1994_

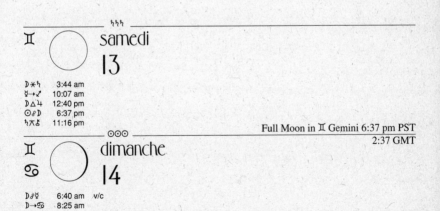

ᚺᚺᚺ

♊ ○ samedi

13

☽✳♄	3:44 am
♂→♐	10:07 am
☽△♃	12:40 pm
☉☍☽	6:37 pm
♄⚹♇	11:16 pm

Full Moon in ♊ Gemini 6:37 pm PST
2:37 GMT

○○○

♊
♋ ○ dimanche

14

| ☽☍♅ | 6:40 am | v/c |
| ☽→♋ | 8:25 am | |

diciembre

〉〉〉

♋ ◗ **lunes**
15

☽□♄ 8:37 am
♂☌♆ 9:19 pm

Woman Gathering #1
▢ Tamara Thiebaux 1994

♂♂♂

♋
♌ ◗ **martes**
16

♄ D 2:29 am
☽☍♆ 12:00 pm
☽☍♂ 12:54 pm v/c
☽→♌ 2:58 pm
☽☍♀ 6:57 pm
☉☌☿ 11:53 pm

☿☿☿

♌ ◖ **miércoles**
17

☽△♇ 2:44 am
☽☍♅ 3:01 am
☿PrG 3:54 am
☽△♄ 4:43 am
♂→♒ 10:37 pm

♃♃♃

♌ ◖ **jueves**
18

☽☍♃ 4:26 am
☽△☿ 11:51 am
☉△☽ 7:34 pm v/c

♀♀♀

♌
♍ ◗ **viernes**
19

☽→♍ 1:00 am
☽□♇ 1:38 pm

All aspects in Pacific Standard Time; add 3 hours for EST; add 8 hours for GMT

Year at a glance CAPRICORN ♑ (Dec. 21–Jan. 19)

Neptune clings tenaciously to the last degrees of Capricorn in 1997. Hang onto your dreams for as long as possible (difficult for such a pragmatic sign). You are a focal point for certain universal values; hold fast to your position. Don't let the inertia of "how it's always been" strangle your convictions. By standing in stark contrast, you may be able to sound a wake-up call to those around you.

Don't lose sight of the territory you explored last year. This year may not be as big for traveling or adventures, but there are ongoing benefits and connections you can use to your advantage. The year may start off in a haze of unrealistic optimism. Your vision clears by February.

Your material and economic situation is unsteady and needs to be set up so it can adapt to unexpected fluctuations. Watch for sudden windfalls and opportunities from unexpected quarters. Capitalize on your ability to drop everything and respond to the moment. In February, watch for a significant opportunity, and take it as far as you can. Don't expect any trend to continue in the same direction for long.

Saturn's placement at the base of your chart suggests it's the right time to seek out roots, to secure a stable base of operations for future accomplishments. You may need to simplify your needs and be creative with your financing to do this. Payments and repairs seem burdensome. Ultimately it is inner nourishment you are attempting to secure. You are proving to yourself that you can care for yourself, parent yourself. You may need to do some work disconnecting yourself from old family roles. Memories from your past come up to be resolved; it is a good time for emotional housecleaning.

¤ Gretchen Lawlor 1996

ħħ

♏  sábado

20

☽□☿   6:23 pm

⊙⊙⊙

♏   domingo   *Solstice*
♎
21
                                                                                    ♑

☿⚹♃   4:02 am
☽△♇   10:42 am   v/c
⊙→♑   12:07 pm   ☽ApG   3:33 pm
☽→♎   1:35 pm   ☽△♂   7:46 pm
⊙□☽   1:43 pm   ☽△♀   8:43 pm

Sun in Capricorn 12:07 pm PST, 20:07 GMT
Waning Half Moon in ♎ Libra 1:43 pm PST, 21:43 GMT

MOON XII

Drawing Water from the Well

I went down to the well, like Leah and Rachel, like Miriam and Rebecca. The women of the Old Testament were always meeting at wells. Things were welling up inside of them, inside of me. I was looking for women with whom I could draw water—quench my thirst, cleanse my soul, mirror even a reflection of myself. Who was I— more than this empty space, this longing, this searching? Like an empty cup, a chalice perhaps, waiting to be filled. I long to bear the libation, a sacrament we raise to our lips. Let us taste the communion.

We are all sometimes women alone, waiting for this chance to come together. It is a marking point on the mythic map of our journey. We have wakened to the calling for something deeper, something we call up from the earth, from our bodies. As women we find ourselves rooted in our bodies. We can't escape them, so we embrace them. And this is the beginning, when we turn inward to draw up water from the well. We will meet at the source.

□ *Julie Weber 1994*

□ *zana 1983*

Winter Solstice: December 21

It is the longest night of the year, the shortest day. We meet to honor the darkness at its peak, reclaiming the night sky and the dark womb as source of light and life. We rejoice in the return of the sun as the light begins to grow. The Goddess is the newborn baby. We honor the birth of the Sun Goddess, Lucina, coming with her crown of lights to disperse the darkness. Amaterasu (Japan) comes out of the dark cave, sees her reflection in a mirror, and lights the world with love from the beauty she sees. Yemaya (Africa) creates the world anew from her womb.

Burn many candles. Light the Yule log. Allow yourself to be still and quiet. Let the darkness bring forth new ideas. Make wishes for the new year. Stay up all night and greet the morning sun. Blessed be!

excerpt © Dánahy Sharonrose 1996

I Am Learning These Blessings

I am learning by heart
what has never before been taught
Tracing hurt with a kissed finger
I find the pattern
in a constellation of scars
and recognize myself there

What was inconceivable is
born like blossoms from the black soil
as light pours warm honey
and something new learns to rise

Holding myself gently,
I turn to my sisters in the circle
We are learning by heart
what cannot be taught
to nurture the miracle of each
as we are born with fists
opening into stars reaching
beyond what we have known

and giving tenderly
what we have yet to receive
We feed each other yeasty bread,
saying "May you never hunger"

We have been unthinking
now we are untangling barbed wire between us
picking up the garbage
knowing there is nowhere we can put it
where it will not be
each agreeing to hold our own

doing the daily work
of making bread and community
Learning by heart

as we pass the chalice, full and trusting
in the wholeness of the circle
it will return from a different direction
with its blessing
"May you never thirst"

December

♎ **Monday**
22

☽✶♇	2:39 am
☽△♅	3:03 am
♀♂♂	1:43 pm
☽☍♄	5:09 pm

♂♂♂

♎ **Tuesday**
23

☽✶♉	2:59 am
☽△♃	7:15 am
☽□♆	11:29 pm v/c

☿☿☿

♎ **Wednesday**
♏ **24**

☽→♏	2:07 am
☉✶☽	7:49 am
☽□♀	9:44 am
☽☌♂	12:18 pm
☽□♅	3:27 pm

♃♃♃

♏ **Thursday**
25

☽□♃	7:10 pm

♀♀♀

♏ **Friday**
♐ **26**

♂✶♇	8:06 am
☽✶♆	9:47 am v/c
☽→♐	12:07 pm
♀ R	1:21 pm
♂♂♅	4:39 pm
☽✶♀	7:29 pm

All aspects in Pacific Standard Time; add 3 hours for EST; add 8 hours for GMT

© *Sandra Stanton 1994-95*

Cinnamon Bark
Cinnamomum zeylanicum

Herbs provide a wonderful way to create sacred space, whether it's in a ceremonial area set aside for that purpose, or in creating it on the spot. I tend to have a wide array of herbs that I have carefully gathered and dried to use in different ways in consecrating sacred space. Cinnamon is a warming, stimulating, generally protective herb, and has the advantages of being available almost everywhere and ready to use. Place it on a burning piece of charcoal or sprinkle it on a wood stove. Cinnamon draws expansive energy wherever it is burned and

 raises the energy vibration in the room. It was used in many Eastern countries for the purpose of temple purification.

© *Colette Gardiner 1996*

 ♐

Saturday
27

☽ ☌ ♇	12:26 am
☽ ⚹ ♅	12:56 am
☽ ⚹ ♂	1:26 am
♉ D	3:41 am
☽ △ ♄	1:24 pm
☽ ☌ ♉	7:40 pm

 ♐
♑

Sunday
28

☽ ⚹ ♃	3:40 am	v/c
☽ → ♑	6:48 pm	

We'Moon: Calendar/Land/Community

We'Moon is not just an appointment book, it is a way of life! It is not just something we do on paper, it is something we create as a small intentional community of we'moon living on land in Oregyn. It is something we create with an international community of womyn who come together on these pages to share the creative expressions of our lives.

We at We'Moon have the special task of interweaving our life on the land with our work on the calendar throughout the year. The publishing of the We'Moon calendar is the main cottage industry supporting we'moon living in our community.

We'moon Gaia Gals got Gaia Rhythm! We dance to the Directions, end our weekly meetings with a Schoom!, celebrate the cycles, grow our food, drink water from the ground, live with fire, breathe! We have check-ins, feelings meetings, work in the garden, do yoga and body work, eat together, take breaks. Each one holds a piece of the truth, we honor the sacred in our work, make altars in the office, name computers after goddesses, bring the theme home, birth **We'Moon** with magic.

Like the moon, we go through our changes and have our differences. While the old cultural divides of class, race, age, culture, nationality, spirituality and sexual identity continue to challenge and teach us—they can also raise our consciousness. Consensus training has helped us to value and work through our differences. As a group, we are learning to survive conflict with love and humor.

We are all beginners at this thing called community—whether we have been doing it for 20 years, or are just passing through—it is a drop in the bucket of patriarchal time. We are re-membering community and creating culture as we'moon loving we'moon. We still have much to learn, but we're committed to keeping on keeping on.

□ *Musawa 1996*

XIII. WE'MOON MOON

□ Linda Meagaen 1995

We'Moon Community Members: Past, Present, and Future
(Back l–r: Lori Katz, Amy Schutzer, Pandora, Carruch, Musawa,
Front: l–r: Linda Meagaen, Beth Freewomon, Marna Hauk)

□ Guida Veronda 1994

We'Moon '96 *Weaving at She Wings, Fly Away Home*

Dezember

♑ ### Montag
29

☉☌☽ 8:57 am
☽□♄ 6:52 pm

We'Moon Schoom!
¤ Linda Meagaen 1995

New Moon in ♑ Capricorn 8:57 am PST, 16:57 GMT

♑ ### Dienstag
≈ ### 30

☽☌♆ 9:07 pm v/c
☽→≈ 10:58 pm

≈ ### Mittwoch
31

☽☌♀ 4:57 am
☽⚹♇ 10:31 am
☽☌♅ 11:07 am
☽☌♂ 5:25 pm
☽⚹♄ 10:26 pm

≈ ### Donnerstag
1

Januar 1998

☽⚹♅ 7:05 am
☽☌♃ 1:07 pm v/c

≈ ### Freitag
♓ ### 2

☽→♓ 1:56 am
☽□♇ 1:29 pm
☉⚹☽ 11:26 pm

All aspects in Pacific Standard Time; add 3 hours for EST; add 8 hours for GMT

To my Land Sisters

First, we want to thank all of you who entered this year's Annual Refrigerator-Cleanout-and-Guess-What-Food-This-Used-To-Be Contest. Carruch, our soul judge this year, said that the entries were fascinating and varied, providing a number of stunning visual, as well as olfactory surprises!! Well done, leftover artists! However, we're sad to report that, since so few of you (in fact, none of you) signed or dated your entries, we're unable to identify the creator of the winning selection, Vegetable?? Medley with Sauce??. So this year's grand prize will go unclaimed.

CALL FOR CONTRIBUTIONS

Next year's contest begins with today's food, so rush your entry now to the Hazel House refrigerator. Because the number of entries was so large this year, we'll be strictly enforcing our documentation rules, meaning that only **signed** and **dated** entries will be considered. If you neglect to sign and date your entry, it will be discarded at the first sign of decay as if it were ordinary decomposing food, regardless of your artistic sensitivities. Please check the bottom shelf of the refrigerator to see if any of this food is a possible entry for next year's contest. The judge especially enjoyed the entry Four and Two-halves Egg Cartons with Less Than Three Eggs Each. While the food inside was still recognizable, she felt this entry had great promise given a few months. Please mark your entries **immediately** so that we can credit you next year. **Thanks again to all the artists!!**

¤ *Carruch 1995*

♓ ☽ Samstag
3

☽PrG 12:32 am
☽□♉ 12:40 pm

♓ ☽ Sonntag
♈ 4

☉□♄ 2:33 am
☽✶♆ 3:08 am v/c
☽→♈ 4:43 am
☽✶♀ 8:41 am   ☽△♇ 4:26 pm
♂✶♄ 2:58 pm   ☽✶♅ 5:11 pm

janvier

♈ **lundi**
5

☽☌♄	4:22 am
☽⚹♂	5:07 am
☉□☽	6:18 am
☽△♅	7:12 pm
☽⚹♃	8:29 pm

Star Tree, Hazel House

© Beth Freewoman 1993

Waxing Half Moon in ♈ Aries 6:18 am PST, 14:18 GMT

♈
♉ **mardi**
6

☽□♆	6:25 am	v/c
☉⚹♀	6:27 am	
☽→♉	7:52 am	
☽□♀	10:28 am	
☿⚹♃	5:20 pm	
☽□♅	8:41 pm	

♉ **mercredi**
7

☽□♂	11:39 am
♂□♀	1:12 pm
☉△☽	1:50 pm

♉
♊ **jeudi**
8

☽□♃	12:56 am	
☽△♆	10:21 am	v/c
☽→♊	11:42 am	
☽△♀	12:37 pm	

♊  **vendredi**
9

☽☍♇	12:00 am
☽△♅	12:57 am
☽⚹♄	12:23 pm
♀→♑	1:03 pm
☽△♂	7:15 pm

All aspects in Pacific Standard Time; add 3 hours for EST; add 8 hours for GMT

© *Beth Freewomon 1993*

Garden Workday Diptych

♄♄♄

♊ | ◐ | samedi
♋ | | 10

☽△♃	6:31 am	
☽☌♂♅	12:45 pm	v/c
☽→♋	4:43 pm	
♀☌♆	7:01 pm	

☉☉☉

♋ | ○ | dimanche
| | 11

☽□♄	6:25 pm

☽☽☽

♋ | ○ | lundi
♌ | | 12

☿→♑	8:20 am	
☉☍☽	9:24 am	
☽☍♀	8:15 pm	
☽☍♆	10:38 pm	v/c
☽→♌	11:45 pm	

Full Moon in ♋ Cancer 9:24 am PST, 17:24 GMT

MOON XIII

HOW TO BECOME A WE'MOON CONTRIBUTOR

We'Moon is an exploration of a world created in Her image. We welcome artwork by, for, and about womyn. Our focus on womyn is an affirmation of the range and richness of a world where womyn are whole unto themselves. Many earth-based cultures traditionally have womyn-only spaces and times, which, through deepening the female experience, are seen to enhance womyn's contributions to the whole of society. We'Moon invites all womyn who love and honor womyn to join us in this spirit, and we offer what we create from such a space for the benefit of all beings.

Now creating (due date: Sept. 21, 1996):
We'Moon '98: Wise Womyn Ways

Now accepting contributions for:
WE'MOON '99: LUNAR POWER
the moon, prophesy, guidance, meditation, divination, oracles, trance, psychic phenomena, mysticism, right brain creativity, inner light, the mysteries, chaos theory, the feminine principle
We welcome your art and brief writings
DUE DATE: SEPTEMBER 21, 1997

If you are interested in being a We'Moon contributor, please send a business-sized SASE (self-addressed stamped #10 envelope) *or* an SAE and 2 international postal coupons. By July 1997, we will send you a Call for Contributions and a Release form (which will include more information about the theme, as well as how to submit your art and writing).

How to Order a We'Moon
- We'Moon '97 is available directly from the publisher
- @ $16.00 each ($13.95 plus $2.05 surface mail)
- Orders of 3 or more to the same address: postage free
- Inquire about additional charges for 1st class or air mail
- When ordering please include the following: a check or money order in U.S. funds made out to Mother Tongue Ink *and* a note listing your name, address, phone number, and quantity ordered.

Mother Tongue Ink
P.O. Box 1395-A, Estacada, OR 97023
503-630-7848 or 1-800-844-1681 or wemoon@teleport.com

WE'MOON NETWORKING

Visit our Web Home Page! Every New Moon, starting January 8, 1997, there will be a new interactive **We'Moon** experience, including astrological updates with Gretchen Lawlor and community musings with Musawa. **URL http://www.teleport.com/~wemoon/**

Snail Mail or **E-Mail**: be sure to indicate on envelope (for snail mail) or subject line (for e-mail) about what subject (e.g., sales, contributor, networking, job inquiries, community) and/or to whom you are writing. If you want a postal response, please enclose an SASE.

Help work on We'Moon! •Weaving Circles: help choose **We'Moon** art/writing •Internships: special projects, community life (2 week min) •Odd jobs: editing, proofing, database •Ongoing positions: We'Moonager/Matrix/Creatrix, Computer/Contributor Hag . . . .

ERRATA

We'd like to apologize to Emma for crediting her art to the wrong artist in **We'Moon '96** (Moons V and VI). Please see p.22 and the May 10th page for this year's republishing of these gorgeous works. We'd also like to apologize for an error of the printer which marred Kit Sugrue's piece, "Return to Mother Earth" (Moon V). Sorry! And lastly, long overdue apologies to Mari Jackson for crediting her art in **We'Moon '94** with ¤ , instead of ©.

COVER NOTES

Front cover photography by Christine Eagon. This work features hands of women artists in a national network of support groups known as "No Limits." Christine is an original member of the Portland, Oregon "No Limits" community and leads an ongoing group in Vancouver, WA.

Back cover photography by Rita DeBellis. "Root Feet" is a product of my work documenting the Root Wy'mn Theatre Company. I photographed them for the first time as they rehearsed for their inaugural production. They took a break, and I found this image as they sat resting in a circle, feet touching. The company has since adopted this image as a symbol—of their connection to each other, to all women, to the earth, to themselves.

ACKNOWLEDGEMENTS

This is the fifth edition of **We'Moon** that I have been involved in and evolved through. I feel it is an honor to do this work. Thank you Musawa for seeing the **We'Moon** through to this point where she can begin to support me and other wimmin to make our livelihoods; I have enjoyed weaving with you. Special appreciation to the wonderful We'Moon staff: Amy for your editing skills and Creatrix work; Linda for your persistent computer, office, and Matrix support; Pandora and Laura for your work with contributors and more; to all my Land sisters, for your year-round love and support which blesses my life; I love you all.

There is an evergrowing number of wimmin who touch the threads that are woven into what you hold in your hand. Thanks to all who helped in the selection/weaving process: Salisha, Ivy, Dorothy, Kia, Beth W., Debrae, Claudia, Patty, Grace, Moje, Carruch, Reeva, Josanna, Sarah, Elana, Dánahy, Stefanie, Heidi, Margarita, Lois, C.J., Linda, Laura, Amy, Lori, Ila, Judith, Mary, Marna, Grace, Celeste, Amanda, Julie, Teresa, Nina, Rosanne, Kim, Cynthia, Bethroot, Madrone, Guida, Becky, and Catherine. Extra thanks to Margarita, Madrone, Bethroot, and Amy for hosting weaving circles.

I also want to thank the production angels: Justine and NíAódágaín for your professional editing, proofing and editing job; Wimmin of Rainbow's End/Other End for sharing your homes during the marathon; Francis, for your pagemaking skill; Maria, Hope, Laura, gani et se, Kristen, Teri and Kathleen for your indispensable proofing work; And to Jaz, for your yummy food and yoga support.

Once again Gisela, Rosemarie, and Monica have put much love into producing the German edition. © *Beth Freewomon 1996*

© COPYRIGHTS ¤ AND CONTACTING CONTRIBUTORS

Contributor Bylines

A. Kimberlin Blackburn (Kapaa, HI): Living, loving, co-creating with the Goddess in paradise. Would be happy to hear from you at 6510 Puupilo Rd., Kapaa, HI 96746.

Alea Brage (Portland, OR): Being a city girl, I must make it my daily practice to feel of the earth through song, dance, ritual and with we'moons' love.

Amarah K. Gabriel (Pender Island, BC, Canada): A founding member of Stella Maris Gallery, artist cooperative, and single mother, I am deeply inspired by nature, animals, and being a wild womon. I create vividly coloured paintings, which reflect my concern for the environment and transformation, and "reawakening" bowls, bones, suitcases, and chairs with exotic designs.

Ann Marie Mitchell (Lafayette, CO): I am a teacher who is amazed at how much there is to learn.

Anndee Hochman (Philadelphia, PA) writes articles, book reviews, essays, short fiction and occasional e-mail from her home in Philadelphia. Her book of essays, *Everyday Acts & Small Subversions: Women Reinventing Family, Community and Home*, was published in 1994 by the Eighth Mountain Press of Portland.

Annie Ocean (Roseburg, OR): A longtime country lesbian, naturalist-herbalist-witch. A quintuplet water sign, age 47, photographing since she was 7, singing since she was born!

Antiga (Minneapolis, MN) is a feminist witch, writer, singer, artist, crone, and outrageous womoon. Antiga turned 60 in 1992 and is finding these years of her life the best (and scariest) yet. She is currently working on a collection of goddess stories, and a collection of poetry, *The Crone and her Cronies*.

Becky Bee (Grants Pass, OR): Teacher of women's Earth home building workshops, mother of three, lesbian, lover of life. For workshop information, contact Groundworks at PO Box 381, Murphy, OR 97527, (541) 471-3470.

Berta Freistadt (London, England): Poet and storyteller. Garden maker, cat companion. Aunty to children. Catcher, so far, of all that life can chuck. Collector of friends and stones—looking for angels.

Beth Freewomon (Estacada, OR): I am feeling my roots and my sense of home and place deepen. I watch and feel Her Earth body and night sky ever change. I am devoted and a bit whacky and I've never written a resume! Blessed be.

Bethroot Gwynn (Myrtle Creek, OR): I have been living on lesbian land for 20 years—growing food, art, poetry, ritual. We offer summer workshops for women in Tai Chi, Personal Theater, Writing. Write for details: Fly Away Home, PO Box 593, Myrtle Creek, OR 97457.

Betty LaDuke (Ashland, OR): An artist-traveler with a passion for research on women and art in third world cultures. Her paintings, resulting from her many travel ventures, are illustrated in color and described in Gloria Orenstein's book, *Multicultural Celebrations: Betty LaDuke's Paintings 1972–1992* (Pomegranate 1993). LaDuke's own works include: *Compañeras: Women, Art, and Social Change in Latin America* (1986), *Africa Through the Eyes of Women Artists* (1990), *Women Artists, Multicultural Visions* (1990), *Africa: Women's Art, Women's Lives* (1996).

Blanche M. Jackson (Auto, WV) is an American-born African, Brooklyn-bred dyke gone country. As founding director of Maat Dompin, Womyn of Color Land Project, & co-proprietor of Market Wimmin, she seeks to bring African earth-centric sensibilities through the present & into the future with appropriate, sustainable technologies & people-centric philosophies.

Camp Sister Spirit (Ovett, MS) is a feminist education retreat and cooperative space for learning non-oppressive lifeways, made available by Sister Spirit Inc., whose mission is to provide information, education, referral, advocacy and meeting space regarding social issues. For further information write to Box 12, Ovett, MS 39464 or e-mail at sisterspir@aol.com.

Carolyn Gage (Santa Rose, CA): A lesbian-feminist playwright, a survivor on her way home.

Carruch (Portland, OR) is a very sexy We'Moon Community Alumna, currently urban-transitional seeking her spiritual/emotional/physical mate. For a good time call 503-795-9426.

Cayce Terrell Moon-Star-Oak (Helen, GA): Storyteller, carpenter, mother, artist, poet, dancer, witch. There are no coincidences. Blessed be!

Christina Baldwin (Whidbey Island, WA) and her partner Ann Linnea hold forth a vision for community they call "PeerSpirit". Based on Christina's book *Calling the Circle*, they teach, learn and network Peer Spirit Circles throughout the US and Canada. Contact PO Box 550, Langley, WA 98260.

Christine Eagon (Vancouver, WA) is a visual artist working primarily in fine art photography for more than a decade, also teaching creative workshops for artists and photographers. She recently taught two masterclasses at the World Congress of Professional Photographers in Dublin, Ireland. Currently Chris is printing images from her trip to the ancient sacred sites of the British Isles.

Christine Pierce (Corvallis, OR): Love of the Earth and Her creatures and of womyn young and old kindles my creative spirit and gives joy, hope, and nourishment to this long-legged Piscean lesbian.

Cilla Ericson (Drottningholm, Sweden): Artist, mother, founder of The Painting Academy for Children in Stockholm. Artists can still see with the eyes of a child.

Colette Gardiner (Eugene, OR) is an herbalist, plant lover, and green witch. She has been working with our green allies for 18 years, is co-owner of Blue Iris Botanicals, and co-founder of the Women's Herbalist Conference. She offers classes, herbwalks, and apprenticeships. She is assisted by her feline companions. To contact: e-mail at coletteg@efn.org or PO Box 10914, Eugene, OR 97440.

Connie Panzarino (Jamaica Plain, MA) is a disabled lesbian writer who has published her autobiography, *The One in the Mirror,* two children's books, numerous essays, poems, and stories.

Cookie Andrews-Hunt (Seattle, WA) is a longtime community photographer and activist, leatherdyke, grandmother and mother, witch artist with a passion for the Goddess and the Two Lands.

Cora Yee (Honolulu, HI): Presently residing in Honolulu. Printmaker and painter.

Dánahy Sharonrose, MA, FCC (Eugene, OR) lives at Asherah Sanctuary, a place of refuge on the edge of the Eugene forest. She is a womanist psychospiritual counselor, sex educator and artist/writer, transforming through her menopausal years. She is committed to facilitating women in re-membering our sacred selves.

Dance Brigade (Oakland, CA) is based in Oakland and performs regularly within the Bay Area and throughout the United States and Canada. Our address is PO Box 2962, Oakland, CA 94609.

Demetra George (Waldport, OR) is author of *Asteroid Goddesses, Astrology for Yourself, Mysteries of the Dark Moon,* and *Finding Our Way through the Dark.* She incorporates mythological archetypes, transpersonal healing therapies, and astrology in her lecturing, writing, and counseling. Demetra teaches internationally and leads pilgrimages to sacred sites in the Mediterranean.

Denman Island Craft Shop (Denman Island, BC, Canada): Members are Anna Lise Haagerup, Bev Severn, Carla Morrison, Cheryl Moreland, Lee Andra Jacobs, Laura Pope, Lynn Thompson, Patti Willis, Phyllis Fabbi, Sudasi Gardner. Contact us at Box 61, Denman Island, BC, V0R 1T0, Canada.

Diana Aleyn Cohen (Portland, OR) is a lesbian poet, carpenter, and mediator. Her book *Grasp: Selected Poems from the First 30 Years* is available for $11.50. Simply send a check to Diana at 4737 N.E. Going St., Portland, OR 97218.

Emma (North London, England): Artist and singer; loves wimmin, meditation, yoga, and (Buddhist) retreats. I am recovering my creativity after a long-term "sentence" in Art School and recovering from addiction one day at a time. May we all be well, happy and free!

Erin Dragonsong (Denman Island, BC, Canada): I'm a poet/mystic/lesbian/witch/counseling student (not necessarily in that order) weaving a web of home, friends, community, work and love in my life. I'm living on a rain foresty island with my family: 1 feline, 1 canine, 1 wonderful humon. And always Goddess. Blessed Be.

Full Circle Temple (Portland, OR): Called to form a container for the witches, the Goddesses, and the priestesses of our times. As we gather, we each bring our small flame to feed a fire filled with fierce Goddess Passion! Feel free to contact us, mail donations, and send prayers: 3125 E. Burnside, Portland, OR 97214, (503) 238-0675.

Gretchen Lawlor (Whidbey Island, WA): Astrologer and naturopath. I do astrological consultations in person or by mail, using appropriate homeopathics and flower essences to support growth and ease challenges. Box 753, Langley, WA 98260 or light@whidbey.com.

Guida Veronda (Yellowstone National Park, WY): Committed to living within the resources of Mother Earth, respecting interconnections, and "interpreting" planet to people in national parks. I am isolated from wimmin's community; correspondence welcome: PO Box 3100, Lake Station, Yellowstone National Park, WY 82190.

Harvest McCampbell (Carmichael, CA) is a poet and herbalist of Native American and northern European descent. She lives and works in Sacramento County, CA.

Hawk Madrone (Fly Away Home, OR): My home is my sanctuary, a women-only hilltop in southern Oregon. With my animal companions nearby, I am a baker, woodworker, gardener, photographer, knitter, teacher, woodswoman, writer.

Ila Suzanne (Portland, OR) lives and writes in Portland, Oregon. She loves water, women, and full moons.

Jan Van Pelt (Seattle, WA) is a mediator and consultant. Through her organization, Building Bridges, she works with individuals and organizations dealing with change and conflict. In September 1995, she joined 40,000 women attending the NGO Forum on Women in China. She describes her participation in the conference as a life-changing experience.

Joey Garcia (Sacramento, CA): My first poem arrived in 1993 on the tail of a dream. I am now devoted to poetry and to following my grandmothers, who were shamans and curanderas in Belize where I was born. I consult by phone or in person and offer workshops and lectures on journaling, yoga/scoliosis, and the shamanic path: 5068 Klondike Way, Cameron Park, CA 95682 (916) 672-9239.

Josée Lafrenière (Montreal, Que., Canada): I am living the contradiction of being a French Canadian graduate student in English. I am an aspiring writer inspired by my relationship with my sisters, both of blood and of spirit.

Joules (Lopez Island, WA): I'm a singer, songwriter, recording artist, Earth-worshipping wild child who makes my home in the woodsy San Juan Islands off the coast of northern Washington. Tapes and CDs of my music are available via: Joules, PO Box 153, Lopez Island, WA 98261.

Juana Maria Gonzalez Paz (Louisa, VA) is a New York Puerto Rican former welfare mom, now the parent of a college student. She's lived at a mixed-gender commune since 1990 & writes regularly about lesbian land, community-based education, & community issues.

Julia Doughty (San Diego, CA) writes poetry and performance art, and explores the wild spaces of the West Coast. She is writer-in-residence at San Diego's The Writing Center.

Julie Weber (Ashland, OR) is a creative writer and witch working for grassroots social change. She is one of the organizers of the Full Moon in June Women's Festival and the Womansource gatherings in southern Oregon.

Kate Ellison (Monticello, KY): I am a pagan carpenter, poet, and yoga instructor living on wimmin's land for 7 years. Pioneer work is difficult, but I love it and I'm committed to being a part of the community we create outside of patriarchy.

Kate Millett (Poughkeepsie, NY): Writer; artist; tree farmer; author of *Sexual Politics, Flying, Sita, Going to Iran, The Basement, The Prositution Papers*; filmmaker *(Three Lives)*; sculptor with about 40 exhibitions of photos, sculpture, drawings, and silkscreens; PhD (Columbia 1970), Oxford First Class Honours.

Katherine (Roseburg, OR): Best friend, lover, mother, grandmother, daughter, sister, aunt, all the relations; lesbian; midwife/healer; writer/poet; dance leader; Sufi; visionary/dreamer.

Kathy Crabbe (Laguna Beach, CA): I am a silk painter living in Laguna Beach. I am deeply interested in metaphysics, especially astrology. I would love to hear from you, so please write me! 122 High Drive, Laguna Beach, CA 92651

Kathy Randel (Jamaica Plain, MA): Photographer and artist revealing the sacred and profound in the everyday. *Daughters of the Moon Tarot* by Ffiona Morgan provided inspiration for this piece. At forty I am coming into my Power—more often happy, peaceful, and whole. Blessed be!

Kia (Inverness, Scotland): I'm an in-love-with-Mother-Nature kinda dyke, gardener, yogi, guilder, on the healing path.

Kristy O'Connor (Perth, Scotland): Artist—slowly re-emerging from a plutonic desent. Excited by "Process Work" and committed to learning to express female sexuality and power in myriad ways.

Kristie Scarazzo (Bridgton, ME): Bushels of bountiful berries and wild spiraling grapevines! Namaste to my sisters and to Life! I am a purple-hearted, moon-worshiping witch and radical feminist. I work as a massage therapist, herbalist, and organic farmer, and do a small bakery. I find peace in the Northeast with my partner Nat and our three cats: Toaster, Violet, and ELMNO.

Laura Irene Wayne (Sacramento, CA) is an African American poet and multi-media artist. Her work has won awards for excellence and has appeared in books, magazines, newspapers, journals, and galleries. She lives with her partner, where they own and operate Womyn Work: A Fine Art Company. You may write or call to schedule a reading or for a catalog of her work: PO Box 221850, Sacramento, CA 95822, (916) 427-4567.

Laurie York (Albion, CA) is a painter who lives on the Mendocino Coast.

Lava (at large, HI) is housesitting in the land of Pele and could errupt at any moment.

Lee Lanning (Serafina, NM) lives at Outland, a Lesbian spirit community in New Mexico. She is editor of *MAIZE: A Lesbian Country Magazine.* Write PO Box 130, Serafina, NM 87569 for info on subscribing to *MAIZE* or living at Outland.

Lena Bartula (Santa Fe, NM): An artist who incorporates dreams, visions and memories to create shrine-like paintings. One of 7 sisters, with 12 years of convent school; past patriarchal concept of God to Divine Feminine. Daughter of the Moon—cohort of the Green Man.

Leslie Foxfire Stager (Walnut Creek, CA): This year I am "breaking free womyn"—leaving behind *all* to travel the world, explore new models of living, and certainly to draw and doodle along the way!

Lin Karmon (San Diego, CA): When I clear my brain and see through my heart all things are Buddha-full. (619) 222-5415.

Linda Meagaen (We'Moon Community, Cascadia): I always wanted to be a country dyke and now here I am, living in the We'Moon community, working on the calendar, and loving life as never before! Soon to be apprenticing in earth house construction with Becky Bee.

Linda Sweatt (Chimayo, NM): As an artist I am seeking to explore and express my highest power. I bring ancient Goddess and Lesbian erotica to the womyn of today to know. My paintings celebrate and honor the power, beauty, and wisdom of womyn! I live in the mountainous desert and hike a lot with my son and daughter.

Lucy Poulin (East Orland, Maine) is a former Carmelite nun, now a farmer and the founder of H.O.M.E., Inc. an extended community for people who have no place to go and want to make the world a better place to be.

Luna Dancing Waters (Yonkers, NY): Yemaya priestess, solitary Wiccan (28 years), singing in the world's greatest opera company. Husband and 11 cats share my life. Hobbies: yoga, meditation, animal shelter volunteering, gardening, ninjutsu, and observing sunsets, moonrise, and the Goddess' creatures from our flower-jammed terrace overlooking the Hudson River. Penpals welcomed.

Lyena Strelkoff (Los Angeles, CA): I'm a teacher, writer, dancer, priestess, and beast who loves cooking, making dolls, and just being FREE.

Lynn Thompson (Denman Island, BC, Canada), photographer, often looks for the whimsical, choosing natural light and comfortable surroundings, especially in portraiture. Through the distribution of prints, cards, and magnets, Lynn shares her passion. She welcomes mail order, portrait, and assignment inquiries, c/o Denman Island Craft Shop (see byline for address).

M. Kiwani (Burns Lake, BC, Canada): Waterdragon living on rented rural land.

Magie Dominic (New York, NY): I am a Newfoundland feminist writer and artist, dedicated to healing the earth. I make magical boxes, with earth things for meditation. Send SASE for info to M. Dominic, 348 W. 21st St. #4R, New York, NY 10011. My poetry has been published in Canada, the US, and India.

Mara Friedman (Lorane, OR) is a Scorpio artist. In the quiet of her forest studio, she creates images that both honor and express the spirit of the sacred feminine. For a catalog of cards and prints write her c/o New Moon Visions; PO Box 23; Lorane, OR 97451.

Marcia Diane (Chandler, AZ): Marcia paints multicultural portraits honoring women & feminine spirituality. Her art appears on magazine & book covers. For print/card catalog, send $3 for shipping & handling. Receive 3 cards worth $6. PO Box 3882, Chandler AZ 85244-3882.

Margaret Copfer (Loveland, OH): I am 47 and a wife, mother, teacher, and painter. I have been responding to my own inner promptings regarding the faces and the spirit of the Goddess for almost ten years. I feel that, at this time, I need to see if these images connect at all with the Goddess images of others.

Mari Susan Selby (Santa Fe, NM): After 23 years as an astrologer and Lesbian, I am still in love with women and nature. I'm available for writing workshops and all forms of readings, astrological, poetry, etc. PO Box 8736, Santa Fe, NM 87504.

Marilyn Murphy (St. Augustine, FL): A feminist activist since 1969, she has taught women's history, and founded education/action groups and rape crisis centers. Her essays appear in many Lesbian and feminist publications. For 13 years, she has written a column, "Lesbianic Logic," for Lesbian News. Her book *Are You Girls Traveling Alone? Adventures in Lesbianic Logic* came out in 1991.

Marita Holdaway (Seattle, WA) owns Benham Studio Gallery in Seattle, Washington. She recieved a grant from the Puffin Foundation that allowed her to attend and photo document the 4th World Conference on Women in China. Visit her web site at http://www.halcyon.com/benham/.

Marsha Gómez (Austin, TX): Clay sculptor, environmental/human rights activist for 20 years. Currently director of Alma de Mujer Retreat Center for Social Change. Contact her at La Madre Productions, PO Box 3870, Austin, TX 78764.

Mary Rowe (Milwaukie, OR): Mother, mediator, reclaiming my voice through poetry, grounded in Pacific Northwest, Gemini.

Mary Sojourner (Flagstaff, AZ) writes for Goddess: *Sisters of the Dream* (a novel), *Sister Raven, Brother Hare* and *Dreamweaving* (journals), and more. She loves and serves Light, Shadow, Juniper, Red Cedar, and Raven. Blessed be.

Megaera (Daylesford, Victoria, Australia) is an Australian-born artist whose images reflect and promote her lesbian-feminist values and vision. Postcards, greeting cards, and catalogue available from PO Box 263, Daylesford, VIC 3460, Australia.

Mikaya Heart (Laytonville, CA) was brought up in Scotland, in a thoroughly dysfunctional family. Writing is one of her many passions. She believes we must refute society's lies by being completely and unashamedly ourselves, in public and private.

Monica Sjöö (Bristol, England): I'm involved, 5 years now, in AMA MAWU/ End of Patriarchy movement, a spirituality & political group. I've recently been exhibiting in UK & United Arab Emirate in women's group exhibitions, as well as in a large show of my work, travelling in northern Sweden, where *God Giving Birth* was bought by the new women's art museum in Skellefteae. I amcoauthor of *The Great Cosmic Mother* & author of *New Age and Armageddon*.

Musawa/Radha/Drolma (Estacada, OR): As We'Moon Crone, I am experiencing what it is like to pass the mother role on to the next generation—with both the *We'Moon* almanac and We'Moon Land/Community. I am enjoying not being as involved in the day-to-day work of raising the offspring of our collective creation, while still being part of the circle to guide and enjoy the fruits.

Nancy Ann Jones (La Crescenta, CA) is a witch, Metis elder, grandmother, artist, and cranky old lady. She hangs out as elder priestess of Virago, a compatible company of contentious crones.

Nancy Bareis (Brooklyn, NY): Aries, artist, and photographer.

Nancy Blair (Melbourne Beach, FL) is the author of *Amulets of the Goddess* and *Goddesses for Every Season*. She lives and works in Florida where she creates the Great Goddess Collection Gift Catalog.

Nett Hart (Minneapolis, MN) is a land dyke and the administrator of Lesbian Natural Resources, Box 8742, Minneapolis, MN 55408.

Ní Aódagaín (Waldport, OR) is a wild, word-wielding warrior/witch who is adventuring into new realms of reality, after 10 years of dedicated daily duty to a land called OWL. Look to the sky and watch her fly. Blessed be!!!

Oriol Dancer (Medstead, Sask., Canada): i am an earth-maintenance artist practicing both "on the wall" and "off the wall" ways of working. i am grateful to the grandmothers for their whispers of wisdom; to this circle of life that nourishes, sustains, supports me on this path of service; to all my relations who give away so that i might bring forth beauty for the good of all.

Pesha Gertler (Seattle, WA) is a Leo, and an apprentice crone in love with the Cascade and Olympic Mt. Muses. Sometimes they evoke poems, sometimes guidelines for the women's creative writing classes she leads. And sometimes they bask in silence.

Phyllis Chesler (Brooklyn, NY) has been active in the radical feminist movement since 1967. She is the author of eight books, including *Women and Madness* and *Mothers on Trial: The Battle for Children and Custody*. Dr. Chesler has been envisioning a feminist government in exile since the late sixties. She is Editor-at-Large of *On the Issues* magazine.

Raggy (Tofino, BC, Canada): I'm called Raggy because I'm intense when I'm on the rag. My real name is Chris Lowther. I live in Clayoquot Sound, a rainforest not quite saved. I'm a writer, and I'm reconnecting with my mother who was killed when I was seven.

Rainbow Williams (St. Augustine, FL) is a crone and member of the Old Lesbian Organizing Committee. She enjoys the ocean and Florida sunshine, does architectural drafting, illustration, cartoons, found object goddesses, and history timelines. She plays dulcimer and is a member of The Amazing Almost All Girl String Band.

Rashani (Na'alehu, Ka'ū, HI): A social activist and spiritual seeker since childhood, Rashani has dedicated her life to personal and collective transformation. She is the founder of Earthsong Community, and when not travelling the world she resides on the Big Island of Hawaii.

Reeva Wortel (Estacada, OR): My inspiration comes from people. The people I love and from Mama Earth; she creates my flow, my natural rhythms in my art.

Rita DeBellis (Austin, TX) is a graphic artist/photographer and proprietor of DeBellis DeSign, a print media/communications company in Austin, Texas.

the root wy'mn theatre company (Austin, TX) is an ensemble of Afrikan-American Wy'mn formed to tour a herstory of Afrikan American Wy'mn's stories through performance, workshops and presentations. Writer/artistic director, Sharon Bridgeforth, and the company, can be contacted at 201 W. Stassney #502, Austin, TX 78745.

Sally-Ann Gray (Bondi Beach, New South Wales, Australia): For more information about the Barouti Beadwear Project please contact me at PO Box 233, Bondi Beach, NSW, 2026, Australia, or call/fax (612) 365-1271

Sandra Calvo (Oakland, CA): I enjoy doing my art to connect to, explore, and express the spiritual/emotional/cultural/sexual dimensions of my life. I am especially fond of collages that let me piece many parts into a cohesive whole.

Sandra Pastorius AKA Laughing Giraffe (Santa Cruz, CA): With awe and inspiration, I continue my practice of astrological counseling, metaphysical bookselling at Gateways Book & Gift, and spiritual/political work with the Holy Hemp Sisters. Write me at PO Box 2344, Santa Cruz, CA 95063.

Sandra Spicer (Ottawa, Ont., Canada): My life is woven with the magic of the Goddess; I have crocuses and pussy willows; warm water at Andrews Cottage; fiery leaves and woodsmoke; and the first snowfall. I share this awe with my husband Peter and hope one day we'll share it with a baby.

Sandra Stanton (Farmington, ME): An artist whose paintings are centered around Goddess mythology—ancient & future & all Her beautiful creatures.

Sekayi (Portsmouth, VA) is a poet, mother, lover, teacher, and artistic collaborator currently working in academia and growing in a loving community in New Mexico and the world.

Sheila Broun (Leeds, West Yorkshire, England): Working with Goddess, sacred trees, and elemental forces.

Shewolf (Covington, LA): A crone caretaking land and networking wimmin's lands. Her directory of wimmin's lands is available (ppd) by sending a $12 money order or check to: Royal T. Pub., 2013 Rue Royal, New Orleans, LA 70116 or contact her at Woman's World, PO Box 655, Madisonville, LA 70447.

Shirley Kishiyama (Portland, OR): My poetry reflects my intense commitment to writing about racism. I usually write in form because of its inherent appeal to the hearing sense in hopes of drawing the listener in to what might otherwise be difficult content.

Shoshana Rothaizer (Flushing, NY): A native New Yorker who connects Mother Nature's rhythms and spirits both in city and country. She hopes that her photography serves as a bridge between people of different lifestyles. Brochure of her postcards available: 147-44 69th Rd., Flushing, NY 11367-1732.

Sierra Lonepine Briano (Gaston, OR): I am a 48-year-old dyke artist moving toward cronehood, reconnecting with the earth, creating the Art Farm space for women to retreat and make art.

Sophia Rosenberg (Victoria, BC, Canada) is both a solitary and a member of many communities (in true Gemini fashion). She is a witch, a Jew, a lesbian, a writer, and an artist and she lives on the beautiful West Coast of Canada.

Stephanie Gaydos (San Diego, CA): While living in New Mexico, I was an interpretive guide: sharing the life of an ancient community with people from all corners of the world. This work I am most reminded of, for it gave me serenity, courage, and wisdom. Presently relocating to Big Sky country, to rekindle old friendships.

Sudie Rakusin (Hillsborough, NC): I am a lesbian and an artist. I live in North Carolina with my three dog companions. I have embarked on an exploration of papier maché, which is taking my painting into a three-dimensional realm where I create the surface and then adorn it. Paralleling my personal journey, there are no rules and no limitations. It is exciting and challenging. I thank the universe for providing me this time to go even deeper.

Sue DuMonde (Lopez Island, WA): I am a mother, photographer, bookbinder, school bus driver, wood chopper, & odd jobber. I photograph the small island community I am a part of, alternative gatherings, & the ironic twists of modern society. Postcards of my work reflecting humorous Northwest themes are available at PO Box 524, Lopez Island, WA 98261.

Susan Levitt (Sausalito, CA) is a fey tarot-reading mermaid priestess living in watery bliss by the sea. She is also a bird gal. Blessed beak.

Suzannah Dalzell (Seattle, WA) : I am a free-lance writer and independent scholar. My passions are feminist philosophy/theology and visioning cultural transformation. Currently I am caught up in the emergence of my daughter as a strong, independent womyn.

Suzanne Benton (Ridgefield, CT) creates metal sculptured masks, collage monoprints, and "secret future works" inspired by world culture. She has gathered tales, exhibited her work, presented mask performances and lectures, and led workships and seminars in the US and 24 other countries. Honors include numberous artist-in-residences and grants worldwide.

Tamara Thiebaux (Wolfville, NS, Canada): Visual magicienne pulls out fantastically, elaborately, subtly potent pictures from blank paper and watercolor paint, in between making yummy love and being goofy with a delightfully affectionate musical magicien, and doing other serious things like hanging out with his 12-year-old marvelous daughter and gardening and general shit disturbing.

Thela Brown (Fauquier, BC, Canada): Photographing, painting and dancing the universal, I live with family and friends on a beautiful mountainside farm here in the Kootenays.

Thsia (Portland OR): Priestess remembering threads from the web of truth. I drink in Mama Earth and speak dirt, I bury broken-winged angels and tend to the brilliant cycles. Receiving Goddess . . . receiving Thsia . . . receiving Wisdom.

Tracy Litterick (Sheffield, South Yorkshire, England): I am a wild woman adventurer, mountain biker, footballer, swimmer, homeopath, astrologer, lesbian, photographer, amphibian. Inspired by connectedness with nature, wildness, belly laughing, and the magic of homeopathy.

Uma Thunder Bear (Madison, WI): I am a daughter of the Mother's Heart, an ancient Records Keeper, writer-artist-healer who is healing soul, walking the Beauty Path of Ascension.

Valerie (Roseburg, OR): Nature lover, reader, writer, artist, craftswomon, womon's health care nurse/healer, gardener, land lesbian, animal-loving recluse.

zana (Tucson, AZ): recovering control freak, learning to take life as it comes. what—me worry?! i'm 49, jewish, disabled, on lesbian land 16 years. my book of poetry and art, *herb womon*, is available for $7 from me at HC4 box 6872-044, tucson, az 85735.

Zelie Kūliaikanuʻu Duvauchelle (Molokaʻi, HI): A recording artist native to Hawaiʻi, I play traditional Hawaiian and original music. I run a retreat home on the beach in Molokaʻi, where I enjoy swimming, making art, working in the garden, and playing with my partner Victoria and our dogs Bone and Little.

Zella Bardsley (Boise, ID) is a writer and artist living in Boise with her two children, Greyhound and crone kitty Max. She has an MA from Boise State University and is a frequent contributor to women's spirituality journals.

RETURN TO SOURCE: MERCURY RETROGRADE ☿ ℞

The cycle of the wing-footed messenger, Mercury, represents our mental and communicative life processes. This companion dancer to the sun (never traveling more than 28° away) inspires mobility and adaptability within our environment. Mercury retrogrades three or four times a year, always in a sign of the same element that the sun is in. During this passage, lasting 20 to 28 days, our attention moves toward unfinished business. Since all backward movement symbolizes a return to source, we can use these times to attend to our inner perceptions, and reconnect with the spiritual source of our thoughts.

As 1997 begins, Mercury is already retrograde. During the year Mercury retraces her steps four times while in earth signs. We have the opportunity to reevaluate our material values and appraise tools according to their ecological soundness. During 1997's first Capricorn retrograde period, from January 1 to 12, we reflect on goals and make serious resolutions for the new year. During Taurus' retrograde period, from April 14 to May 8, we can go back through our wintry accumulations and spring clean! From August 17 to September 9, when Mercury is in Virgo, we can work on a community level and clean up our act together. She retrogrades again while in Capricorn from December 7 to 27. We wrap up the year's loose ends, reconsider our social commitments, and rise to collective occasions.

© *Sandra Pastorius 1996*

ECLIPSES 1997

A solar eclipse is a conjunction of the sun and the moon. This occurs only at the time of the new moon. A solar eclipse can be partial, total, or annular. An annular eclipse occurs when the moon is at apogee and the surface of the moon is not large enough to completely block out the sun. As a result, the sun leaves a light ring around the moon.

A lunar eclipse is an opposition of the sun and the moon. This occurs only during the time of the full moon. A lunar eclipse occurs 14 days before or after a solar eclipse. Total, partial, and appulse eclipses are the forms of lunar eclipse. During an appulse eclipse, the body of the moon only receives the light of the sun from one side of the earth. This produces a darkening of the moon's surface.

During the time of the eclipse, a crack in ordinary reality appears. Eclipses bring us in touch with our dark side: fears, wild woman selves, emotional patterns, animal natures. We can use this information to create a window for change, on any level, and specifically to evolve our emotional consciousness. 1997 eclipses occur March 8, March 23, September 1, and September 16. © *Mari Susan Selby 1993*

EVOLUTIONARY COMMUNITY
OUTER PLANETARY REVOLUTIONS: TAKING OUR PLACE IN SPACE

The recent planetary revolutions of Pluto, into the sign of Sagittarius (until 2008), and Uranus, into the sign of Aquarius (until 2003), sound urgent calls for truth and freedom. Emerging from the insecurities of the trying and deeply purging years of Pluto in Scorpio (1984–1995), we now apply the lessons we've learned, bringing our medicine into the public forum. Pluto in Sagittarius, symbolized by Persephone's ascent from the underworld, externalizes a spontaneous truthfulness that allows our spirits to surge with "conscious optimism."

We have the power to choose whether our spiritual beliefs become a wedge between us or the bonding agent for our common good. As the struggle between church and state intensifies, our passions run high and our righteous indignations get mirrored. The evolving civil war of values is of the old paradigm. If we are to loosen the grip of global greed and stop the exploitation and pollution of nature, we must transform these old belief systems. We are finding that the boundaries between us are speculative and can be rearranged for our changing purposes.

The Aquarian vision of Uranus opens our eyes and telescopes onto the heavens, revealing a vastness so rich we see the very seedbed of the universe, the womb of the Great Mother. We are discovering new planets and radically changing our perceptions of what we think we know. Telecommunication links, space travel, and an awakening collective intuition expand our realms of knowledge.

These planetary energies are helping us to create the connections necessary to form a critical mass consciousness that can coalesce into sustainable, evolutionary communities worldwide. Everything we do, or don't do, as individuals becomes part of our strategy. It is time to become millennial activists. It will be our acts of joyful participation in the sorrows of the world that bring a healing balm to our ailing planet. Watch creativity leap off the planet as linear frameworks crumble and the new chaos within the divine mind opens everything up! This mythos of liberation is the torch we (all immigrants into the next millenium) carry, willing to take our place in space.

© *Sandra Pastorius 1996*

ASTEROIDS

The asteroids, a belt of planetary bodies orbiting in the solar system mostly between Mars and Jupiter, were discovered in the early 1800's. Since the sighting of new planets in the solar system corresponds to the activation of new centers of consciousness in the human psyche, the discovery of these planetary bodies, carrying the names of hundreds of goddesses, points to an awakening of a feminine-defined principle.

Because traditional astrology uses a ten-planet system (and only two of these symbols, the Moon and Venus, represent feminine archetypes) astrology by default has not had a set of symbols by which to describe other avenues of feminine expression. It has tried to fit all other women's experiences into masculine-defined archetypes.

The asteroids signify new archetypal symbols in the astrological language and they specifically address the current psychological and social issues that are arising in today's world due to the activation of the feminine principle. Synchronistic with the publication of the asteroid goddess ephemeris, the forefront of the women's movement emerged into society. At this time new aspects of feminine expression began to enter into human consciousness. Women became imbued with the seed possibilities of feminine creativity and intelligence that expanded and transcended the traditional roles of wife and mother (Venus and the Moon). This also marked a time of the rediscovery of women's ancient history, the growth of women's culture and sexuality independent of men, and the rebirth of the Goddess in women's spirituality.

On the following page the mandala of asteroid goddesses can help us to better understand the meaning of Ceres, Pallas, Juno and Vesta (the first four asteroids discovered). The large circle in the mandala represents the Moon, which is the foundation of the feminine principle and contains potential expressions of the feminine nature. Behind the Moon resides the Sun. The union of these two energies gives rise to what mystics define as "oneness." In the center of the mandala resides Venus, the core essence of the feminine nature in her activated form, who embodies the well-spring of feminine creative, magnetic, sexual, reproductive vital life force. Venus is surrounded by Ceres, Pallas, Vesta and Juno who represent the primary relation-ships of a woman's life, that of mother, daughter, sister and partner, respectively. Each asteroid utilizes the creative sexual energy of Venus at the center of the circle in her own unique way, as she expresses various functions and activities of the feminine principle. They are placed at the four cardinal directions of the mandala. In the horoscope this fourfold division is designated by the four angles: the Ascendent and Descendent, which define the line of the horizon, and the Midheaven and Nadir, which mark the meridian line.

Ceres, as the Great Mother and Goddess of agriculture, gives birth to the world of physical form; she births children and provides food for their survival. As the Nadir (IC) she represents a point of foundation, roots, and family.

Pallas Athene, as the daughter and the Goddess of Wisdom, generates mental and artistic creations from her mind. At the Midheaven (MC), where visible and socially useful accomplishments are realized, she represents the principle of creative intelligence.

Vesta, as the Sister, is the Temple Priestess and is a virgin in the original sense of being whole and complete in oneself. As the Ascendant (ASC.), Vesta corresponds to the Self. She signifies the principle of spiritual focus and devotion to following one's calling.

Juno, as the Goddess of Marriage, fosters and sustains union with a partner. Placed at the Descendant (DESC.), the point of one-to-one relationships, Juno symbolizes the principle of relatedness and commitment to the other.

© Demetra George 1996 excerpted and reprinted from Asteroid Goddesses Natal Report (a software program published by Astrolabe)

SOUTH

Goddess of Wisdom & Warrior Queen
Courage and Will

MC

air

Pallas Athene
daughter

MOON (Sun)

MOON (Sun)

Temple Priestess

VENUS

VENUS

Goddess of Marriage

EAST

fire

ASC.

Vesta
sister

MOON • VENUS •

− ♀ +

0 ASTEROIDS

water

DESC.

Juno
partner

WEST

Clarity and Insight

Compassion and Healing

MOON (Sun)

(Sun) MOON

earth

Ceres
mother

IC

Great Mother
Silence and Strength

**The Mandala of the
Asteroid Goddesses**

© Demetra George 1995

NORTH

1997 Asteroid Ephemeris

Reprinted with permission from Astro Communications Services, Inc.

1997	Ceres 1	Pallas 2	Juno 3	Vesta 4
JAN 1	18♏51.7	27♐30.3	14♈40.4	27♍08.8
11	22 51.0	01♑35.4	18 26.5	02≈22.0
21	26 50.2	05 35.4	22 38.9	07 34.8
31	00♐48.2	09 29.2	27 12.2	12 46.5
FEB 10	04 44.2	13 15.5	02♉02.3	17 56.7
20	08 37.1	16 52.8	07 06.3	23 04.6
MAR 2	12 25.9	20 19.3	12 21.0	28 09.6
12	16 09.7	23 33.2	17 44.3	03♓11.2
22	19 47.0	26 32.3	23 13.4	08 05.5
APR 1	23 16.8	29 14.2	28 46.8	13 01.0
11	26 37.5	01≈35.9	04♊23.2	17 48.0
21	29 47.5	03 34.2	10 01.2	22 28.6
MAY 1	02♑45.1	05 05.5	15 39.1	27 02.0
11	05 28.0	06 05.9	21 16.5	01♈27.3
21	07 53.7	06 31.4	26 52.4	05 43.1
31	09 59.5	06♑19.1	02♋26.1	09 48.2
JUN 10	11 42.3	05 26.6	07 56.8	13 41.1
20	12 58.4	03 55.1	13 24.1	17 19.4
30	13 44.8	01 49.3	18 47.7	20 41.3
JUL 10	13♑57.9	29♐18.2	24 07.2	23 43.6
20	13 35.8	26 35.8	29 21.8	26 22.9
30	12 38.5	23 57.1	04♌31.4	28 35.5
AUG 9	11 08.6	21 36.8	09 35.8	00♉16.6
19	09 13.1	19 46.0	14 34.5	01 21.4
29	07 02.8	18 30.9	19 26.7	01 45.4
SEP 8	04 51.0	17 53.7	24 12.4	01♉24.7
18	02 51.7	17D53.5	28 50.6	00 18.8
28	01 16.4	18 27.2	03♍20.8	28♈31.7
OCT 8	00 13.2	19 31.1	07 41.8	26 12.7
18	29≈46.4	21 01.2	11 52.7	23 38.5
28	29D58.1	22 53.7	15 52.4	21 08.0
NOV 7	00♐40.8	25 05.3	19 38.9	18 59.8
17	01 57.5	27 32.7	23 10.4	17 27.7
27	03 42.2	00≈13.4	26 24.7	16 39.0
DEC 7	05 51.7	03 05.0	29 19.0	16D35.6
17	08 22.1	06 05.4	01≈50.1	17 15.1
27	11 10.4	09 12.8	03 54.4	18 33.0
JAN 6	14♐13.9	12≈25.8	05♍27.7	20♉24.5

1997	Sappho 80	Amor 1221	Pandora 55	Icarus 1566
JAN 1	13♏51.5	27≈45.7	05R47.1	26♏03.8
11	19 30.0	01♓47.6	05♓00.9	00≈32.7
21	25 13.2	05 51.0	04D58.1	05 10.1
31	01≈00.7	09 55.1	05 36.5	09 57.1
FEB 10	06 52.0	13 59.4	06 52.2	14 55.7
20	12 46.5	18 03.1	08 40.5	20 08.3
MAR 2	18 43.5	22 05.5	10 56.0	25 38.4
12	24 42.6	26 06.2	13 34.2	01♓31.0
22	00♓42.9	00♈04.6	16 31.2	07 52.7
APR 1	06 43.9	04 00.0	19 43.3	14 53.2
11	12 44.9	07 52.1	23 07.8	22 46.4
21	18 44.9	11 40.0	26 42.3	01♈51.7
MAY 1	24 43.2	15 23.1	00♈24.5	12 37.4
11	00♈38.9	19 00.9	04 13.0	25 42.7
21	06 30.6	22 32.3	08 06.3	12♉00.3
31	12 17.5	25 56.5	12 03.1	02♊50.9
JUN 10	17 58.2	29 12.2	16 02.7	29 43.1
20	23 30.8	02♉18.1	20 03.9	20♋39.7
30	28 53.9	05 12.6	24 06.1	14♌37.4
JUL 10	04♉05.4	07 53.5	28 05.7	13♍10.2
20	09 02.5	10 18.2	02♊10.5	08♎19.7
30	13 42.8	12 24.0	06 11.3	26 00.5
AUG 9	18 02.3	14 06.9	10 10.5	08♏08.1
19	21 56.8	15 22.8	14 07.2	17 01.8
29	25 21.5	16 06.8	18 00.7	24 05.1
SEP 8	28 09.8	16R13.7	21 50.2	00♐04.3
18	00♊15.1	15 38.7	25 34.8	05 24.4
28	01 30.5	14 18.8	29 13.4	10 20.0
OCT 8	01R49.2	12 14.1	02♋44.7	15 00.3
18	01 08.6	09 30.9	06 07.3	19 30.7
28	29♉32.3	06 21.9	09 19.5	23 54.8
NOV 7	27 12.7	03 05.8	12 19.3	28 15.2
17	24 32.8	00 03.7	15 04.3	02♑33.5
27	21 59.5	27♈33.6	17 31.9	06 50.8
DEC 7	19 57.6	25 47.6	19 38.8	11 08.2
17	18 43.7	24 51.2	21 21.7	15 26.1
27	18D23.6	24D43.8	22 36.8	19 45.3
JAN 6	18♉56.4	25♈22.3	23♊20.4	24♑06.3

1997	Psyche 16	Eros 433	Lilith 1181	Toro 1685
JAN 1	18♏05.1	18♏39.7	01♎28.1	19♎38.2
11	18R11.7	24 37.0	02 39.4	23 13.6
21	17 43.4	00≈33.2	03 13.1	25 54.4
31	16 41.2	06 28.6	03R06.6	27 31.8
FEB 10	15 08.7	12 23.7	02 18.8	27R53.7
20	13 13.6	18 18.7	00 52.3	26 48.3
MAR 2	11 06.9	24 13.8	28♍54.6	24 08.9
12	09 01.1	00♓09.6	26 37.1	20 00.1
22	07 08.8	06 06.2	24 15.4	14 48.7
APR 1	05 39.7	12 04.3	22 05.0	09 21.2
11	04 40.1	18 04.4	20 18.9	04 27.5
21	04 13.1	24 06.9	19 05.8	00 43.9
MAY 1	04D18.4	00♈12.6	18 29.4	28♍23.1
11	04 54.2	06 22.1	18D29.6	27 21.3
21	05 57.8	12 36.2	19 04.5	27D28.1
31	07 25.7	18 55.8	20 10.0	28 30.1
JUN 10	09 14.8	25 21.8	21 42.4	00♎16.6
20	11 22.1	01♉55.2	23 37.9	02 38.3
30	13 44.9	08 37.2	25 52.8	05 28.0
JUL 10	16 20.8	15 29.0	28 24.2	08 40.5
20	19 07.8	22 31.6	01♎09.4	12 11.8
30	22 04.1	29 46.6	04 05.9	15 58.6
AUG 9	25 08.2	07♊15.0	07 12.2	19 59.1
19	28 18.8	14 57.8	10 26.5	24 11.4
29	01♐34.5	22 56.2	13 47.2	28 34.4
SEP 8	04 54.5	01♋10.7	17 13.4	03♏07.5
18	08 17.6	09 41.2	20 43.7	07 49.9
28	11 42.9	18 27.7	24 17.2	12 41.5
OCT 8	15 08.4	27 28.6	27 53.1	17 42.4
18	18 36.1	06♌41.8	01♏30.3	22 52.5
28	22 02.1	16 05.1	05 07.9	28 12.2
NOV 7	25 26.4	25 34.3	08 45.1	03♐42.1
17	28 47.6	05♍05.2	12 20.8	09 22.9
27	02♑04.7	14 33.9	15 54.0	15 15.5
DEC 7	05 16.3	23 55.0	19 23.7	21 21.2
17	08 20.7	03♎03.9	22 48.5	27 41.3
27	11 16.2	11 56.4	26 07.2	04♑17.7
JAN 6	14♑00.9	20♎26.8	29♏16.2	11♑12.7

1997	Diana 78	Hidalgo 944	Urania 30	Chiron 2060
JAN 1	23≈27.8	05♐01.0	15♓34.5	00♏12.6
11	26 49.4	06 04.2	20 17.8	00 56.9
21	00♓18.8	07 00.6	25 12.0	01 30.7
31	03 54.4	07 48.9	00♈15.0	01 53.3
FEB 10	07 35.3	08 27.7	05 25.6	02 04.1
20	11 20.1	08 55.9	10 42.0	02R03.2
MAR 2	15 07.8	09 12.5	16 03.1	01 50.7
12	18 57.7	09R16.6	21 27.8	01 27.6
22	22 48.6	09 07.7	26 55.2	00 55.4
APR 1	26 40.0	08 45.9	02♉24.3	00 15.9
11	00♈30.9	08 11.5	07 54.6	29♎31.5
21	04 20.5	07 25.8	13 25.3	28 45.0
MAY 1	08 08.0	06 30.4	18 55.7	27 59.1
11	11 52.7	05 27.5	24 25.4	27 16.5
21	15 33.4	04 20.2	29 53.9	26 39.6
31	19 09.1	03 11.4	05♊20.6	26 10.6
JUN 10	22 38.7	02 04.4	10 45.2	25 50.8
20	26 00.5	01 02.3	16 07.1	25 41.4
30	29 13.1	00 07.7	21 25.9	25D42.9
JUL 10	02♉14.2	29♏22.8	26 41.1	25 55.4
20	05 01.4	28 49.1	01♋52.2	26 18.7
30	07 31.9	28 27.7	06 58.6	26 52.2
AUG 9	09 41.9	28 18.8	11 59.5	27 35.3
19	11 27.5	28D22.5	16 54.4	28 27.1
29	12 44.1	28 38.3	21 42.2	29 26.7
SEP 8	13 26.5	29 05.4	26 21.8	00♏33.2
18	13R30.4	29 43.0	00♌51.9	01 45.3
28	12 52.9	00♐29.9	05 10.9	03 02.2
OCT 8	11 33.6	01 25.0	09 16.8	04 22.6
18	09 38.0	02 27.2	13 07.2	05 45.6
28	07 17.3	03 35.1	16 39.5	07 09.9
NOV 7	04 48.3	04 47.5	19 50.0	08 34.5
17	02 30.6	03 00.3	22 34.6	09 58.2
27	00 42.1	07 20.5	24 48.7	11 19.7
DEC 7	29♈34.8	08 35.8	26 26.6	12 38.0
17	29D14.9	09 55.7	27 23.2	13 51.7
27	29 42.6	11 10.7	27R33.7	14 59.6
JAN 6	00♉55.6	12♐22.2	26♌54.9	16♏00.7

Giving the positions of asteroids every
ten days in LONGITUDE at 00:00 GMT

Noon Ephemeris: GMT*

January 1997

Day	Sid.Time	☉	0 hr ☽	Noon ☽	True ☊	☿	♀	♂	♃	♄	♅	♆	♇
1 W	18 44 42	11♑ 7 2	28♍44 16	4♎44 46	2♎26.3	12♑26.3	19♐ 4.3	29♍24.2	25♑17.1	1♈21.7	3♒17.8	26♑50.8	4♐24.1
2 Th	18 48 39	12 8 12	10♎48 38	16 56 34	2R26.3	11R 4.9	20 19.4	29 43.8	25 31.0	1 24.8	3 21.2	26 53.0	4 26.1
3 F	18 52 36	13 9 22	23 9 15	29 27 20	2 25.3	9 44.1	21 34.5	0♎ 3.0	25 44.9	1 28.0	3 24.5	26 55.2	4 28.1
4 Sa	18 56 32	14 10 32	5♏51 26	12♏22 5	2 22.4	8 26.6	22 49.5	0 21.9	25 58.9	1 31.2	3 27.9	26 57.5	4 30.1
5 Su	19 0 29	15 11 42	18 59 43	25 44 38	2 16.9	7 14.5	24 4.6	0 40.3	26 12.8	1 34.6	3 31.3	26 59.7	4 32.0
6 M	19 4 25	16 12 53	2♐37 0	9♐36 45	2 8.7	6 9.7	25 19.8	0 58.3	26 26.8	1 38.1	3 34.7	27 2.0	4 33.9
7 Tu	19 8 22	17 14 4	16 43 40	23 57 17	1 58.3	5 13.6	26 34.9	1 15.9	26 40.8	1 41.7	3 38.1	27 4.2	4 35.8
8 W	19 12 18	18 15 15	1♑16 57	8♑41 45	1 46.8	4 26.9	27 50.0	1 33.0	26 54.8	1 45.4	3 41.5	27 6.5	4 37.7
9 Th	19 16 15	19 16 25	16 10 39	23 42 26	1 35.5	3 50.1	29 5.1	1 49.7	27 8.9	1 49.2	3 44.9	27 8.7	4 39.5
10 F	19 20 11	20 17 35	1♒15 49	8♒49 30	1 25.7	3 23.3	0♑20.3	2 6.0	27 22.9	1 53.0	3 48.4	27 11.0	4 41.3
11 Sa	19 24 8	21 18 45	16 22 12	23 52 44	1 18.4	3 6.3	1 35.4	2 21.7	27 37.0	1 57.0	3 51.8	27 13.3	4 43.1
12 Su	19 28 5	22 19 55	1♓20 3	8♓43 18	1 13.9	2D58.7	2 50.5	2 37.0	27 51.1	2 1.0	3 55.3	27 15.5	4 44.9
13 M	19 32 1	23 21 3	16 1 47	23 15 1	1 12.0	2 59.8	4 5.7	2 51.8	28 5.2	2 5.1	3 58.8	27 17.8	4 46.7
14 Tu	19 35 58	24 22 11	0♈22 42	7♈24 41	1D11.9	3 9.2	5 20.8	3 6.2	28 19.3	2 9.3	4 2.2	27 20.1	4 48.4
15 W	19 39 54	25 23 19	14 21 0	21 11 46	1R12.3	3 26.1	6 35.9	3 20.0	28 33.4	2 13.6	4 5.7	27 22.4	4 50.1
16 Th	19 43 51	26 24 25	27 57 12	4♉37 36	1 12.1	3 49.9	7 51.1	3 33.3	28 47.5	2 18.0	4 9.2	27 24.6	4 51.8
17 F	19 47 47	27 25 31	11♉13 16	17 44 34	1 10.0	4 19.9	9 6.2	3 46.0	29 1.6	2 22.5	4 12.7	27 26.9	4 53.4
18 Sa	19 51 44	28 26 36	24 11 51	0♊35 26	1 5.5	4 55.7	10 21.4	3 58.3	29 15.7	2 27.0	4 16.2	27 29.2	4 55.0
19 Su	19 55 40	29 27 40	6♊55 40	13 12 48	0 58.3	5 36.6	11 36.5	4 10.0	29 29.9	2 31.7	4 19.7	27 31.5	4 56.6
20 M	19 59 37	0♒28 43	19 27 8	25 38 52	0 48.8	6 22.1	12 51.6	4 21.2	29 44.0	2 36.4	4 23.3	27 33.7	4 58.2
21 Tu	20 3 34	1 29 46	1♋48 14	7♋55 23	0 37.6	7 11.8	14 6.8	4 31.7	29 58.1	2 41.2	4 26.8	27 36.0	4 59.7
22 W	20 7 30	2 30 48	14 0 28	20 3 39	0 25.8	8 5.2	15 21.9	4 41.8	0♒12.2	2 46.0	4 30.3	27 38.3	5 1.2
23 Th	20 11 27	3 31 49	26 5 4	2♌ 4 50	0 14.5	9 2.1	16 37.1	4 51.2	0 26.4	2 51.0	4 33.8	27 40.6	5 2.7
24 F	20 15 23	4 32 49	8♌ 3 7	14 0 5	0 4.5	10 2.1	17 52.2	5 0.0	0 40.5	2 56.0	4 37.3	27 42.8	5 4.2
25 Sa	20 19 20	5 33 48	19 55 55	25 50 50	29♍56.7	11 4.8	19 7.3	5 8.3	0 54.6	3 1.1	4 40.9	27 45.1	5 5.6
26 Su	20 23 16	6 34 47	1♍45 6	7♍39 1	29 51.4	12 10.1	20 22.5	5 15.9	1 8.7	3 6.3	4 44.4	27 47.4	5 7.0
27 M	20 27 13	7 35 45	13 32 56	19 27 13	29 48.6	13 17.7	21 37.6	5 22.9	1 22.8	3 11.5	4 47.9	27 49.6	5 8.4
28 Tu	20 31 9	8 36 42	25 22 19	1♎18 43	29D47.9	14 27.3	22 52.8	5 29.2	1 36.9	3 16.8	4 51.4	27 51.9	5 9.7
29 W	20 35 6	9 37 38	7♎16 56	13 17 31	29 48.7	15 39.0	24 7.9	5 34.9	1 50.9	3 22.2	4 54.9	27 54.1	5 11.0
30 Th	20 39 3	10 38 34	19 21 4	25 28 12	29 50.0	16 52.4	25 23.0	5 39.9	2 5.0	3 27.7	4 58.4	27 56.3	5 12.3
31 F	20 42 59	11 39 29	1♏39 31	7♏55 40	29R50.9	18 7.4	26 38.2	5 44.2	2 19.0	3 33.2	5 1.9	27 58.6	5 13.5

Longitude

February 1997

Day	Sid.Time	☉	0 hr ☽	Noon ☽	True ☊	☿	♀	♂	♃	♄	♅	♆	♇
1 Sa	20 46 56	12♒40 23	14♏17 15	20♏44 50	29♍50.6	19♑24.0	27♑53.3	5♎47.8	2♒33.1	3♈38.8	5♒ 5.4	28♑ 0.8	5♐14.7
2 Su	20 50 52	13 41 17	27 18 56	3♐59 59	29R48.6	20 42.0	29 8.5	5 50.8	2 47.1	3 44.5	5 8.9	28 3.0	5 15.9
3 M	20 54 49	14 42 10	10♐48 17	17 44 1	29 44.6	22 1.4	0♒23.6	5 53.0	3 1.1	3 50.2	5 12.4	28 5.2	5 17.1
4 Tu	20 58 45	15 43 2	24 47 10	1♑57 35	29 38.9	23 22.0	1 38.7	5 54.5	3 15.1	3 56.0	5 15.9	28 7.4	5 18.2
5 W	21 2 42	16 43 53	9♑14 49	16 38 16	29 32.2	24 43.8	2 53.9	5 55.3	3 29.1	4 1.8	5 19.4	28 9.6	5 19.3
6 Th	21 6 38	17 44 43	24 7 6	1♒40 16	29 25.4	26 6.8	4 9.0	5R55.3	3 43.0	4 7.8	5 22.9	28 11.8	5 20.3
7 F	21 10 35	18 45 32	9♒16 35	16 54 43	29 19.5	27 30.8	5 24.2	5 54.5	3 57.0	4 13.7	5 26.3	28 14.0	5 21.4
8 Sa	21 14 32	19 46 19	24 33 20	2♓11 3	29 15.1	28 55.9	6 39.3	5 53.1	4 10.9	4 19.8	5 29.8	28 16.1	5 22.3
9 Su	21 18 28	20 47 5	9♓46 34	17 18 42	29 12.7	0♒22.0	7 54.4	5 50.8	4 24.7	4 25.9	5 33.2	28 18.3	5 23.3
10 M	21 22 25	21 47 50	24 46 27	2♈ 8 57	29D 12.2	1 49.1	9 9.5	5 47.8	4 38.6	4 32.0	5 36.6	28 20.4	5 24.2
11 Tu	21 26 21	22 48 33	9♈25 35	16 35 53	29 13.1	3 17.1	10 24.6	5 44.0	4 52.4	4 38.2	5 40.0	28 22.5	5 25.1
12 W	21 30 18	23 49 14	23 39 38	0♉36 44	29 14.6	4 46.1	11 39.7	5 39.4	5 6.2	4 44.5	5 43.4	28 24.6	5 26.0
13 Th	21 34 14	24 49 54	7♉27 16	14 11 24	29 16.0	6 16.0	12 54.8	5 34.0	5 19.9	4 50.8	5 46.8	28 26.7	5 26.8
14 F	21 38 11	25 50 32	20 49 27	27 21 44	29R 16.4	7 46.8	14 9.8	5 27.9	5 33.7	4 57.2	5 50.2	28 28.8	5 27.6
15 Sa	21 42 7	26 51 9	3♊48 42	10♊10 47	29 15.5	9 18.5	15 24.9	5 21.0	5 47.4	5 3.6	5 53.5	28 30.9	5 28.3
16 Su	21 46 4	27 51 43	16 28 25	22 42 4	29 13.1	10 51.1	16 40.0	5 13.3	6 1.0	5 10.1	5 56.9	28 32.9	5 29.0
17 M	21 50 1	28 52 16	28 52 12	4♋59 14	29 9.3	12 24.6	17 55.0	5 4.8	6 14.6	5 16.6	6 0.2	28 35.0	5 29.7
18 Tu	21 53 57	29 52 48	11♋ 3 34	17 5 36	29 4.5	13 59.1	19 10.0	4 55.6	6 28.2	5 23.2	6 3.5	28 37.0	5 30.4
19 W	21 57 54	0♓53 17	23 5 41	29 4 9	28 59.3	15 34.4	20 25.1	4 45.6	6 41.8	5 29.8	6 6.8	28 39.0	5 31.0
20 Th	22 1 50	1 53 45	5♌ 1 18	10♌57 24	28 54.2	17 10.7	21 40.1	4 34.8	6 55.3	5 36.5	6 10.1	28 41.0	5 31.6
21 F	22 5 47	2 54 11	16 52 45	22 47 34	28 49.9	18 47.9	22 55.1	4 23.2	7 8.7	5 43.2	6 13.3	28 43.0	5 32.1
22 Sa	22 9 43	3 54 35	28 42 7	4♍36 37	28 46.6	20 26.0	24 10.1	4 10.9	7 22.1	5 49.9	6 16.5	28 44.9	5 32.6
23 Su	22 13 40	4 54 58	10♍31 19	16 26 29	28 44.7	22 5.1	25 25.1	3 57.8	7 35.5	5 56.7	6 19.7	28 46.9	5 33.1
24 M	22 17 36	5 55 19	22 22 20	28 19 11	28D 44.0	23 45.1	26 40.1	3 44.0	7 48.8	6 3.5	6 22.9	28 48.8	5 33.5
25 Tu	22 21 33	6 55 38	4♎17 19	10♎17 3	28 44.5	25 26.1	27 55.0	3 29.5	8 2.1	6 10.4	6 26.1	28 50.7	5 34.0
26 W	22 25 30	7 55 56	16 18 45	22 22 47	28 45.7	27 8.2	29 10.0	3 14.3	8 15.3	6 17.3	6 29.2	28 52.6	5 34.3
27 Th	22 29 26	8 56 12	28 29 33	4♏39 28	28 47.3	28 51.2	0♓24.9	2 58.3	8 28.5	6 24.2	6 32.3	28 54.4	5 34.7
28 F	22 33 23	9 56 27	10♏52 59	17 10 33	28 48.9	0♓35.2	1 39.9	2 41.7	8 41.6	6 31.2	6 35.4	28 56.3	5 35.0

Ephemeris reprinted with permission from Astro Communications Services, Inc.

Each planet's retrograde period is shaded gray.

*Giving the positions of planets daily at noon, in LONGITUDE Greenwich Mean Time

NOON EPHEMERIS: GMT*

MARCH 1997

Day	Sid.Time	☉	0 hr ☽	Noon ☽	True ☊	☿	♀	♂	♃	♄	♅	♆	♇
1 Sa	22 37 19	10♓56 41	23♏32 37	29♏59 39	28♍49.9	2♓20.3	2♓54.8	2♎24.4	8♒54.7	6♈38.2	6♒38.5	28♑58.1	5♐35.2
2 Su	22 41 16	11 56 53	6♐32 2	13♐10 9	28R50.2	4 6.4	4 9.8	2R 6.5	9 7.7	6 45.3	6 41.5	28 59.9	5 35.5
3 M	22 45 12	12 57 3	19 54 20	26 44 48	28 49.8	5 53.6	5 24.7	1 48.0	9 20.7	6 52.4	6 44.5	29 1.7	5 35.7
4 Tu	22 49 9	13 57 12	3♑41 40	10♑44 57	28 48.6	7 41.8	6 39.6	1 28.8	9 33.6	6 59.5	6 47.5	29 3.4	5 35.8
5 W	22 53 5	14 57 19	17 54 30	25 9 59	28 47.0	9 31.1	7 54.5	1 9.2	9 46.5	7 6.6	6 50.5	29 5.1	5 35.9
6 Th	22 57 2	15 57 25	2♒30 56	9♒56 40	28 45.3	11 21.5	9 9.4	0 48.9	9 59.3	7 13.8	6 53.4	29 6.9	5 36.0
7 F	23 0 58	16 57 29	17 26 22	24 59 3	28 43.9	13 13.0	10 24.3	0 28.2	10 12.0	7 21.0	6 56.3	29 8.5	5 36.1
8 Sa	23 4 55	17 57 31	2♓33 36	10♓ 8 51	28 42.9	15 5.5	11 39.2	0 7.0	10 24.7	7 28.3	6 59.2	29 10.2	5R36.1
9 Su	23 8 52	18 57 32	17 43 36	25 16 38	28D42.5	16 59.0	12 54.0	29♍45.4	10 37.3	7 35.5	7 2.0	29 11.9	5 36.1
10 M	23 12 48	19 57 30	2♈46 48	10♈13 5	28 42.6	18 53.6	14 8.9	29 23.4	10 49.8	7 42.8	7 4.9	29 13.5	5 36.0
11 Tu	23 16 45	20 57 26	17 34 35	24 50 32	28 43.1	20 49.1	15 23.7	29 1.0	11 2.3	7 50.1	7 7.6	29 15.1	5 36.0
12 W	23 20 41	21 57 21	2♉ 0 22	9♉ 3 41	28 43.8	22 45.5	16 38.5	28 38.4	11 14.7	7 57.4	7 10.4	29 16.6	5 35.8
13 Th	23 24 38	22 57 13	16 0 16	22 50 4	28 44.4	24 42.8	17 53.3	28 15.5	11 27.0	8 4.8	7 13.1	29 18.2	5 35.7
14 F	23 28 34	23 57 3	29 33 8	6♊ 9 41	28 44.8	26 40.8	19 8.1	27 52.3	11 39.3	8 12.1	7 15.8	29 19.7	5 35.5
15 Sa	23 32 31	24 56 51	12♊40 2	19 4 33	28 45.0	28 39.5	20 22.9	27 29.1	11 51.5	8 19.5	7 18.5	29 21.2	5 35.3
16 Su	23 36 27	25 56 36	25 23 42	1♋37 59	28R45.0	0♈38.7	21 37.6	27 5.6	12 3.6	8 26.9	7 21.1	29 22.6	5 35.0
17 M	23 40 24	26 56 19	7♋47 54	13 54 2	28 44.9	2 38.2	22 52.4	26 42.1	12 15.6	8 34.3	7 23.7	29 24.1	5 34.7
18 Tu	23 44 21	27 56 0	19 56 54	25 57 3	28 44.8	4 37.9	24 7.1	26 18.6	12 27.6	8 41.8	7 26.2	29 25.5	5 34.4
19 W	23 48 17	28 55 39	1♌55 1	7♌51 18	28D44.8	6 37.6	25 21.8	25 55.1	12 39.5	8 49.2	7 28.7	29 26.9	5 34.0
20 Th	23 52 14	29 55 15	13 46 22	19 40 42	28 44.9	8 36.9	26 36.5	25 31.6	12 51.2	8 56.7	7 31.2	29 28.2	5 33.7
21 F	23 56 10	0♈54 49	25 34 44	1♍28 50	28 45.1	10 35.6	27 51.1	25 8.2	13 3.0	9 4.1	7 33.6	29 29.5	5 33.2
22 Sa	0 0 7	1 54 22	7♍23 23	13 18 44	28 45.3	12 33.4	29 5.8	24 45.0	13 14.6	9 11.6	7 36.0	29 30.8	5 32.8
23 Su	0 4 3	2 53 51	19 15 10	25 12 59	28R45.4	14 29.8	0♈20.4	24 21.9	13 26.1	9 19.1	7 38.4	29 32.1	5 32.3
24 M	0 8 0	3 53 19	1♎12 27	7♎13 47	28 45.4	16 24.7	1 35.0	23 59.1	13 37.6	9 26.6	7 40.7	29 33.4	5 31.8
25 Tu	0 11 56	4 52 45	13 17 15	19 23 1	28 45.0	18 17.4	2 49.6	23 36.5	13 49.0	9 34.1	7 43.0	29 34.6	5 31.2
26 W	0 15 53	5 52 9	25 31 19	1♏42 20	28 44.3	20 7.7	4 4.2	23 14.2	14 0.2	9 41.6	7 45.3	29 35.7	5 30.6
27 Th	0 19 50	6 51 31	7♏56 16	14 13 19	28 43.3	21 55.0	5 18.8	22 52.3	14 11.4	9 49.1	7 47.5	29 36.9	5 30.0
28 F	0 23 46	7 50 51	20 33 41	26 57 32	28 42.2	23 39.1	6 33.4	22 30.8	14 22.5	9 56.6	7 49.7	29 38.0	5 29.4
29 Sa	0 27 43	8 50 9	3♐25 6	9♐56 34	28 41.0	25 19.3	7 47.9	22 9.6	14 33.6	10 4.2	7 51.8	29 39.1	5 28.7
30 Su	0 31 39	9 49 26	16 32 8	23 11 57	28 40.1	26 55.5	9 2.5	21 48.9	14 44.5	10 11.7	7 53.9	29 40.2	5 28.0
31 M	0 35 36	10 48 41	29 56 11	6♑44 56	28D39.6	28 27.1	10 17.0	21 28.8	14 55.3	10 19.2	7 55.9	29 41.2	5 27.3

LONGITUDE

APRIL 1997

Day	Sid.Time	☉	0 hr ☽	Noon ☽	True ☊	☿	♀	♂	♃	♄	♅	♆	♇
1 Tu	0 39 32	11♈47 54	13♑38 19	20♑36 19	28♍39.7	29♈53.9	11♈31.5	21♍ 9.1	15♒ 6.0	10♈26.7	7♒57.9	29♑42.2	5♐26.5
2 W	0 43 29	12 47 5	27 38 53	4♒45 54	28 40.4	1♉15.5	12 46.0	20R49.9	15 16.6	10 34.3	7 59.9	29 43.2	5R25.7
3 Th	0 47 25	13 46 15	11♒57 6	19 12 11	28 41.5	2 31.6	14 0.4	20 31.4	15 27.1	10 41.8	8 1.8	29 44.2	5 24.9
4 F	0 51 22	14 45 22	26 30 39	3♓51 58	28 42.6	3 42.0	15 14.9	20 13.5	15 37.6	10 49.3	8 3.7	29 45.1	5 24.0
5 Sa	0 55 18	15 44 28	11♓15 26	18 40 17	28 43.4	4 46.5	16 29.4	19 56.1	15 47.9	10 56.8	8 5.5	29 45.9	5 23.1
6 Su	0 59 15	16 43 32	26 5 40	3♈30 39	28R43.5	5 44.9	17 43.8	19 39.5	15 58.1	11 4.3	8 7.3	29 46.8	5 22.2
7 M	1 3 12	17 42 34	10♈54 18	18 15 42	28 42.8	6 36.9	18 58.2	19 23.5	16 8.2	11 11.8	8 9.1	29 47.6	5 21.3
8 Tu	1 7 8	18 41 34	25 33 55	2♉48 9	28 41.0	7 22.6	20 12.6	19 8.3	16 18.1	11 19.3	8 10.8	29 48.4	5 20.3
9 W	1 11 5	19 40 32	9♉57 39	17 1 49	28 38.3	8 1.7	21 27.0	18 53.7	16 28.0	11 26.8	8 12.4	29 49.2	5 19.3
10 Th	1 15 1	20 39 28	24 0 11	0♊52 25	28 35.2	8 34.2	22 41.3	18 39.9	16 37.8	11 34.3	8 14.1	29 49.9	5 18.3
11 F	1 18 58	21 38 22	7♊38 21	14 17 56	28 32.0	9 0.2	23 55.7	18 26.9	16 47.4	11 41.8	8 15.6	29 50.6	5 17.3
12 Sa	1 22 54	22 37 13	20 51 17	27 18 36	28 29.3	9 19.5	25 10.0	18 14.6	16 56.9	11 49.2	8 17.2	29 51.2	5 16.2
13 Su	1 26 51	23 36 2	3♋40 12	9♋56 31	28 27.4	9 32.2	26 24.3	18 3.1	17 6.3	11 56.6	8 18.6	29 51.8	5 15.1
14 M	1 30 47	24 34 49	16 8 0	22 15 13	28D26.6	9R38.6	27 38.6	17 52.3	17 15.6	12 4.1	8 20.1	29 52.4	5 14.0
15 Tu	1 34 44	25 33 34	28 18 43	4♌19 6	28 26.9	9 38.6	28 52.8	17 42.4	17 24.8	12 11.5	8 21.4	29 53.0	5 12.9
16 W	1 38 41	26 32 16	10♌17 0	16 13 1	28 28.1	9 32.5	0♉ 7.1	17 33.2	17 33.8	12 18.8	8 22.8	29 53.5	5 11.7
17 Th	1 42 37	27 30 56	22 7 47	28 1 53	28 29.9	9 20.6	1 21.3	17 24.9	17 42.7	12 26.2	8 24.1	29 54.0	5 10.5
18 F	1 46 34	28 29 34	3♍55 55	9♍50 24	28 31.6	9 3.3	2 35.5	17 17.3	17 51.5	12 33.6	8 25.3	29 54.5	5 9.3
19 Sa	1 50 30	29 28 10	15 45 52	21 42 49	28 32.8	8 40.9	3 49.7	17 10.5	18 0.2	12 40.9	8 26.5	29 54.9	5 8.1
20 Su	1 54 27	0♉26 43	27 41 39	3♎42 47	28R32.8	8 14.0	5 3.8	17 4.5	18 8.7	12 48.2	8 27.6	29 55.3	5 6.8
21 M	1 58 23	1 25 15	9♎46 33	15 53 15	28 31.5	7 43.2	6 18.0	16 59.3	18 17.1	12 55.5	8 28.7	29 55.7	5 5.5
22 Tu	2 2 20	2 23 44	22 3 6	28 16 18	28 28.5	7 8.9	7 32.1	16 54.9	18 25.4	13 2.7	8 29.8	29 56.0	5 4.2
23 W	2 6 16	3 22 12	4♏32 59	10♏53 12	28 24.0	6 32.0	8 46.2	16 51.3	18 33.5	13 10.0	8 30.8	29 56.3	5 2.9
24 Th	2 10 13	4 20 38	17 17 1	23 44 24	28 18.3	5 53.1	10 0.3	16 48.4	18 41.5	13 17.2	8 31.7	29 56.5	5 1.6
25 F	2 14 10	5 19 2	0♐15 19	6♐49 40	28 12.1	5 13.0	11 14.4	16 46.3	18 49.4	13 24.4	8 32.6	29 56.8	5 0.2
26 Sa	2 18 6	6 17 25	13 27 24	20 8 21	28 6.2	4 32.4	12 28.4	16 44.9	18 57.1	13 31.5	8 33.5	29 57.0	4 58.8
27 Su	2 22 3	7 15 46	26 52 26	3♑39 31	28 1.1	3 52.1	13 42.5	16D44.3	19 4.7	13 38.7	8 34.3	29 57.1	4 57.5
28 M	2 25 59	8 14 5	10♑29 29	17 22 12	27 57.6	3 12.8	14 56.5	16 44.5	19 12.1	13 45.8	8 35.1	29 57.3	4 56.1
29 Tu	2 29 56	9 12 23	24 17 35	1♒15 30	27 55.8	2 35.1	16 10.5	16 45.4	19 19.4	13 52.8	8 35.8	29 57.4	4 54.6
30 W	2 33 52	10 10 39	8♒15 52	15 18 32	27D55.6	1 59.6	17 24.5	16 47.0	19 26.6	13 59.9	8 36.4	29 57.4	4 53.2

*Giving the positions of planets daily at noon,
in LONGITUDE Greenwich Mean Time

Noon Ephemeris: GMT* May 1997

Day	Sid.Time	☉	0 hr ☽	Noon ☽	True ☊	☿	♀	♂	♃	♄	♅	♆	♇
1 Th	2 37 49	11♉ 8 54	22♒23 23	29♒30 13	27♍56.5	1♉27.0	18♉38.5	16♍49.3	19♒33.6	14♈ 6.9	8♒37.0	29♑57.5	4♐51.7
2 F	2 41 45	12 7 7	6♓38 51	13♓49 0	27 57.7	0R57.7	19 52.4	16 52.4	19 40.5	14 13.9	8 37.6	29R57.5	4R50.3
3 Sa	2 45 42	13 5 19	21 0 20	28 12 28	27R58.3	0 32.1	21 6.4	16 56.1	19 47.2	14 20.8	8 38.1	29 57.4	4 48.8
4 Su	2 49 39	14 3 29	5♈24 56	12♈37 12	27 57.4	0 10.5	22 20.3	17 0.6	19 53.7	14 27.7	8 38.5	29 57.4	4 47.3
5 M	2 53 35	15 1 38	19 48 41	26 58 46	27 54.5	29♈53.2	23 34.2	17 5.7	20 0.1	14 34.6	8 39.0	29 57.3	4 45.8
6 Tu	2 57 32	15 59 45	4♉ 6 47	11♉12 4	27 49.4	29 40.4	24 48.1	17 11.6	20 6.4	14 41.4	8 39.3	29 57.1	4 44.2
7 W	3 1 28	16 57 51	18 14 1	25 12 0	27 42.3	29 32.2	26 2.0	17 18.1	20 12.4	14 48.2	8 39.6	29 57.0	4 42.7
8 Th	3 5 25	17 55 55	2♊ 5 33	8♊54 13	27 34.1	29D28.6	27 15.9	17 25.2	20 18.4	14 54.9	8 39.9	29 56.8	4 41.1
9 F	3 9 21	18 53 57	15 37 40	22 15 43	27 25.5	29 29.8	28 29.7	17 33.0	20 24.1	15 1.6	8 40.1	29 56.6	4 39.6
10 Sa	3 13 18	19 51 58	28 48 17	5♋15 24	27 17.5	29 35.6	29 43.6	17 41.5	20 29.7	15 8.3	8 40.2	29 56.3	4 38.0
11 Su	3 17 14	20 49 57	11♋37 12	17 53 57	27 11.0	29 46.1	0♊57.4	17 50.6	20 35.2	15 14.9	8 40.4	29 56.0	4 36.4
12 M	3 21 11	21 47 54	24 6 1	0♌13 48	27 6.5	0♉ 1.1	2 11.2	18 0.3	20 40.5	15 21.5	8 40.4	29 55.7	4 34.8
13 Tu	3 25 8	22 45 49	6♌17 50	12 18 40	27 4.0	0 20.6	3 25.0	18 10.6	20 45.6	15 28.0	8R40.4	29 55.3	4 33.2
14 W	3 29 4	23 43 42	18 16 54	24 13 10	27D 3.4	0 44.5	4 38.7	18 21.5	20 50.5	15 34.5	8 40.4	29 54.9	4 31.6
15 Th	3 33 1	24 41 33	0♍ 8 9	6♍ 2 29	27 3.9	1 12.6	5 52.5	18 33.0	20 55.3	15 41.0	8 40.3	29 54.5	4 30.0
16 F	3 36 57	25 39 23	11 56 51	17 51 54	27 4.8	1 44.8	7 6.2	18 45.0	20 59.9	15 47.4	8 40.1	29 54.1	4 28.4
17 Sa	3 40 54	26 37 11	23 48 16	29 46 35	27R 5.1	2 21.1	8 19.9	18 57.6	21 4.3	15 53.7	8 40.0	29 53.6	4 26.8
18 Su	3 44 50	27 34 58	5♎47 25	11♎51 17	27 3.9	3 1.1	9 33.5	19 10.7	21 8.6	15 60.0	8 39.7	29 53.1	4 25.1
19 M	3 48 47	28 32 42	17 58 39	24 9 55	27 0.6	3 45.0	10 47.2	19 24.4	21 12.7	16 6.2	8 39.4	29 52.5	4 23.5
20 Tu	3 52 43	29 30 26	0♏25 26	6♏45 25	26 54.9	4 32.4	12 0.8	19 38.6	21 16.6	16 12.4	8 39.1	29 52.0	4 21.9
21 W	3 56 40	0♊28 8	13 10 1	19 39 19	26 46.9	5 23.3	13 14.5	19 53.3	21 20.3	16 18.5	8 38.7	29 51.4	4 20.2
22 Th	4 0 36	1 25 48	26 13 15	2♐51 43	26 37.1	6 17.7	14 28.1	20 8.5	21 23.9	16 24.6	8 38.3	29 50.7	4 18.6
23 F	4 4 33	2 23 28	9♐34 28	16 21 13	26 26.5	7 15.3	15 41.7	20 24.2	21 27.2	16 30.6	8 37.8	29 50.1	4 17.0
24 Sa	4 8 30	3 21 6	23 11 35	0♑ 5 9	26 16.1	8 16.1	16 55.2	20 40.4	21 30.5	16 36.8	8 37.3	29 49.4	4 15.3
25 Su	4 12 26	4 18 43	7♑ 1 29	14 0 7	26 6.9	9 20.1	18 8.8	20 57.1	21 33.5	16 42.5	8 36.7	29 48.7	4 13.7
26 M	4 16 23	5 16 19	21 0 36	28 2 30	25 60.0	10 27.1	19 22.3	21 14.2	21 36.3	16 48.4	8 36.1	29 47.9	4 12.0
27 Tu	4 20 19	6 13 54	5♒ 5 27	12♒ 9 5	25 55.6	11 37.0	20 35.9	21 31.8	21 39.0	16 54.2	8 35.4	29 47.2	4 10.4
28 W	4 24 16	7 11 28	19 13 7	26 17 20	25 53.5	12 49.8	21 49.4	21 49.8	21 41.5	16 59.9	8 34.7	29 46.4	4 8.7
29 Th	4 28 12	8 9 1	3♓21 31	10♓25 32	25D53.1	14 5.5	23 2.9	22 8.2	21 43.7	17 5.6	8 34.0	29 45.6	4 7.1
30 F	4 32 9	9 6 33	17 29 15	24 32 32	25R53.3	15 23.9	24 16.4	22 27.1	21 45.8	17 11.2	8 33.2	29 44.7	4 5.4
31 Sa	4 36 6	10 4 5	1♈35 16	8♈37 19	25 52.9	16 45.1	25 29.8	22 46.4	21 47.8	17 16.7	8 32.3	29 43.8	4 3.8

Longitude June 1997

Day	Sid.Time	☉	0 hr ☽	Noon ☽	True ☊	☿	♀	♂	♃	♄	♅	♆	♇
1 Su	4 40 2	11♊ 1 36	15♈38 31	22♈38 38	25♍50.6	18♉ 9.0	26♊43.3	23♍ 6.1	21♒49.5	17♈22.2	8♒31.4	29♑42.9	4♐ 2.2
2 M	4 43 59	11 59 6	29 37 26	6♉34 38	25R45.7	19 35.6	27 56.7	23 26.2	21 51.0	17 27.7	8R30.5	29R42.0	4R 0.5
3 Tu	4 47 55	12 56 35	13♉29 52	20 22 48	25 38.1	21 4.9	29 10.1	23 46.8	21 52.4	17 33.0	8 29.5	29 41.0	3 58.9
4 W	4 51 52	13 54 4	27 13 2	4♊ 0 12	25 27.9	22 36.8	0♋23.6	24 7.7	21 53.5	17 38.3	8 28.5	29 40.0	3 57.3
5 Th	4 55 48	14 51 31	10♊43 56	17 23 53	25 16.1	24 11.3	1 37.0	24 29.0	21 54.5	17 43.5	8 27.4	29 39.0	3 55.7
6 F	4 59 45	15 48 58	23 59 47	0♋31 25	25 3.6	25 48.4	2 50.3	24 50.7	21 55.3	17 48.7	8 26.3	29 38.0	3 54.1
7 Sa	5 3 41	16 46 24	6♋58 39	13 21 26	24 51.9	27 28.1	4 3.7	25 12.7	21 55.8	17 53.8	8 25.1	29 36.9	3 52.5
8 Su	5 7 38	17 43 48	19 39 49	25 53 56	24 41.7	29 10.4	5 17.1	25 35.2	21 56.2	17 58.8	8 23.9	29 35.9	3 50.9
9 M	5 11 35	18 41 12	2♌ 3 59	8♌10 18	24 34.0	0♊55.3	6 30.4	25 58.0	21R56.4	18 3.7	8 22.7	29 34.7	3 49.3
10 Tu	5 15 31	19 38 35	14 13 15	20 13 19	24 28.8	2 42.7	7 43.7	26 21.1	21 56.4	18 8.6	8 21.4	29 33.6	3 47.7
11 W	5 19 28	20 35 56	26 11 0	2♍ 6 52	24 26.1	4 32.6	8 57.0	26 44.6	21 56.2	18 13.4	8 20.1	29 32.5	3 46.2
12 Th	5 23 24	21 33 17	8♍ 1 33	13 55 40	24 25.2	6 25.0	10 10.3	27 8.4	21 55.9	18 18.1	8 18.7	29 31.3	3 44.6
13 F	5 27 21	22 30 36	19 49 56	25 45 0	24 25.1	8 19.8	11 23.5	27 32.5	21 55.3	18 22.7	8 17.3	29 30.1	3 43.1
14 Sa	5 31 17	23 27 55	1♎41 34	7♎40 19	24 24.8	10 16.9	12 36.7	27 57.0	21 54.5	18 27.3	8 15.8	29 28.9	3 41.6
15 Su	5 35 14	24 25 13	13 41 54	19 46 59	24 23.2	12 16.2	13 50.0	28 21.7	21 53.6	18 31.7	8 14.4	29 27.6	3 40.0
16 M	5 39 10	25 22 30	25 56 7	2♏ 9 52	24 19.5	14 17.7	15 3.1	28 46.8	21 52.4	18 36.2	8 12.8	29 26.4	3 38.5
17 Tu	5 43 7	26 19 46	8♏28 39	14 52 52	24 13.4	16 21.2	16 16.3	29 12.2	21 51.1	18 40.5	8 11.3	29 25.1	3 37.0
18 W	5 47 4	27 17 2	21 22 45	27 58 28	24 4.7	18 26.5	17 29.5	29 37.8	21 49.6	18 44.7	8 9.7	29 23.8	3 35.6
19 Th	5 51 0	28 14 16	4♐40 0	11♐27 14	23 54.1	20 33.4	18 42.6	0♎ 3.8	21 47.8	18 48.9	8 8.1	29 22.5	3 34.1
20 F	5 54 57	29 11 31	18 19 54	25 17 36	23 42.5	22 41.7	19 55.7	0 30.0	21 46.0	18 53.0	8 6.4	29 21.2	3 32.7
21 Sa	5 58 53	0♋ 8 45	2♑19 48	9♑25 52	23 31.0	24 51.2	21 8.8	0 56.6	21 43.9	18 57.0	8 4.7	29 19.8	3 31.2
22 Su	6 2 50	1 5 58	16 35 6	23 46 43	23 21.0	27 1.5	22 21.8	1 23.4	21 41.6	19 0.9	8 3.0	29 18.5	3 29.8
23 M	6 6 46	2 3 11	0♒59 58	8♒14 4	23 13.2	29 12.5	23 34.9	1 50.4	21 39.1	19 4.8	8 1.2	29 17.1	3 28.4
24 Tu	6 10 43	3 0 24	15 28 19	22 42 3	23 8.1	1♋23.9	24 47.9	2 17.7	21 36.5	19 8.5	7 59.4	29 15.7	3 27.1
25 W	6 14 39	3 57 37	29 54 43	7♓ 5 51	23 5.6	3 35.3	26 0.9	2 45.3	21 33.7	19 12.2	7 57.6	29 14.3	3 25.7
26 Th	6 18 36	4 54 50	14♓15 5	21 22 9	23D 4.9	5 46.5	27 13.9	3 13.2	21 30.7	19 15.8	7 55.8	29 12.8	3 24.4
27 F	6 22 33	5 52 3	28 26 51	5♈29 5	23R 5.0	7 57.2	28 26.9	3 41.3	21 27.5	19 19.3	7 53.9	29 11.4	3 23.0
28 Sa	6 26 29	6 49 16	12♈28 46	19 25 53	23 4.5	10 7.2	29 39.9	4 9.6	21 24.1	19 22.7	7 51.9	29 9.9	3 21.7
29 Su	6 30 26	7 46 29	26 20 25	3♉12 21	23 2.4	12 16.3	0♌52.8	4 38.2	21 20.6	19 26.0	7 50.0	29 8.5	3 20.4
30 M	6 34 22	8 43 42	10♉ 1 42	16 48 25	22 57.9	14 24.2	2 5.7	5 7.0	21 16.8	19 29.2	7 48.0	29 7.0	3 19.2

*Giving the positions of planets daily at noon, in LONGITUDE Greenwich Mean Time

Noon Ephemeris: GMT* — July 1997

Day	Sid.Time	☉	0 hr ☽	Noon ☽	True ☊	☿	♀	♂	♃	♄	♅	♆	♇
1 Tu	6 38 19	9♋40 55	23♉32 27	0♊13 43	22♍50.6	16♋30.9	3♌18.6	5♎36.1	21♒12.9	19♈32.4	7♒46.0	29♑ 5.5	3♐17.9
2 W	6 42 15	10 38 8	6♊52 9	13 27 37	22R41.0	18 36.0	4 31.5	6 5.4	21R 8.9	19 35.4	7R44.0	29R 4.0	3R16.7
3 Th	6 46 12	11 35 22	20 0 0	26 29 12	22 29.7	20 39.6	5 44.4	6 34.9	21 4.6	19 38.4	7 41.9	29 2.4	3 15.5
4 F	6 50 8	12 32 35	2♋55 5	9♋17 35	22 17.8	22 41.5	6 57.2	7 4.7	21 0.2	19 41.2	7 39.9	29 0.9	3 14.3
5 Sa	6 54 5	13 29 49	15 36 38	21 52 15	22 6.5	24 41.7	8 10.0	7 34.7	20 55.6	19 44.0	7 37.8	28 59.4	3 13.2
6 Su	6 58 2	14 27 2	28 4 27	4♌13 22	21 56.7	26 40.0	9 22.8	8 4.9	20 50.9	19 46.7	7 35.6	28 57.8	3 12.0
7 M	7 1 58	15 24 16	10♌19 7	16 21 58	21 49.1	28 36.5	10 35.6	8 35.3	20 46.0	19 49.3	7 33.5	28 56.3	3 10.9
8 Tu	7 5 55	16 21 29	22 22 11	28 20 8	21 44.1	0♌31.0	11 48.3	9 6.0	20 41.0	19 51.8	7 31.3	28 54.7	3 9.8
9 W	7 9 51	17 18 42	4♍16 12	10♍10 52	21 41.5	2 23.6	13 1.1	9 36.8	20 35.8	19 54.1	7 29.1	28 53.1	3 8.8
10 Th	7 13 48	18 15 56	16 4 38	21 58 4	21D40.8	4 14.3	14 13.8	10 7.9	20 30.4	19 56.4	7 26.9	28 51.5	3 7.7
11 F	7 17 44	19 13 9	27 51 47	3♎46 24	21 41.2	6 3.1	15 26.4	10 39.2	20 24.9	19 58.6	7 24.7	28 49.9	3 6.7
12 Sa	7 21 41	20 10 22	9♎42 33	15 40 57	21R41.8	7 49.9	16 39.1	11 10.7	20 19.3	20 0.7	7 22.5	28 48.3	3 5.7
13 Su	7 25 37	21 7 35	21 42 14	27 47 4	21 41.7	9 34.7	17 51.7	11 42.3	20 13.5	20 2.7	7 20.2	28 46.7	3 4.8
14 M	7 29 34	22 4 48	3♏56 8	10♏10 0	21 40.0	11 17.6	19 4.3	12 14.2	20 7.6	20 4.6	7 17.9	28 45.1	3 3.9
15 Tu	7 33 31	23 2 1	16 29 16	22 54 23	21 36.3	12 58.6	20 16.8	12 46.2	20 1.5	20 6.4	7 15.6	28 43.5	3 3.0
16 W	7 37 27	23 59 14	29 25 46	6♐ 3 41	21 30.5	14 37.6	21 29.4	13 18.5	19 55.3	20 8.1	7 13.3	28 41.9	3 2.1
17 Th	7 41 24	24 56 28	12♐48 17	19 39 35	21 22.9	16 14.6	22 41.9	13 50.9	19 49.0	20 9.7	7 11.0	28 40.3	3 1.2
18 F	7 45 20	25 53 42	26 37 25	3♑41 26	21 14.4	17 49.8	23 54.3	14 23.5	19 42.6	20 11.2	7 8.7	28 38.6	3 0.4
19 Sa	7 49 17	26 50 56	10♑51 8	18 5 51	21 6.0	19 22.9	25 6.8	14 56.3	19 36.1	20 12.7	7 6.3	28 37.0	2 59.6
20 Su	7 53 13	27 48 10	25 24 46	2♒46 59	20 58.5	20 54.1	26 19.2	15 29.2	19 29.4	20 14.0	7 4.0	28 35.4	2 58.8
21 M	7 57 10	28 45 25	10♒11 30	17 37 17	20 52.9	22 23.3	27 31.5	16 2.3	19 22.7	20 15.2	7 1.6	28 33.8	2 58.1
22 Tu	8 1 6	29 42 41	25 3 18	2♓28 37	20 49.4	23 50.6	28 43.9	16 35.6	19 15.8	20 16.3	6 59.3	28 32.2	2 57.4
23 W	8 5 3	0♌39 57	9♓52 18	17 13 37	20D48.1	25 15.8	29 56.2	17 9.1	19 8.9	20 17.3	6 56.9	28 30.5	2 56.7
24 Th	8 9 0	1 37 14	24 31 54	1♈46 37	20 48.4	26 39.0	1♍ 8.4	17 42.7	19 1.8	20 18.2	6 54.5	28 28.9	2 56.1
25 F	8 12 56	2 34 32	8♈57 23	16 3 57	20 49.5	28 0.1	2 20.7	18 16.5	18 54.7	20 19.0	6 52.1	28 27.3	2 55.4
26 Sa	8 16 53	3 31 51	23 6 9	0♉ 3 55	20R50.2	29 19.1	3 32.9	18 50.5	18 47.5	20 19.6	6 49.7	28 25.7	2 54.9
27 Su	8 20 49	4 29 11	6♉57 18	13 46 20	20 49.9	0♍35.9	4 45.1	19 24.6	18 40.2	20 20.2	6 47.3	28 24.1	2 54.3
28 M	8 24 46	5 26 32	20 31 9	27 11 53	20 47.8	1 50.5	5 57.2	19 58.9	18 32.8	20 20.7	6 44.9	28 22.4	2 53.8
29 Tu	8 28 42	6 23 54	3♊48 42	10♊21 45	20 43.8	3 2.9	7 9.4	20 33.3	18 25.4	20 21.1	6 42.5	28 20.8	2 53.3
30 W	8 32 39	7 21 18	16 51 11	23 17 9	20 38.1	4 12.9	8 21.4	21 7.9	18 17.9	20 21.4	6 40.2	28 19.2	2 52.8
31 Th	8 36 35	8 18 42	29 39 47	5♋59 14	20 31.2	5 20.5	9 33.5	21 42.7	18 10.3	20 21.6	6 37.8	28 17.6	2 52.4

Longitude — August 1997

Day	Sid.Time	☉	0 hr ☽	Noon ☽	True ☊	☿	♀	♂	♃	♄	♅	♆	♇
1 F	8 40 32	9♌16 7	12♋15 36	18♋29 1	20♍23.8	6♍25.6	10♍45.5	22♎17.6	18♒ 2.7	20♈21.6	6♒35.4	28♑16.0	2♐52.0
2 Sa	8 44 29	10 13 33	24 39 36	0♌47 28	20R16.8	7 28.1	11 57.5	22 52.7	17R55.0	20R21.6	6R33.0	28R14.5	2R51.6
3 Su	8 48 25	11 11 0	6♌52 46	12 55 40	20 10.8	8 27.9	13 9.5	23 27.9	17 47.3	20 21.5	6 30.6	28 12.9	2 51.2
4 M	8 52 22	12 8 28	18 56 21	24 55 1	20 6.3	9 24.8	14 21.4	24 3.3	17 39.6	20 21.2	6 28.2	28 11.3	2 50.9
5 Tu	8 56 18	13 5 57	0♍51 55	6♍47 20	20 3.6	10 18.8	15 33.3	24 38.8	17 31.8	20 20.9	6 25.8	28 9.7	2 50.7
6 W	9 0 15	14 3 26	12 41 35	18 35 2	20D 2.6	11 9.7	16 45.1	25 14.5	17 24.0	20 20.4	6 23.4	28 8.2	2 50.4
7 Th	9 4 11	15 0 57	24 28 5	0♎21 10	20 3.1	11 57.4	17 56.9	25 50.4	17 16.2	20 19.9	6 21.1	28 6.7	2 50.2
8 F	9 8 8	15 58 28	6♎14 45	12 9 22	20 4.5	12 41.6	19 8.7	26 26.3	17 8.4	20 19.2	6 18.7	28 5.1	2 50.0
9 Sa	9 12 4	16 56 0	18 5 34	24 3 54	20 6.2	13 22.2	20 20.4	27 2.4	17 0.5	20 18.5	6 16.4	28 3.6	2 49.9
10 Su	9 16 1	17 53 33	0♏ 4 59	6♏ 9 24	20 7.6	13 59.1	21 32.1	27 38.7	16 52.7	20 17.6	6 14.0	28 2.1	2 49.8
11 M	9 19 58	18 51 7	12 17 46	18 30 41	20R 8.2	14 32.0	22 43.7	28 15.1	16 44.9	20 16.7	6 11.7	28 0.6	2 49.7
12 Tu	9 23 54	19 48 42	24 48 43	1♐12 25	20 7.6	15 0.6	23 55.3	28 51.6	16 37.1	20 15.6	6 9.4	27 59.1	2 49.6
13 W	9 27 51	20 46 18	7♐42 15	14 18 37	20 5.7	15 24.9	25 6.9	29 28.3	16 29.3	20 14.5	6 7.1	27 57.6	2D49.6
14 Th	9 31 47	21 43 55	21 1 49	27 52 0	20 2.8	15 44.6	26 18.4	0♏ 5.1	16 21.5	20 13.2	6 4.8	27 56.2	2 49.6
15 F	9 35 44	22 41 32	4♑49 13	11♑53 19	19 59.2	15 59.4	27 29.8	0 42.0	16 13.7	20 11.8	6 2.5	27 54.7	2 49.7
16 Sa	9 39 40	23 39 11	19 4 0	26 20 44	19 55.4	16 9.1	28 41.2	1 19.0	16 6.0	20 10.4	6 0.3	27 53.3	2 49.8
17 Su	9 43 37	24 36 51	3♒42 53	11♒ 9 35	19 52.1	16R13.6	29 52.5	1 56.2	15 58.4	20 8.8	5 58.0	27 51.9	2 49.9
18 M	9 47 33	25 34 32	18 39 51	26 12 36	19 49.7	16 12.6	1♎ 3.8	2 33.5	15 50.7	20 7.2	5 55.8	27 50.5	2 50.1
19 Tu	9 51 30	26 32 15	3♓46 40	11♓20 52	19 48.5	16 6.1	2 15.1	3 10.9	15 43.2	20 5.4	5 53.6	27 49.1	2 50.2
20 W	9 55 27	27 29 58	18 54 3	26 25 9	19D48.4	15 53.8	3 26.2	3 48.5	15 35.6	20 3.6	5 51.4	27 47.8	2 50.5
21 Th	9 59 23	28 27 44	3♈53 9	11♈17 13	19 49.2	15 35.7	4 37.4	4 26.2	15 28.2	20 1.6	5 49.3	27 46.4	2 50.7
22 F	10 3 20	29 25 31	18 36 39	25 50 54	19 50.5	15 11.9	5 48.5	5 4.0	15 20.8	19 59.6	5 47.1	27 45.1	2 51.0
23 Sa	10 7 16	0♍23 19	2♉59 34	10♉ 2 27	19 51.7	14 42.4	6 59.5	5 41.9	15 13.5	19 57.5	5 45.0	27 43.8	2 51.3
24 Su	10 11 13	1 21 10	16 59 24	23 50 28	19 52.5	14 7.5	8 10.5	6 19.9	15 6.2	19 55.2	5 42.9	27 42.5	2 51.7
25 M	10 15 9	2 19 2	0♊35 44	7♊15 26	19R52.6	13 27.4	9 21.4	6 58.1	14 59.1	19 52.9	5 40.9	27 41.2	2 52.1
26 Tu	10 19 6	3 16 56	13 49 48	20 19 8	19 51.9	12 42.7	10 32.3	7 36.4	14 52.0	19 50.5	5 38.8	27 40.0	2 52.5
27 W	10 23 2	4 14 52	26 43 47	3♋ 4 5	19 50.5	11 53.9	11 43.1	8 14.8	14 45.0	19 48.0	5 36.8	27 38.7	2 52.9
28 Th	10 26 59	5 12 50	9♋20 24	15 33 6	19 48.6	11 1.8	12 53.9	8 53.3	14 38.1	19 45.4	5 34.8	27 37.5	2 53.4
29 F	10 30 56	6 10 49	21 42 31	27 49 0	19 46.6	10 7.3	14 4.6	9 32.0	14 31.3	19 42.8	5 32.9	27 36.3	2 54.0
30 Sa	10 34 52	7 8 50	3♌52 52	9♌54 26	19 44.7	9 11.3	15 15.3	10 10.7	14 24.6	19 40.0	5 30.9	27 35.2	2 54.5
31 Su	10 38 49	8 6 53	15 53 59	21 51 50	19 43.1	8 15.0	16 25.9	10 49.6	14 18.1	19 37.1	5 29.0	27 34.0	2 55.1

*Giving the positions of planets daily at noon, in LONGITUDE Greenwich Mean Time

NOON EPHEMERIS: GMT* SEPTEMBER 1997

Day	Sid.Time	☉	0 hr ☽	Noon ☽	True ☊	☿	♀	♂	♃	♄	♅	♆	♇
1 M	10 42 45	9♍ 4 58	27♌48 14	3♍43 28	19♍42.1	7♍19.6	17♎36.5	11♏28.6	14♒11.6	19♈34.2	5♒27.1	27♑32.9	2♐55.7
2 Tu	10 46 42	10 3 4	9♍37 48	15 31 31	19D41.7	6R26.3	18 47.0	12 7.8	14R 5.3	19R31.2	5R25.3	27R31.8	2 56.4
3 W	10 50 38	11 1 12	21 24 53	27 18 12	19 41.7	5 36.2	19 57.4	12 47.0	13 59.1	19 28.1	5 23.5	27 30.7	2 57.1
4 Th	10 54 35	11 59 21	3♎11 47	9♎ 5 56	19 42.2	4 50.7	21 7.8	13 26.3	13 53.0	19 24.9	5 21.7	27 29.7	2 57.8
5 F	10 58 31	12 57 32	15 1 1	20 57 23	19 42.8	4 10.7	22 18.1	14 5.8	13 47.0	19 21.6	5 20.0	27 28.6	2 58.5
6 Sa	11 2 28	13 55 45	26 55 27	2♏55 36	19 43.5	3 37.2	23 28.3	14 45.4	13 41.2	19 18.3	5 18.3	27 27.6	2 59.3
7 Su	11 6 24	14 53 59	8♏58 17	15 3 58	19 44.1	3 11.1	24 38.5	15 25.1	13 35.6	19 14.9	5 16.6	27 26.7	3 0.1
8 M	11 10 21	15 52 14	21 13 7	27 26 12	19 44.4	2 53.0	25 48.6	16 4.8	13 30.1	19 11.4	5 14.9	27 25.7	3 1.0
9 Tu	11 14 18	16 50 32	3♐43 43	10♐ 6 8	19 44.6	2 43.5	26 58.6	16 44.7	13 24.7	19 7.8	5 13.3	27 24.8	3 1.9
10 W	11 18 14	17 48 51	16 33 53	23 7 24	19R44.8	2D42.9	28 8.6	17 24.8	13 19.5	19 4.2	5 11.8	27 23.9	3 2.8
11 Th	11 22 11	18 47 11	29 47 1	6♑33 2	19 44.6	2 51.3	29 18.5	18 4.9	13 14.4	19 0.5	5 10.2	27 23.0	3 3.7
12 F	11 26 7	19 45 33	13♑25 37	20 24 51	19D44.5	3 8.9	0♏28.3	18 45.1	13 9.5	18 56.8	5 8.7	27 22.2	3 4.7
13 Sa	11 30 4	20 43 56	27 30 39	4♒42 48	19 44.6	3 35.6	1 38.0	19 25.4	13 4.8	18 52.9	5 7.3	27 21.4	3 5.7
14 Su	11 34 0	21 42 21	12♒ 0 55	19 24 25	19 44.7	4 11.0	2 47.6	20 5.8	13 0.2	18 49.1	5 5.9	27 20.6	3 6.8
15 M	11 37 57	22 40 48	26 52 36	4♓24 32	19 44.9	4 55.0	3 57.2	20 46.3	12 55.9	18 45.1	5 4.5	27 19.8	3 7.8
16 Tu	11 41 53	23 39 16	11♓59 14	19 35 31	19R45.0	5 47.1	5 6.6	21 26.9	12 51.6	18 41.1	5 3.2	27 19.1	3 8.9
17 W	11 45 50	24 37 46	27 12 13	4♈48 6	19 44.9	6 46.9	6 16.0	22 7.6	12 47.6	18 37.0	5 1.9	27 18.4	3 10.1
18 Th	11 49 47	25 36 19	12♈21 58	19 52 42	19 44.5	7 53.7	7 25.3	22 48.4	12 43.7	18 32.9	5 0.6	27 17.7	3 11.2
19 F	11 53 43	26 34 53	27 19 15	4♉40 46	19 43.8	9 7.0	8 34.5	23 29.3	12 40.0	18 28.7	4 59.4	27 17.1	3 12.4
20 Sa	11 57 40	27 33 29	11♉56 33	19 6 3	19 43.0	10 26.2	9 43.6	24 10.4	12 36.5	18 24.5	4 58.3	27 16.5	3 13.6
21 Su	12 1 36	28 32 8	26 8 54	3♊ 4 57	19 42.1	11 50.7	10 52.6	24 51.5	12 33.1	18 20.2	4 57.1	27 15.9	3 14.9
22 M	12 5 33	29 30 49	9♊54 8	16 36 35	19 41.5	13 19.8	12 1.5	25 32.7	12 30.0	18 15.9	4 56.1	27 15.3	3 16.2
23 Tu	12 9 29	0♎29 32	23 12 33	29 42 20	19D41.2	14 53.0	13 10.4	26 14.0	12 27.0	18 11.6	4 55.0	27 14.8	3 17.5
24 W	12 13 26	1 28 18	6♋ 6 21	12♋25 3	19 41.4	16 29.5	14 19.1	26 55.4	12 24.2	18 7.2	4 54.0	27 14.3	3 18.8
25 Th	12 17 22	2 27 5	18 38 58	24 48 36	19 42.2	18 9.0	15 27.8	27 36.9	12 21.6	18 2.7	4 53.1	27 13.9	3 20.2
26 F	12 21 19	3 25 55	0♌54 28	6♌57 8	19 43.3	19 50.8	16 36.3	28 18.4	12 19.2	17 58.2	4 52.2	27 13.5	3 21.6
27 Sa	12 25 16	4 24 47	12 57 5	18 54 49	19 44.6	21 34.5	17 44.7	29 0.1	12 17.0	17 53.7	4 51.3	27 13.1	3 23.0
28 Su	12 29 12	5 23 42	24 50 50	0♍45 34	19 45.9	23 19.7	18 53.1	29 41.9	12 14.9	17 49.2	4 50.5	27 12.7	3 24.5
29 M	12 33 9	6 22 38	6♍39 26	12 32 50	19 46.7	25 6.0	20 1.3	0♐23.8	12 13.1	17 44.6	4 49.8	27 12.4	3 26.0
30 Tu	12 37 5	7 21 36	18 26 8	24 19 39	19R46.7	26 53.1	21 9.4	1 5.8	12 11.5	17 40.0	4 49.0	27 12.1	3 27.5

LONGITUDE OCTOBER 1997

Day	Sid.Time	☉	0 hr ☽	Noon ☽	True ☊	☿	♀	♂	♃	♄	♅	♆	♇
1 W	12 41 2	8♎20 37	0♎13 42	6♎ 8 35	19♍45.9	28♍40.7	22♏17.4	1♐47.8	12♒10.0	17♈35.4	4♒48.4	27♑11.8	3♐29.0
2 Th	12 44 58	9 19 39	12 4 32	18 1 49	19R44.1	0♎28.6	23 25.3	2 30.0	12R 8.8	17R30.7	4R47.8	27R11.5	3 30.6
3 F	12 48 55	10 18 44	24 0 41	0♏ 1 22	19 41.3	2 16.6	24 33.1	3 12.2	12 7.8	17 26.0	4 47.2	27 11.3	3 32.1
4 Sa	12 52 51	11 17 51	6♏ 4 5	12 9 5	19 37.9	4 4.5	25 40.7	3 54.6	12 6.9	17 21.3	4 46.7	27 11.2	3 33.8
5 Su	12 56 48	12 16 59	18 16 35	24 26 52	19 34.3	5 52.1	26 48.3	4 37.0	12 6.3	17 16.6	4 46.2	27 11.0	3 35.4
6 M	13 0 44	13 16 10	0♐40 11	6♐56 49	19 30.8	7 39.4	27 55.6	5 19.5	12 5.8	17 11.9	4 45.8	27 10.9	3 37.1
7 Tu	13 4 41	14 15 22	13 17 2	19 41 8	19 27.9	9 26.3	29 2.9	6 2.1	12 5.6	17 7.2	4 45.4	27 10.9	3 38.8
8 W	13 8 38	15 14 36	26 9 26	2♑42 13	19 26.1	11 12.6	0♐10.0	6 44.8	12D 5.6	17 2.4	4 45.1	27D10.8	3 40.5
9 Th	13 12 34	16 13 52	9♑19 46	16 2 21	19D25.5	12 58.3	1 17.0	7 27.6	12 5.7	16 57.7	4 44.8	27 10.8	3 42.2
10 F	13 16 31	17 13 9	22 50 11	29 43 25	19 26.1	14 43.5	2 23.8	8 10.5	12 6.1	16 53.0	4 44.6	27 10.9	3 44.0
11 Sa	13 20 27	18 12 28	6♒42 10	13♒46 26	19 27.3	16 28.0	3 30.4	8 53.4	12 6.6	16 48.2	4 44.4	27 10.9	3 45.8
12 Su	13 24 24	19 11 49	20 56 5	28 10 53	19 28.8	18 11.8	4 36.9	9 36.4	12 7.4	16 43.5	4 44.3	27 11.0	3 47.6
13 M	13 28 20	20 11 12	5♓30 27	12♓54 14	19R29.8	19 54.9	5 43.2	10 19.6	12 8.4	16 38.8	4 44.2	27 11.1	3 49.4
14 Tu	13 32 17	21 10 37	20 21 34	27 51 36	19 29.7	21 37.4	6 49.3	11 2.7	12 9.5	16 34.0	4D44.2	27 11.3	3 51.2
15 W	13 36 13	22 10 3	5♈23 22	12♈55 47	19 28.1	23 19.1	7 55.3	11 46.0	12 10.9	16 29.3	4 44.2	27 11.5	3 53.1
16 Th	13 40 10	23 9 31	20 27 43	27 58 1	19 24.8	25 0.2	9 1.0	12 29.3	12 12.4	16 24.6	4 44.3	27 11.7	3 55.0
17 F	13 44 7	24 9 2	5♉25 32	12♉49 12	19 20.1	26 40.6	10 6.6	13 12.8	12 14.1	16 20.0	4 44.4	27 12.0	3 56.9
18 Sa	13 48 3	25 8 34	20 8 4	27 21 19	19 14.7	28 20.3	11 12.0	13 56.2	12 16.1	16 15.3	4 44.6	27 12.3	3 58.9
19 Su	13 52 0	26 8 9	4♊28 19	11♊28 36	19 9.1	29 59.4	12 17.2	14 39.8	12 18.2	16 10.7	4 44.8	27 12.6	4 0.8
20 M	13 55 56	27 7 46	18 21 54	25 8 8	19 4.3	1♏37.9	13 22.2	15 23.5	12 20.6	16 6.0	4 45.1	27 13.0	4 2.8
21 Tu	13 59 53	28 7 26	1♋47 22	8♋19 49	19 0.7	3 15.7	14 26.9	16 7.2	12 23.1	16 1.5	4 45.5	27 13.4	4 4.8
22 W	14 3 49	29 7 7	14 45 49	21 5 50	18 58.8	4 53.0	15 31.5	16 51.0	12 25.8	15 56.9	4 45.9	27 13.8	4 6.8
23 Th	14 7 46	0♏ 6 51	27 20 23	3♌30 2	18D58.5	6 29.6	16 35.8	17 34.9	12 28.7	15 52.4	4 46.3	27 14.3	4 8.8
24 F	14 11 42	1 6 37	9♌35 24	15 37 9	18 59.4	8 5.7	17 39.9	18 18.9	12 31.8	15 47.9	4 46.8	27 14.8	4 10.9
25 Sa	14 15 39	2 6 26	21 35 55	27 32 20	19 1.0	9 41.2	18 43.8	19 2.9	12 35.1	15 43.4	4 47.3	27 15.3	4 12.9
26 Su	14 19 36	3 6 16	3♍27 3	9♍20 40	19 2.4	11 16.2	19 47.4	19 47.0	12 38.6	15 39.0	4 47.9	27 15.9	4 15.0
27 M	14 23 32	4 6 9	15 13 45	21 6 51	19R 2.8	12 50.6	20 50.7	20 31.2	12 42.2	15 34.6	4 48.5	27 16.5	4 17.1
28 Tu	14 27 29	5 6 3	27 0 28	2♎55 2	19 1.6	14 24.6	21 53.8	21 15.5	12 46.1	15 30.3	4 49.2	27 17.1	4 19.2
29 W	14 31 25	6 6 0	8♎50 58	14 48 38	18 58.3	15 58.1	22 56.7	21 59.8	12 50.1	15 26.0	4 50.0	27 17.8	4 21.4
30 Th	14 35 22	7 5 59	20 48 19	26 50 17	18 52.7	17 31.1	23 59.2	22 44.2	12 54.3	15 21.8	4 50.8	27 18.5	4 23.5
31 F	14 39 18	8 6 0	2♏54 45	9♏ 1 51	18 45.0	19 3.6	25 1.5	23 28.7	12 58.7	15 17.6	4 51.6	27 19.2	4 25.7

*Giving the positions of planets daily at noon, in LONGITUDE Greenwich Mean Time

Noon Ephemeris: GMT*

November 1997

Day	Sid.Time	☉	0 hr ☽	Noon ☽	True ☊	☿	♀	♂	♃	♄	♅	♆	♇
1 Sa	14 43 15	9♏ 6 2	15♏11 44	21♏24 29	18♍35.8	20♏35.7	26♐ 3.4	24♐13.3	13♒ 3.3	15♈13.4	4♒52.5	27♑20.0	4♐27.8
2 Su	14 47 11	10 6 7	27 40 8	3♐58 45	18R26.0	22 7.3	27 5.1	24 57.9	13 8.1	15R 9.4	4 53.5	27 20.8	4 30.0
3 M	14 51 8	11 6 13	10♐20 21	16 44 57	18 16.5	23 38.5	28 6.4	25 42.6	13 13.1	15 5.3	4 54.4	27 21.6	4 32.2
4 Tu	14 55 5	12 6 21	23 12 35	29 43 16	18 8.2	25 9.2	29 7.4	26 27.3	13 18.2	15 1.4	4 55.5	27 22.5	4 34.5
5 W	14 59 1	13 6 31	6♑17 5	12♑54 5	18 2.0	26 39.5	0♑ 8.0	27 12.2	13 23.5	14 57.5	4 56.6	27 23.4	4 36.7
6 Th	15 2 58	14 6 42	19 34 22	26 18 0	17 58.2	28 9.4	1 8.2	27 57.1	13 29.0	14 53.7	4 57.7	27 24.3	4 38.9
7 F	15 6 54	15 6 55	3♒ 5 7	9♒55 50	17D 56.6	29 38.8	2 8.1	28 42.0	13 34.6	14 49.9	4 58.9	27 25.3	4 41.2
8 Sa	15 10 51	16 7 9	16 50 13	23 48 22	17 56.7	1♐ 7.8	3 7.5	29 27.0	13 40.5	14 46.2	5 0.2	27 26.2	4 43.4
9 Su	15 14 47	17 7 24	0♓50 17	7♓55 56	17 57.4	2 36.3	4 6.6	0♑12.1	13 46.5	14 42.6	5 1.5	27 27.3	4 45.7
10 M	15 18 44	18 7 41	15 5 12	22 17 51	17R 57.6	4 4.3	5 5.2	0 57.3	13 52.6	14 39.0	5 2.8	27 28.3	4 48.0
11 Tu	15 22 40	19 8 0	29 33 33	6♈51 50	17 56.1	5 31.8	6 3.4	1 42.5	13 58.9	14 35.6	5 4.2	27 29.4	4 50.3
12 W	15 26 37	20 8 19	14♈12 6	21 33 38	17 52.2	6 58.7	7 1.0	2 27.7	14 5.4	14 32.2	5 5.6	27 30.5	4 52.6
13 Th	15 30 33	21 8 41	28 55 37	6♉17 7	17 45.6	8 25.1	7 58.2	3 13.0	14 12.1	14 28.8	5 7.1	27 31.6	4 54.9
14 F	15 34 30	22 9 4	13♉37 12	20 54 53	17 36.6	9 50.9	8 54.9	3 58.4	14 18.9	14 25.6	5 8.6	27 32.8	4 57.2
15 Sa	15 38 27	23 9 28	28 9 14	5♊19 22	17 26.1	11 16.0	9 51.1	4 43.8	14 25.9	14 22.4	5 10.2	27 34.0	4 59.5
16 Su	15 42 23	24 9 55	12♊24 31	19 24 4	17 15.1	12 40.3	10 46.7	5 29.3	14 33.0	14 19.4	5 11.8	27 35.3	5 1.8
17 M	15 46 20	25 10 23	26 17 32	3♋ 4 37	17 4.9	14 3.9	11 41.8	6 14.9	14 40.3	14 16.4	5 13.5	27 36.5	5 4.2
18 Tu	15 50 16	26 10 53	9♋45 10	16 19 13	16 56.5	15 26.5	12 36.2	7 0.4	14 47.7	14 13.5	5 15.2	27 37.8	5 6.5
19 W	15 54 13	27 11 24	22 46 55	29 8 35	16 50.5	16 48.1	13 30.1	7 46.1	14 55.3	14 10.7	5 17.0	27 39.1	5 8.9
20 Th	15 58 9	28 11 57	5♌24 39	11♌35 35	16 47.1	18 8.6	14 23.3	8 31.8	15 3.1	14 7.9	5 18.8	27 40.5	5 11.2
21 F	16 2 6	29 12 32	17 41 59	23 44 29	16 45.7	19 27.8	15 15.9	9 17.6	15 11.0	14 5.3	5 20.6	27 41.8	5 13.6
22 Sa	16 6 3	0♐13 9	29 43 45	5♍40 29	16D 45.7	20 45.6	16 7.8	10 3.4	15 19.0	14 2.7	5 22.5	27 43.2	5 15.9
23 Su	16 9 59	1 13 48	11♍35 23	17 29 10	16R 45.9	22 1.7	16 59.0	10 49.3	15 27.2	14 0.3	5 24.5	27 44.7	5 18.3
24 M	16 13 56	2 14 28	23 22 30	29 16 3	16 45.2	23 16.0	17 49.4	11 35.2	15 35.5	13 57.9	5 26.5	27 46.1	5 20.6
25 Tu	16 17 52	3 15 9	5♎10 28	11♎ 6 20	16 42.6	24 28.1	18 39.1	12 21.2	15 44.0	13 55.7	5 28.5	27 47.6	5 23.0
26 W	16 21 49	4 15 52	17 4 11	23 4 31	16 37.4	25 37.7	19 28.0	13 7.2	15 52.6	13 53.5	5 30.5	27 49.1	5 25.4
27 Th	16 25 45	5 16 37	29 7 44	5♏14 12	16 29.4	26 44.6	20 16.1	13 53.3	16 1.3	13 51.4	5 32.7	27 50.7	5 27.7
28 F	16 29 42	6 17 23	11♏24 12	17 37 54	16 18.6	27 48.3	21 3.3	14 39.4	16 10.2	13 49.5	5 34.8	27 52.2	5 30.1
29 Sa	16 33 38	7 18 11	23 55 27	0♐16 52	16 5.8	28 48.3	21 49.6	15 25.6	16 19.3	13 47.6	5 37.0	27 53.8	5 32.5
30 Su	16 37 35	8 19 0	6♐42 7	13 11 6	15 52.0	29 44.2	22 34.9	16 11.8	16 28.4	13 45.8	5 39.2	27 55.4	5 34.8

Longitude

December 1997

Day	Sid.Time	☉	0 hr ☽	Noon ☽	True ☊	☿	♀	♂	♃	♄	♅	♆	♇
1 M	16 41 32	9♐19 50	19♐43 40	26♐19 37	15♍38.5	0♑35.3	23♑19.3	16♑58.1	16♒37.7	13♈44.2	5♒41.5	27♑57.1	5♐37.2
2 Tu	16 45 28	10 20 41	2♑58 41	9♑40 38	15R 26.5	1 21.0	24 2.7	17 44.4	16 47.1	13R 42.6	5 43.8	27 58.7	5 39.6
3 W	16 49 25	11 21 34	16 25 13	23 12 11	15 17.2	2 0.6	24 45.0	18 30.7	16 56.7	13 41.2	5 46.2	28 0.4	5 41.9
4 Th	16 53 21	12 22 27	0♒ 1 19	6♒52 27	15 10.8	2 33.4	25 26.2	19 17.1	17 6.4	13 39.8	5 48.6	28 2.1	5 44.3
5 F	16 57 18	13 23 21	13 45 27	20 40 12	15 7.4	2 58.4	26 6.2	20 3.6	17 16.2	13 38.6	5 51.0	28 3.9	5 46.6
6 Sa	17 1 14	14 24 15	27 36 38	4♓34 43	15 6.3	3 14.9	26 45.0	20 50.1	17 26.1	13 37.4	5 53.5	28 5.6	5 49.0
7 Su	17 5 11	15 25 11	11♓34 26	18 35 44	15 6.2	3R 22.0	27 22.5	21 36.6	17 36.1	13 36.4	5 56.0	28 7.4	5 51.3
8 M	17 9 7	16 26 7	25 38 36	2♈42 57	15 5.7	3 18.9	27 58.7	22 23.1	17 46.3	13 35.5	5 58.5	28 9.2	5 53.7
9 Tu	17 13 4	17 27 3	9♈48 38	16 55 29	15 3.6	3 4.9	28 33.5	23 9.7	17 56.6	13 34.7	6 1.1	28 11.0	5 56.0
10 W	17 17 1	18 28 1	24 3 13	1♉11 27	14 58.8	2 39.6	29 6.9	23 56.4	18 7.0	13 34.0	6 3.7	28 12.8	5 58.3
11 Th	17 20 57	19 28 58	8♉19 45	15 27 35	14 51.1	2 2.9	29 38.8	24 43.0	18 17.5	13 33.4	6 6.3	28 14.7	6 0.6
12 F	17 24 54	20 29 57	22 34 21	29 39 26	14 40.6	1 14.9	0♒ 9.1	25 29.7	18 28.1	13 32.9	6 9.0	28 16.6	6 2.9
13 Sa	17 28 50	21 30 57	6♊42 8	13♊41 49	14 28.3	0 16.4	0 37.8	26 16.4	18 38.8	13 32.5	6 11.7	28 18.5	6 5.2
14 Su	17 32 47	22 31 57	20 37 51	27 29 41	14 15.3	29♐ 8.7	1 4.9	27 3.2	18 49.6	13 32.3	6 14.5	28 20.4	6 7.5
15 M	17 36 43	23 32 58	4♋16 51	10♋58 58	14 3.1	27 53.5	1 30.2	27 50.0	19 0.6	13 32.1	6 17.3	28 22.3	6 9.8
16 Tu	17 40 40	24 33 59	17 35 48	24 7 14	13 52.7	26 33.1	1 53.7	28 36.8	19 11.6	13D 32.1	6 20.1	28 24.3	6 12.1
17 W	17 44 36	25 35 2	0♌33 17	6♌54 2	13 44.9	25 10.3	2 15.3	29 23.6	19 22.8	13 32.1	6 22.9	28 26.3	6 14.4
18 Th	17 48 33	26 36 5	13 9 46	19 20 49	13 39.9	23 47.9	2 35.0	0♒10.5	19 34.0	13 32.3	6 25.8	28 28.3	6 16.6
19 F	17 52 30	27 37 9	25 27 37	1♍30 40	13 37.4	22 28.5	2 52.8	0 57.4	19 45.3	13 32.6	6 28.7	28 30.3	6 18.9
20 Sa	17 56 26	28 38 14	7♍30 32	13 27 52	13D 36.8	21 14.6	3 8.4	1 44.4	19 56.8	13 33.0	6 31.6	28 32.3	6 21.1
21 Su	18 0 23	29 39 20	19 23 19	25 17 34	13R 37.0	20 8.4	3 22.0	2 31.3	20 8.3	13 33.5	6 34.6	28 34.3	6 23.3
22 M	18 4 19	0♑40 26	1♎11 20	7♎ 5 17	13 36.9	19 11.4	3 33.4	3 18.3	20 20.0	13 34.1	6 37.5	28 36.4	6 25.5
23 Tu	18 8 16	1 41 34	13 0 9	18 56 36	13 35.4	18 24.5	3 42.5	4 5.3	20 31.7	13 34.8	6 40.6	28 38.5	6 27.7
24 W	18 12 12	2 42 41	24 55 17	0♏56 49	13 31.7	17 48.4	3 49.4	4 52.4	20 43.5	13 35.6	6 43.6	28 40.5	6 29.9
25 Th	18 16 9	3 43 50	7♏ 1 45	13 10 35	13 25.4	17 23.1	3 53.9	5 39.5	20 55.4	13 36.6	6 46.7	28 42.6	6 32.1
26 F	18 20 5	4 44 59	19 23 44	25 41 33	13 16.5	17 8.3	3R 56.1	6 26.6	21 7.4	13 37.6	6 49.7	28 44.8	6 34.2
27 Sa	18 24 2	5 46 8	2♐ 4 16	8♐32 2	13 5.6	17D 3.6	3 55.8	7 13.7	21 19.5	13 38.8	6 52.9	28 46.9	6 36.4
28 Su	18 27 59	6 47 19	15 4 50	21 42 37	12 53.6	17 8.3	3 53.1	8 0.8	21 31.6	13 40.0	6 56.0	28 49.0	6 38.5
29 M	18 31 55	7 48 29	28 25 11	5♑12 13	12 41.9	17 21.7	3 47.9	8 48.0	21 43.9	13 41.4	6 59.2	28 51.2	6 40.6
30 Tu	18 35 52	8 49 39	12♑ 3 20	18 58 5	12 31.4	17 43.1	3 40.2	9 35.2	21 56.2	13 42.9	7 2.3	28 53.3	6 42.7
31 W	18 39 48	9 50 50	25 55 57	2♒56 24	12 23.2	18 11.8	3 30.0	10 22.4	22 8.6	13 44.5	7 5.6	28 55.5	6 44.8

*Giving the positions of planets daily at noon,
in LONGITUDE Greenwich Mean Time

January - Januar - janvier - enero

Monday	Tuesday	Wednesday	Thursday	Friday	Saturday	Sunday
		1	2	3	4	5
6	7	8	9	10	11	12
13	14	15	16	17	18	19
20	21	22	23	24	25	26
27	28	29	30	31		

INANNA

February – Februar – février – febrero

Monday	Tuesday	Wednesday	Thursday	Friday	Saturday	Sunday
		FREYA			1	2
3	4	5	6	7	8	9
10	11	12	13	14	15	16
17	18	19	20	21	22	23
24	25	26	27	28		

March - März - mars - marzo

PELE

	Monday	Tuesday	Wednesday	Thursday	Friday	Saturday	Sunday
						1	2
	3 / 24	4	5	6	7	8	9
	10	11	12	13	14	15	16
	17	18	19	20	21	22	23
	24 / 31	25	26	27	28	29	30

April - April - avril - abril

Monday	Tuesday	Wednesday	Thursday	Friday	Saturday	Sunday	
	1	2	3	4	5	6	
7	8	9	10	11	12	13	**TARA**
14	15	16	17	18	19	20	
21	22	23	24	25	26	27	
28	29	30					

May - Mai - mai - mayo

	Monday	Tuesday	Wednesday	Thursday	Friday	Saturday	Sunday
	SAPPHO			1	2	3	4
	5	6	7	8	9	10	11
	12	13	14	15	16	17	18
	19	20	21	22	23	24	25
	26	27	28	29	30	31	

June - Juni - juin - junio

KWAN-YIN

Monday	Tuesday	Wednesday	Thursday	Friday	Saturday	Sunday
						1
2	3	4	5	6	7	8
9	10	11	12	13	14	15
16	17	18	19	20	21	22
23	24	25	26	27	28	29
30						

July - Juli - juilliet - julio

Monday	Tuesday	Wednesday	Thursday	Friday	Saturday	Sunday
	1	2	3	4	5	6
7	8	9	10	11	12	13
14	15	16	17	18	19	20
21	22	23	24	25	26	27
28	29	30	31			

OSHUN

August - August - août - agosto

Monday	Tuesday	Wednesday	Thursday	Friday	Saturday	Sunday
		ARTEMIS		1	2	3
4	5	6	7	8	9	10
11	12	13	14	15	16	17
18	19	20	21	22	23	24
25	26	27	28	29	30	31

September -septembre-septiembre

	Monday	Tuesday	Wednesday	Thursday	Friday	Saturday	Sunday
	1	2	3	4	5	6	7
	8	9	10	11	12	13	14
	15	16	17	18	19	20	21
	22	23	24	25	26	27	28
	29	30					

ISIS

October - Oktober - octobre - octubre

Monday	Tuesday	Wednesday	Thursday	Friday	Saturday	Sunday
		1	2	3	4	5
6	7	8	9	10	11	12
13	14	15	16	17	18	19
20	21	22	23	24	25	26
27	28	29	30	31		

KALI

November - novembre - noviembre

BUFFALO WOMON

Monday	Tuesday	Wednesday	Thursday	Friday	Saturday	Sunday
					1	2
3	4	5	6	7	8	9
10	11	12	13	14	15	16
17	18	19	20	21	22	23
24	25	26	27	28	29	30

December - décembre - diciembre

Monday	Tuesday	Wednesday	Thursday	Friday	Saturday	Sunday
1	2	3	4	5	6	7
8	9	10	11	12	13	14
15	16	17	18	19	20	21
22	23	24	25	26	27	28
29	30	31				

LILITH

Signs and Symbols at a Glance

Planets

Personal Planets are the ones closest to Earth.

☿ **Mercury**: communication, conscious thought, inventiveness

♀ **Venus**: relationship, love, sense of beauty and sensuality, empathy

♂ **Mars**: will to act, initiative, ambition

Asteroids are found between Mars and Jupiter, bridging the personal and the social planets. They reflect the rebirth of the goddess and the awakening of feminine-defined energy centers in human consciousness. See "Asteroids" (p.201).

Social Planets are in between the personal planets and the outer planets.

♃ **Jupiter**: expansion, opportunities, leadership

♄ **Saturn**: limits, structure, discipline

⚷ **Chiron**: a small planetary body between Saturn and Uranus bridging the social and transpersonal planets; represents the wounded healer, the core wound that leads us to our path of service.

Transpersonal Planets are the outer planets. They are slow-moving and influence generational issues.

♅ **Uranus**: revolutionary change, cosmic consciousness

♆ **Neptune**: spiritual awakening, cosmic love, all one

♇ **Pluto**: death and rebirth, purification, takes us to the depths where total change is necessary/possible

Zodiac Signs	
♈	Aries
♉	Taurus
♊	Gemini
♋	Cancer
♌	Leo
♍	Virgo
♎	Libra
♏	Scorpio
♐	Sagittarius
♑	Capricorn
♒	Aquarius
♓	Pisces

Aspects

Aspects show the angle between planets in the 360° zodiac. This relationship informs how the planets influence each other as they circle the sky. The **We'Moon** lists only the 'significant aspects':

♂ CONJUNCTION (planets are 0–5° apart)
linked together, energy of aspected planets is mutually enhancing

⚹ SEXTILE (planets are 60° apart)
cooperative, energies of this aspect blend well

□ SQUARE (planets are 90° apart)
challenging, energies of this aspect are different from each other

△ TRINE (planets are 120° apart)
harmonizing, energies of this aspect are in the same element

☍ OPPOSITION (planets are 180° apart)
polarizing or complementing, energies are diametrically opposite

⚻ QUINCUNX (planets are 150° apart)
variable, energies of this aspect combine contrary elements

223